The
Liberal State
&
the Politics of
Virtue

The
Liberal State
&
the Politics of
Virtue

Ludvig Beckman

Transaction Publishers
New Brunswick (U.S.A.) and London (U.K.)

This volume was made available to the English-reading public through a grant from the Zoryan Institute for Contemporary Armenian Research and Documentation, Cambridge, Massachusetts; Toronto, Ontario.

This study was first published in 2000 as a report in the EVSOC program (Ethics, Virtues, and Social Capital in Sweden) at the City University of Stockholm.

Library of Congress Catalog Number: 00-066964
ISBN: 0-7658-0086-1
Printed in the United States of America

Library of Congress Cataloging-in-Publication Data

Beckman, Ludvig.
    The liberal state and the politics of virtue / Ludvig Beckman.
        p. cm.
    Includes bibliographical references and index.
    ISBN 0-7658-0086-1 (cloth : alk. paper)
        1. Liberalism. 2. Liberalism—Moral and ethical aspects. 3. Political ethics. I. Title.

JC574 .B4 2001
320.51—dc21

                                                                00-066964

Contents

Acknowledgments   vii

1. Liberalism and Virtue: The Beginning of an Argument   1

2. Virtue in Liberal Thought: A Primer   19

3. The Liberal Way of Life: Dworkin on Virtue   41

4. The Liberal Citizen: Rawls on Virtue   63

5. Rights and Virtues: In Conflict?   83

6. Dimensions of Neutrality: The Neutral State as an Ideal   115

7. Neutral Aims: Dworkin and the Liberal State   135

8. Neutral Reasons: The Liberal State Justified   187

9. Liberalism and Dogmatism   241

10. Conclusions: The Liberal's Predicament   257

Bibliography   265

Index   279

Acknowledgements

Without the virtuous colleagues and friends whom I have had the privilege of knowing during these years, this book would not have been what it is. I am greatly indebted to my supervisor, Jörgen Hermansson, who has given me invaluable support and advice—and countless comments—throughout all these years. Mats Lundström, my vice-supervisor, has provided me with a steady stream of callous and incisive observations that meant a lot for the final manuscript. I owe a special thanks to Emil Uddhammar, who initiated a research project on virtues that constituted a constant source of inspiration. At a decisive stage of my wrestling with the liberal and the virtuous I was a visiting graduate at St Catherine's College, Oxford, England. This stimulating milieu and especially the generous weekly supervision provided by Lord Raymond Plant had an immense importance for the direction of my work.

Helpful comments from my colleagues in Uppsala have been a more constant source of challenge and comfort. Thank you Karl-Göran Algotsson, Stefan Björklund, Barry Holmström, and Johan Tralau. Thanks also to Professor John Dunn, whose thorough reading of the manuscript gave me the courage to complete it. I am also grateful for the comments provided by John Barry, Matthew Liao, and Simon Clarke on different versions of chapters four and six. Stefan Olsson and Anna-Carin Svensson deserve a special mentioning simply because we were in this together. Thank you also to Theresa England who checked my spelling. Finally I am deeply grateful to Uppsala University, Thun's scholarship, Sven & Dagmar Salén's foundation and Axel & Margaret Ax:son Johnson's foundation for generous economic support.

I dedicate this book to Ewa and Amanda (my girls), not because they're cute, but because they joined me on this journey and beyond.

Ludvig Beckman
Uppsala and Stockholm
March 2000

1

Liberalism and Virtue: The Beginning of an Argument

This book is about the idea of the state being able to make people virtuous, good or better. Its focus is on the dominant ideology in the Western world today, liberalism. According to common interpretations of this doctrine the state should not try to make people virtuous or good. The state should allow people to live good lives and should not enforce standards of the good life. This view represents the typical liberal response. The aim of this study is to examine the rationale for this view. This involves investigating the beliefs and arguments of liberal writers in order to establish the extent to which the common interpretation of liberalism is in fact justified. Is liberalism committed to the view that the state must not try to teach, foster, inculcate or encourage some specific idea of virtue and the good life? And if so, are there good arguments for accepting this view?

The question of how political authority should deal with claims of virtue has been the focus of academic and public debate since the Reformation. Statesmen, scholars and philosophers have dwelt on whether a state committed to the protection of liberty and rights can legitimately take a stand on questions about virtue and goodness. Are the ends of liberty compatible with the ends of virtue? Are liberal values consistent with conceptions of virtue? Apparently these questions are not new. I will attempt, however, to discuss some of them in relation to recent liberal theories. Moreover, I will propose distinctions that will allow us to understand the alleged conflict between liberalism and virtue in new and original ways. By carefully delineating and specifying the issue this study aims to contribute to this debate. The first chapter is devoted to an attempt to specify the meaning of "liberalism" in this context; the second chapter brings in and attempts to make more specific the notion of "virtue."

1

Liberalism's relation to what might be called *the politics of virtue*[1] is a moral, political and social issue that pertains to a number of phenomena in contemporary society. A few cases will illustrate how and why claims based on notions of virtues and the good life challenge liberal institutions and values.

First and foremost, in the last few decades there has been a growing awareness of the fact that traditional political institutions and ideologies did not correspond to the demands and aspirations held by many individuals and groups. Ideals and interests previously without much impact on the political debate now gained access to the public arena. These new claims include demands for recognition of homosexuals and their rights, affirmation of the particularities of indigenous peoples, sensitivity to the cultures and languages of immigrants, respect for children and their needs, solidarity with the people of the developing countries and their fight for independence, care for nature, animals and the "biosphere," attention to the social status of women, and so on. These new claims have been met to various degrees by the institutions of the liberal democratic state. The point is, however, that these claims are in an important respect concerned with the recognition of life forms and their respective virtues.[2] As a consequence, many governments now regulate and support many different conceptions of the good life and its virtues.

Secondly, there is the more traditional claim to the effect that the state should secure fundamental norms for society. The state has, according to this view, a responsibility for the ideas and values transmitted in schools and by the practices of art and culture. Thus, guidelines for public education have always established that certain attitudes and virtues are desirable and more valuable than others.[3] Similarly, public support for literature and film in Sweden is, as recent research has shown, invested with a multiplicity of choices between good and bad taste and the virtues that are to be served by these activities.[4] Thus the state frequently decides what virtues should be encouraged and promoted.

The state undoubtedly does deal with virtues. But whether the state *should* do so remains disputed. The question I ask and intend to answer is whether liberalism provides conclusive arguments to the effect that the state should not articulate or recognize some set of virtues. The idea that I will defend is that contemporary liberal theories do not provide any such conclusive argument.

Thus, the argument of this study is that the common view, that there is a conflict between liberal values and the idea of a politics of virtue, is unjustified. Bringing the limitations of liberal arguments to the fore is not, however, the same as explaining the basis for this misconception. In other words, I do not propose giving an account of the beliefs, presuppositions or prejudices that have produced the widespread belief in liberalism's denial of virtue. Yet this work has been inspired by recent observations about the difficulty to include concepts of virtue and the good life into modern discourse. As Bernard Williams observes, the term virtue has, for the most part "acquired comic or otherwise undesirable associations."[5]

In an attempt to account for this, writers like Alasdair MacIntyre and Charles Taylor point to the ambiguous effects of prevalent conceptions of individualism and rationality. They believe that the reason why virtue terms are so hard for us to accept, both philosophically and politically, is that they appear to be in conflict with these ideas.[6] Yet I do not intend to take sides on this issue. Rather, the focus here is on the preceding question: is there a conflict between notions of virtue and liberal values and principles? In the following I will explore a number of possible and actual responses from a liberal perspective.

Definitions and Theories

Liberalism and virtue are the two central concepts in this study. Presumably, then, these concepts should be carefully defined before embarking on the inquiry. A common belief is that the meaning of the concepts involved in a question has to be clarified before it can be answered. Though there is some truth in this, my belief is that we should hesitate to accept that definitions are needed in order to clarify the meaning of concepts. There is no reason to assume by default that definitions are necessary in order to identify relevant and specific questions of research.

Like most political concepts, liberalism refers to a considerable number of ideas. Not every idea or value called liberal at one time or another could plausibly be included in a definition of liberalism. But similarly, no singular value, like equality or liberty, is likely to be accepted by all liberals as the exclusive concern of liberalism.[7] In fact, there is no one person with the authority to judge what is a truly liberal position and what is not. Such authority could only hinge on the fact of this person being a "true" liberal or on the fact of this person somehow knowing how to define liberalism. Whether or not a person claims to be a true liberal or to know what liberalism is, this provides no solution to our problem. How would we know whether a person knows what liberalism is unless we already had recourse to the definition of liberalism that we are looking for?

This is not to say that definitions are useless. My point is rather to argue that there are sometimes better ways of clarifying a subject than that of stating definitions.[8] It may in fact be the case, as has been suggested, that liberalism should be regarded more as a tradition of discourse than as a single set of coherent principles and that it does not, therefore, permit one exhaustive definition.[9] Anyway, my belief is that nothing is gained by defining liberalism—even by stipulation—as this or that kind of doctrine. I believe that, instead, I should devote my endeavors to relevant liberal *theories*.

This is the approach defended by Karl Popper in scientific undertakings. We should, Popper argued, not be "concerned with the question of a meaning of a term, but rather with the truth of a theory."[10] Popper's suspicions of definitions derived from his critique of metaphysics and mysticism. Obsessive attention to definitions, coupled with the ambition to make definite the "essential" meaning of all concepts, were considered by Popper to be facets of pre-modern science (*viz* that of Aristotle and Hegel). In the modern context these methods are not only inadequate but also dangerous.[11] However, my concerns are not Popper's.

In my view, the advantage of beginning by a description of theories rather than of definitions is that it makes the basis of the investigation more explicit. Theories are clusters of arguments, and to identify which theories are relevant and which are not will consequently make clear which arguments are challenged and which are not. The focus of this study is on certain claims (theories) not on certain uses of language (terms).[12]

Liberal Possibilities

The question I propose to tackle is whether a liberal state can legitimately pursue conceptions of virtues. Now this question is ambiguous in a way that is not always appreciated. The ambiguity is evident from the fact that one possible argument for the state not to accept the idea of a politics of virtue is that this is the best way of making people virtuous. This view assumes that people develop their character and virtue best in a society where the state does not interfere. However, this view is justified with reference to the value of virtues.

There are, in other words, two questions at stake here. The first one is whether liberalism approves of a state promoting virtue. The other is whether the liberal doctrine includes virtues or ideals of the good life. The second question is distinct from the first since it concerns the extent to which liberalism speaks or argues in terms of virtues and not the extent to which the state should promote them. Hence, a negative answer to the first question need not imply a negative answer to the second. In other words, the statement "the state should not encourage virtues" does not imply that virtues and the good life are considered to be of no importance. I believe the importance of this distinction is not always appreciated.

When there are two distinct questions there are, in analytical terms, four possible answers. To begin with, liberalism could ignore questions concerning the good life and, at the same time, deny that the state has any authority to pursue virtues. This is the "no-no" option. The opposite view is to accept that liberalism is about the realization of virtues and to accept that the state has the authority to pursue them. This is the "yes-yes" option. There are then two more possibilities, less symmetrical and harmonious it would seem. Liberalism could accept that some virtues are more valuable than others but deny that the state has the authority to actively promote what is good. This is the "yes-no" option. The final position, the "no-yes" position, is a possible, though not perhaps very attractive, position. In this view, liberalism is inconsistently affirming both the view that virtues are not relevant and the view that the state may, in any case, promote them.

Figure 1.1
Liberalism and Virtue: Four Possible Positions

Should the liberal state
promote virtues?

		Yes	*No*
Are there liberal virtutes?	Yes	Yes-Yes	Yes-No
	No	No-Yes	No-No

The aim of this work is to study the relation between liberalism and the idea of a politics of virtue. It is now clear that this issue involves two questions: are there liberal virtues and should the liberal state promote virtues? Consequently, there are two alternative arguments to the effect that the state should not accept or support any particular doctrine of virtue and the good life (the "yes-no" and the "no-no" position). They both prefer a neutral state as regards virtues but they do not agree on how to evaluate virtues as such.

We have now examined possible liberal positions. Next we need to know what actual positions there are. What is the liberal response to the idea of a politics of virtue? What kind of considerations have been invoked in order to rebut the suggestion that the state should be devoted to the furtherance of virtue?

The Liberal Paradox

The traditional liberal position with regard to virtue has been that of the skeptic. Virtues and lofty ideals about how life should be led have been treated as bogus metaphysical ideas. The skeptic liberal claims that such beliefs are likely to be false or that they are even beyond truth and falsity in that they are mere expressions of emotion. "Good" and "bad" virtues or modes of life simply do not exist.[13] The skeptical rejection of virtue is found in the writings of Thomas Hobbes in the seventeenth century. Hobbes dismissed virtues as mere words with different meanings to everyone: "And therefore such names can never be true grounds of any ratiocination."[14] To Hobbes, virtues were just words and as such not part of the fabric of the universe that the scientific liberal ought to deal with. The state should be based on principles about what *is*. In a similar spirit of doubt, Bertrand Russell in the twentieth century characterized virtue and the corresponding claims of good and bad character as conceptions with "no scientific justification."[15] To say that this or that virtue is good or bad would, Russell argued, amount to nothing more than an expression of the emotions of the speaker himself.

However, recent academic debate has made increasingly clear the dilemma—the "liberal paradox"—associated with skeptical liberalism. The paradox consists of the fact that skepticism not only undermines non-liberal virtues and doctrines; a liberalism committed to the subjectivity of value will run the risk of depriving itself of validity.[16] A liberal might find it comfortable to appeal to skepticism when he or she confronts people who think they know the truth about the good life. However, they may be less comforted when faced with the difficult task of defending their own position from a skeptical point of view. In contrast to what liberals through the ages have argued, skepticism does not give liberalism its exclusive support. Tolerance is no more justified than intolerance by the skeptic's claim that there are no true values.[17] If you believe that political values cannot be justified, if you deny that there may be principles that are more justified than others, there does not seem to be a basis for preferring liberal institutions to non-liberal. The preference for a fascist government is no less justified than the preference for a liberal-democratic regime from the perspective of moral skepticism.[18]

The liberal paradox tells us that moral skepticism does not give liberalism its exclusive support and therefore cannot be invoked successfully in an argument to rebut the idea of a politics of virtue. If you believe that terms like virtue and goodness are just "sounds" or feelings, no more justified than other emotions, you run the risk of arriving at the same conclusion concerning other evaluative terms. If "goodness" was just a feeling then this would seem to apply to "rightness" and "justice" too. Thus, skepticism is not the exclusive ally of liberalism. In fact, these views do not seem to go readily together because, as pointed out by Susan Mendus; "liberalism asserts what skepticism denies—that some values are superior to others."[19]

The paradoxes of liberal skepticism are well established in recent scholarly contributions. Frequently too the skeptical route is rejected by writers endeavoring to erect a theoretical defense for the liberal state. The contemporary legal philosopher Ronald Dworkin has argued, for example, that skepticism does not produce the answers which a liberal would look for.

> Because if the moral majority is wrong, and each person should be free to choose personal ideals for himself, then this is surely because the choice of one sort of life over another is a matter of supreme importance, not because it is of no importance at all.[20]

Dworkin's point is the now familiar one: that moral skepticism denies what liberalism affirms. In contrast to the skeptic the liberal should accept that the choice of virtue and the ideals of the good life is of great importance to the individual. Thus Dworkin—just like most recent liberals—is keen to avoid the consequences of the liberal paradox. This fact seems to be a good reason for beginning where this debate leaves off.

Liberalism Today: Escaping the Paradox

Recent liberals do not appeal to skepticism. They pursue other argumentative strategies in order to defend the idea that politics should not be concerned with virtue and the good life. In my view, there are only two interesting alternatives. The first is political liberalism, rejecting the idea of a politics of virtue for political reasons; the second is ethical liberalism, rejecting the idea of a politics of virtue for ethical reasons. However, it is sometimes argued that there is a third, and distinct, argument. In this view, the idea of a politics of virtue should be rejected simply because this idea is impracticable. I will briefly discuss this third version of liberalism only in order to defend the conclusion that it does not constitute a distinct argument.[21]

The first view accepts that there are conceptions of virtue and ideas of the good life that are real and important. The skeptical view is thus rejected. Instead, it is argued that the state should reject the idea of a politics of virtue for political reasons: ideas of virtue and the good life are incompatible with the ideal of political justification. The basic idea is that defending a conception of political life is a special kind of activity. Justifications of that kind should be distinguished from others that we frequently undertake (e.g., justifying our personal choices concerning friends, work, etc). Political institutions are coercive and shape our life in a fundamental sense. This is why justifying political institutions is a special kind of activity that should conform to certain norms of reasoning. Political discourse requires legitimacy of a kind that does not pertain to other forms of discourse. Now, according to John Rawls, the idea of a politics of virtue is incompatible with these norms of political justification. The notion of a politics of virtue is rejected because it conflicts with the requirement of *political liberalism*.[22]

In the second view, just like the first, the existence of ethical ideals and virtues is accepted. However, the problem with most such ideas, according to the liberal, is that they include the wrong set of virtues. It is assumed that there is a set of liberal virtues, e.g., individual responsibility and reflection. Nevertheless, according to *ethical liberalism* the state should not actively support these virtues. It is believed that liberal virtues grow and realize themselves only when individuals find out for themselves what is good and bad in life. This reasoning, found in the writings of the contemporary liberal Ronald Dworkin, rejects the politics of virtue but justifies this view by appealing to the value of certain virtues. This argument is thus *ethical*. The politics of virtue is rejected, according to ethical liberalism, because the pursuit of virtue would undermine the liberal way of life.

The third, and last, alternative is to argue that the idea of a politics of virtue should be rejected because it challenges the stability and peace of society. Ideals of virtues and of the good life are controversial and often disputed. A state that engages these issues will consequently run the risk of provoking social conflicts in society. The notion of a "liberalism of fear" captures the basic intuition on which this idea is based: we prefer liberal and neutral institutions because they appear to be less costly in terms of human suffering.[23] Arguably, arguments like these are rather frequent in political life. But is this position distinct from those already presented? I doubt it.

In fact, I believe there is something bogus about justifying principles or institutions negatively, by appealing to the bad things that alternative solutions might bring, and not to the good they themselves create. The claim that conflicts need to be avoided can only be justified by the claim that peace, and the structure of society implied by this peace, is a better alternative. But if a peaceful society is good this must be because of its distinct virtues such as justice, respect for rights or happiness. Peace is not in itself a description of a way of life though it may include one. Now, the values included will be either political or ethical: they are either political values such as equality and justice, or ethical values that define a distinct liberal ideal of the good life. If peace includes no such virtues it will be unclear why it is desirable.[24] Thus, my contention is that the claim that liberal neutrality is justified merely by the fact that it works or constitutes a viable *modus vivendi* (peaceful coexistence) is fundamentally incomplete and unsatisfactory or that it surreptitiously relies on values covered by the previous categories of ethical and political liberalism.

I began by asking whether there are good reasons why liberals should reject the idea of a politics of virtue. In order to answer this question in a systematic way we need to know what is meant by "liberalism." Yet, I argued that a definitional course is not necessarily the most appropriate and that it might be more fruitful to devote our attention to existing liberal theories. I argued, further, that the liberal answer to the question "should the state promote virtues?" might be couched in either skeptical, political or ethical terms. However, my conclusion in the previous section is that recent research has established that the skeptical alternative is unfruitful. Only the remaining theories, the political and the ethical, successfully escape these problems and present moral reasons.

We are now ready to bring together possibilities and theories. By relating these distinctions to each other we are provided with a good view of which positions we need to investigate.

Thus a comprehensive investigation of liberalism's relation to the idea of a politics of virtue calls for a reply to four distinct questions. The first two questions deal with the extent to which liberals believe that there are liberal virtues and a corresponding liberal idea of the good life. At this level, we are faced with two different replies. Political liberals deny that considerations of which virtues are good or bad are of relevance to the liberal ideal. By contrast, ethical liberals believe that liberalism is essentially about the realization of virtue and the good.

At the next level, two more questions emerge. Here, the focus is not on the liberal doctrine but on the liberal state. Should the liberal state promote virtues or not? In contrast to what should be expected on the first level, political and ethical liberalism do not diverge on this issue. Both reject the idea of a politics of virtue. That is, political and ethical liberalism defend similar positions but they do it in different ways. Hence, my task will be to assess the force of these positions. Are they convincing? Do ethical and political liberalism give

Figure 1.2
Liberal Possibilities and Theories Combined

	Political liberalism	Ethical liberalism
Are there liberal virtues?	No	Yes
May the state promote virtues?	No	Yes

us good reasons to reject the idea of a politics of virtue? However, before embarking on these issues the nature of these questions will have to be investigated further. It is necessary to clarify the notion of virtue and to relate the present study to previous research—a task that I will undertake in chapter two.

The Nature of Normative Research

The aim of this study is in one sense to assess the cogency of a political view. This involves rejecting or affirming beliefs and arguments about what the state ought or ought not to do. The aim of this study is thus normative. An investigation to the effect that this or that *should* be the case is different from an investigation to the effect that this or that *is* the case. Yet I do not think the differences should be overstated: a few points are necessary to make this clear. The task of the researcher is to assess the validity of particular arguments and interpretations. This is so whether the question at stake concerns what *is* (descriptive research) or what *should* be (normative research). Normative research, just like other kinds of research and ordinary thinking as well, is about assessing the power of arguments.[25]

What the researcher cannot do, of course, is to prove that a given value has absolute validity. Although this is obvious, the implications of this claim are sometimes misunderstood. Thus critics draw the further conclusion that normative research lacks objectivity and rests on insecure foundations. To support this claim it is frequently pointed out that what is morally right or wrong only reflects the speaker's own convictions or emotions. If ethical and moral claims are subjective, or just emotive, normative research will produce nothing but subjective or emotive conclusions. I call this claim "the argument from subjectivity."[26]

However, the argument from subjectivity provides no valid objection to normative research. Although it is true that an examination of normative political theories will involve "values," this is no less true for any descriptive or explicative analysis of social phenomena. As has long been recognized, values are involved in the choice of what to study, which theories to consider, as well as in the assessment of evidence. The argument from subjectivity will thus constitute an objection to the objectivity of social sciences in general, and not merely to normative research, if understood thus. To

make intersubjective the basis of the researcher's choices and decisions is necessary—and possible—for all kinds of research.[27]

The skeptic may insist that there is a decisive difference between
normative and non-normative investigations. When conclusions from
descriptive or explicative research are drawn they are typically expressed in the form of statements about what is. This or that is now
seen to be, or not to be, the case. Such statements refer to what has
been observed or computed. By contrast, normative conclusions are
expressed in terms of what should or should not be the case. But
these statements do not refer to anything "out there." Propositions
about what should be the case (e.g., fascism is wrong) cannot be
true or false in a sense that descriptive or explicative propositions
can. The subjectivity of normative research is thus revealed by the
fact that normative conclusions are mere opinions without truth-value.

Yet, as has been made abundantly clear by Stefan Björklund, the
metaphysical basis of normative assertions is no more uncertain than
that of descriptive assertions.[28] In neither case does the researcher
have clear or unmediated access to reality as it is: scientific results
do not mirror the world in a simple way. Descriptions, just like recommendations, are dependent on assumptions about the use of
words, concepts and values in order for them to be valid. In order to
demonstrate that there is a fork on my table I have to assume that
everyone knows what "fork" means. Moreover, I have to assume
that everyone accepts my observations as an adequate source of
knowledge—which would not happen in sciences where direct
observation clearly can establish nothing whatsoever (e.g.,
microbiology or quantum mechanics). Scientific research consequently presupposes that a number of assumptions are taken for
granted and not put into question. This does not mean that assumptions cannot or should not themselves be discussed or examined.
However, it does mean that even such an investigation presupposes
some (other) set of assumptions. Not everything can be examined or
criticized at the same time.[29]

The point is that both normative and descriptive examinations
depend on which assumptions are made in the first place. That many
people tend to be more suspicious of normative investigations might
perhaps be explained by their failure to appreciate that even empirical research is based on a number of assumptions. Critics compare
the assumptions concerning values of normative approaches with

the theories used in empirical or descriptive research, and conclude that since only the latter are based on evidence the former are not really "scientific." But this is to commit the "fallacy of disparateness."[30] The ultimate assumptions of normative investigations are compared with assumptions of empirical research which are not ultimate but intermediate. There is in other words a disparity of levels that accounts for the misleading result. If the comparison had been made correctly—taking the ultimate assumptions in both cases—it would have been obvious that neither rests on solid ground.[31]

Another reason why normative arguments are commonly regarded as more dubious is perhaps that it is easier to establish agreement about empirical assumptions than about normative. The false impression that normative conclusions are generally less justified is then explained by the fact, pointed out by Björklund, that "we, in our culture, accept as undisputed many empirical but few moral and even fewer aesthetical assumptions."[32] It is consequently harder, in general, to establish a consensus on what can be taken for granted in normative research. This means that the results of normative investigations will perhaps be more controversial compared to those arrived at through empirical research. Yet the degree to which conclusions are controversial does not necessarily depend on the degree to which they are valid. A normative conclusion can be valid in the sense that it follows from the assumptions made initially even when it is controversial. Quite frequently, this is the case with empirical conclusions too.

An Outline of This Study

Schematically, this book has two parts. The purpose of the first, comprising chapters two, three and four, is to establish whether liberalism does recognize virtues or not. Is there a basis for the claim that liberals ignore the political importance of virtues? The second part, comprising chapters five, six, seven, eight and nine, is concerned with assessing the power of liberal arguments. Are there good arguments against the politics of virtue? What arguments are used in order to demonstrate that the state should not support or promote some particular conception of virtue?

The investigation begins in chapter two with a general assessment of recent accounts of the relation between virtues and liberalism. The ambition is to delimit my investigation primarily with regard to the kind of virtues that are interesting and fruitful to analyze in the context of liberalism. I argue that the interesting question is not *whether* liberals recognize virtues but which virtues they do accept. In particular, I contend that the crucial issue is whether liberals recognize virtues as political ends and not merely as political means. In order to substantiate this idea I examine a number of typical liberal virtues, such as the willingness to compromise and the idea of tolerance.

In chapters three and four I assess ethical and political liberalism as exemplified by the writings of Ronald Dworkin and John Rawls. It is a common belief that Dworkin and Rawls do not include any virtues in their liberal ideal. The liberal state, as conceived by them, does not defend any specific conception of the good life. The liberal state cares only for the rights of individuals. My aim, at this stage, is to establish to what extent these claims are true.

Chapter five marks the beginning of the examination of liberal arguments against a politics of virtue. It has been argued that the idea of a politics of virtue conflicts with the idea of individual rights. The argument from rights can, moreover, be seen as common to different liberal theories. Whatever the basis of liberalism may be (e.g., ethical or political) the institution of individual rights is at its heart. Now, there is a frequent claim to the effect that any political ideal aspiring to make men virtuous produces terror and violence. This claim is analyzed and subsequently challenged.

The liberal state protects the rights of individuals. Ideally, the liberal state is also neutral with respect to questions concerning virtue and the good life. The idea of neutrality is in other words a distinct value. However the doctrine of neutrality is controversial. In what sense could the state be neutral? What does the idea of a neutral state refer to? An answer to these questions is given in chapter six.

In chapter seven I explore three different arguments for the neutral state as found in the work of Ronald Dworkin. The core of liberalism is the value of equality according to Dworkin. The state has an obligation to treat citizens as equals, and this is why the state should not adopt doctrines of virtue. I discuss the meaning and implications of the claim that equality justifies neutrality. I contend that arguments based on equality, important as they are for liberalism, do not justify the idea of a neutral state.

My analysis of the idea of the neutral state is continued in chapter eight where the theory of John Rawls is put under scrutiny. Rawls endeavors to establish an ideal about how the state and its institutions should be justified in a public and reasoned way. The constraints imposed by this ideal debar considerations of virtue and goodness from the political scenery according to Rawls. The idea of a politics of virtue does in other words conflict with the liberal ideal of legitimate government. In this chapter I intend to demonstrate why this conclusion does not bear examination.

The last argument for the neutral state assessed in this work relies on a modified version of moral skepticism. The reason why we must not accept the responsibility of the state for questions about the good life is, from this standpoint, that we cannot have adequate knowledge of which virtues are really good. In this chapter—chapter nine—I explain why the attempt to justify the neutral state by referring to this modified skepticism must fail.

In the last and tenth chapter of this book I summarize the answers to the two questions posed initially. The first question is to what extent liberalism recognizes the value of virtues. The second question is whether the liberal's case for the neutral state is convincing or not. The conclusion I arrive at concerning the first question is that it depends. Liberalism is not hostile to all virtues. However my conclusion is that some virtues, when dependent on a certain vision of the good life, are generally hard to accommodate within a liberal framework. With regard to the second question the answer is less ambiguous. In my view, liberal principles and values do not provide a conclusive case for the neutrality of the state. This leaves the liberal in the troublesome position of having to choose whether to remain faithful to the principle of neutrality or to believe that the liberal ideal is rational.

Notes

1.   For this term see, among others, John Norton, 1991, p 199.
2.   "In the past decade or two, conflicts have developed in advanced Western societies that deviate in various ways from the welfare-state patterns of institutionalized conflict resolution . . . These new conflicts arise in domains of cultural reproduction, social integration, and socialization; they are carried out in sub-institutional—or at least extraparliamentary—forms of protest . . . The issue is not primarily one of compensations that the welfare state can provide, but of defending and restoring ways of life. In short, the new conflicts are not ignited by distribution problems but by questions having to do with the grammar of forms of life." Jürgen Habermas, 1987 [1981], p 392.
3.   See Thomas Englund, 1986. A more general discussion about education and character is found in Eamond Callan, 1997, and in David C Paris, 1991.

4.   Li Bennich-Björkman, 1991, pp 58f, 322; Roger Blomgren, 1998, esp chapter 8.
5.   Bernard Williams, 1985, p 9.
6.   See Alasdair MacIntyre, 1985, chapters 2–9; Charles Taylor, 1994, pp 20–25.
7.   As Susan Mendus observes, a definition of a liberal as a person who believes in liberty is saying both too much and too little. It says too much, since many famous liberals have based their ideology on other values (e.g., equality or progress). It says too little, because the meaning of "liberty" is far from unambiguous. See Susan Mendus, 1989, pp 71–74. On further difficulties involved in defining liberalism see, John Zvesper, 1987, p 285.
8.   This is to say that better definitions are not necessarily conducive to the clarification of obscurities in meaning or to solve disputes among conflicting interpretations. "[D]efintions are not always needed, and, in most cases, issues do not turn upon the way in which words are defined." Robert Fogelin, 1987, p 85.
9.   D J Manning, 1976, pp 58f.
10.   Karl Popper, 1995 [1945], p 250.
11.   Popper claimed that the demand for definitions will produce an infinite regress: once a definition is asked for we may always ask for a definition of the terms used in this definition. Popper also observed that much faith in the need for definitions allows people (especially politicians, according to Popper) to achieve credibility of their ideas simply by presenting a definition however good or bad it is. Popper 1995, pp 246ff.
12.   See also David Miller's claim that, "arguments about the proper interpretation of a political idea cannot fruitfully remain as arguments about language, but must become more general debates about the relative merits of different ways of conceiving society." D Miller, 1976, p 10.
13.   The denial of the existence of values should be distinguished from skepticism in the classical sense: the idea that we cannot know anything about values (although values may exist). This latter form of skepticism is epistemological (i.e., about knowledge) and not ontological (i.e., about what is). See Lars Bergström, 1990, pp 64–68; and David O Brink, 1989, pp 14–22, 32ff and *passim*.
14.   Thomas Hobbes, 1985 [1651], chap 4, p 109. See also Peter Berkowitz, 1999, pp 40f.
15.   Bertrand Russell, 1957, p 49.
16.   The liberal paradox is described as such in a number of works. See, for example, James Fishkin, 1986, p 227; Mats Lundström, 1993, p 179; Charles Taylor, 1991, pp 38f. The expression "the liberal paradox" occasionally refers to the distinct problem of tolerance (should we tolerate the intolerant?). For example, see Jean Hampton, 1989a, p 103.
17.   Gordon Graham, 1996, pp 47ff; Herbert Tingsten, 1933, pp 26–29.
18.   Tingsten, 1933, p 102.
19.   Mendus, 1989, p 78.
20.   Ronald Dworkin, 1983, p 47. The insufficiency of skepticism for liberal purposes is also emphasized by Will Kymlicka who argues that "if all ways of life are equally valuable then no one can complain when the government chooses a particular way of life for the community." Will Kymlicka, 1990, p 202.
21.   My belief is that these categories capture the most influential and challenging conceptions of liberalism in contemporary thought. Yet I do not pretend that it captures every possible liberal perspective. Arguably, there are other alternatives such as, for example, the "contingent" liberalism worked out by Richard Rorty. In this view liberalism "can only be something local and ethnocentric—the tradition of a particular political community." That is, the only defense for liberal ideas is that we happen

to have them. Whether true or not, it seems to me that this view is theoretically not very interesting. Richard Rorty, 1991, pp 176 and 190.

22. The expression "political liberalism" is occasionally used simply in contrast to economic liberalism; where the main concern of the first is the individual and that of the latter is the prosperity of society. See, for this view, Russell Hardin, 1999, p 43. Following Hardin's terminology both versions of liberalism identified by me (ethical and political) are political liberalisms.

23. Judith Shklar, 1989, pp 33f.

24. Michael Walzer elegantly argues against the view that liberalism can be negatively defined in Michael Walzer, 1996, pp 17–24. See also H J McCloskey, 1974, pp 17f.

25. The importance of arguments in everyday reasoning as well as in science is made clear in Deanne Kuhn, 1991, pp 2–10 and chap 10.

26. The classic formula is that science can study, but not establish, values. See Arnold Brecht 1959, pp 117–162. In Sweden this idea was influentially stated by Axel Hägerström (1966). Also Jörgen Westerståhl, 1993, pp 279–282.

27. A different view is to say that values that cause the researcher to pursue this or that perspective does not really affect how the investigation is pursued. Descriptions or explanations may remain value free even though there were values involved in the initial design of the investigation. See Evert Vedung, 1981, pp 197ff.

28. Stefan Björklund, 1993, pp 82f.

29. Stefan Björklund, 1991, pp 51–54, 107–110.

30. Alan Gewirth, 1960, pp. 313ff.

31. Gilbert Harman makes a similar point, arguing that "observational evidence" does not seem to explain normative conclusions (e.g., that "equality is incompatible liberty") in the same sense that it helps to explain descriptive conclusions (e.g., that "heat may produce dehydration"). Gilbert Harman, 1977, chapter 1. Together with the propensity to believe that only observational evidence can justify knowledge this idea might to some extent explain why we are more suspicious of normative than descriptive statements—their shared metaphysical uncertainty notwithstanding.

32. Björklund, 1991, p 109.

2

Virtue in Liberal Thought: A Primer

The claim that the government ought to promote virtue is frequently understood as an objection to liberal principles and values. The alleged defect of liberalism is that it denies the relevance of virtues to political life. As I have argued, this assertion should be broken down into two distinct claims. First, there is the normative issue whether liberal arguments against a politics of virtue are good or not. Second, there is the descriptive issue about whether or not liberalism reasons in terms of virtue. In the first chapter I dealt with the former issue; in this chapter I am concerned with the latter.

However, the purpose is not to provide a definitive answer as to how liberals through the ages have reasoned about virtue. Rather, the aim is to indicate more precisely what a potential answer should be concerned with. Before we can be in a position to assess the various claims about the extent to which liberals recognize virtues as politically relevant, we need to know what is meant by "virtue" in this context. In fact, a weakness of recent critique of liberalism is that it seldom states explicitly which theories or conceptions of virtue that are in question. My aim in this chapter is to compensate for some of these failings, by making more specific the virtues at stake in the debate about the ethical and moral status of liberalism.

The aim of this chapter is, in other words, to establish which conceptions of virtue that constitute a challenge and which conceptions do not. The conclusion drawn here will then be related to the distinctions suggested in chapter one between ethical and political liberal theories. At that point we will, finally, be in a position to characterize the aim of this study as a whole.

The Problem of Liberalism and Virtue: Previous Research

A number of scholars have recently drawn attention to the complicated liberal attitude vis-à-vis virtues and conceptions of the good life. They note that liberals have generally been unfavorably disposed towards the idea that the government might make decisions on the basis of which virtues are good and bad. The conclusions drawn by these scholars do not converge, however. There is, in fact, a certain amount of confusion about the liberal position. More precisely, the *extension* of the liberal distrust of virtue is in dispute. There are writers who claim that *all* liberals reject virtues. Some writers who claim that only *some* liberals reject virtues. And, of course, there are writers who claim that *no* liberals reject virtues.

Thus it has been argued that the rejection of a politics of virtue is fundamental to the liberal ideal. Notions of virtue are simply incompatible with the liberal way of conceiving political relations. Ideas about the individual, rights and liberty loom large in liberal thought and they tend to exclude the idea of a political community engaged in the pursuit of virtue and goodness. Consequently, no liberal writers of prominence have managed to incorporate virtues in their understanding of political life: liberals have never accepted that the state should take responsibility for the good life. Liberalism is confined, it is argued, to a narrow conception of the state as concerned exclusively with the protection of individual rights.[1]

Now other recent writers have contested this view. They reject the view that the liberal tradition as a whole should be considered hostile to notions of virtue. Instead, they suggest that liberalism's failure to appreciate the need for virtue is peculiar to contemporary liberal thought. So-called "classical" liberals, John Locke and John Stuart Mill for example, did not dismiss the beneficial effects of virtue. A more positive attitude to virtue is to be found in the historical texts of the liberal tradition.[2] Though the assessments of classical liberalism diverge, there is consequently a certain agreement about how to understand contemporary liberal thought.

Yet even on this point all judgements do not converge. Contemporary liberal ideas about individual rights and social justice do in fact, it is argued, rest on the affirmation of certain virtues.[3] The liberal citizen has to be tolerant, cooperative and has to accept that other people are entitled to respect and justice. Certainly no liberal society could exist without these virtues.

In sum, recent contentions about liberalism and the politics of virtue can be divided into two distinct disputes: Did liberals, historically, reject the idea of a politics of virtue? Do liberals today reject the idea of a politics of virtue? I will not focus my investigation on the debate about the historical meaning of the liberal tradition. The important issue, as I see it, is not whether liberals *did* but whether they *do* reject the idea of a politics of virtue. This means that only the second question is relevant to my purpose.

Some recent writers, like Stephen Macedo, argue that liberalism does depend on the cultivation of certain virtues, and that this is fully recognized in liberal writings. Other recent writers, such as Alasdair MacIntyre and Thomas Spragens deny that this is the case. Now, I suspect that these claims about the place of virtue within contemporary liberal thought are confused, to a certain extent, when it comes to the *kind* of virtues disputed. I am inclined to think, in other words, that the virtues those defending liberalism recognize are not the ones critics are looking for.

The Prevalence of Instrumental Virtue

Although dismissive about the idea that government should promote the good life, Thomas Hobbes was clear about the political need for some set of virtues. The state should, in the Hobbesian conception, be directed exclusively towards securing peace and safety for its citizens. Though the ends of safety and peace were not themselves the expression of a doctrine of virtue Hobbes clearly saw that some virtues could help citizens and the state to achieve these ends. Virtue thus has its place in political life.

> Appetite is the measure of Good, and Evill: and consequently all men agree on this, that peace is Good, and therefore also the way, or the means of Peace, which are Justice, Gratitude, Modesty, Equity, Mercy, & the rest of the Laws of Nature, are good; that is to say, Morall Vertues.[4]

One peculiar aspect of Hobbes's argument is that virtues are considered merely as "means of Peace" and not as themselves worthy of attention or appraisal.[5] A citizen attentive to the virtues of "Justice" or "Mercy" is good not because these virtues are good but because these virtues are means by which another good, that of peace, will be promoted.

I believe the example of Hobbes suggests that we should distinguish between cases where virtues are valued as a means and cases where virtues are valued as ends. In effect, this corresponds to William Galston's idea that virtues might be regarded as either instrumental or intrinsic values.[6] On the one hand we may think some particular virtue is valuable when it contributes to something else that has a value. This is the Hobbesian version according to which virtues are valuable only because they are necessary in order to establish peace. On the other hand some virtues may be considered valuable because they are valuable in themselves.

Take the example of the virtue of honesty—that of speaking the truth. Most people would probably agree that to be honest is in most cases an important virtue. But to say that people agree on the value of honesty is not the same as saying that most people agree on the reasons for esteeming honesty. One person could say that honesty is desirable because it is essential to a smooth market economy: honesty facilitates the making of contracts by reducing the cost of transactions. Another person could say that honesty is desirable because it is a mark of a good human being: to deceive or lie are reprehensible actions in themselves. The latter view is distinct from the first in that it does not appeal to the consequences or effects of honesty on other values (e.g., that honesty is a good because it gives you more friends, or because it facilitates the making of contracts). The latter view contends that the virtue of honesty is good irrespective of whether honesty is prudent or not. That virtue is simply a mark of a good person. Virtues may consequently be regarded as ends and not merely as means or instrumental values.[7] There is nothing mysterious in such claims: No controversial or supra-natural assumptions are needed in order to realize that the idea of intrinsic virtue is part of ordinary experience.[8]

As is testified by the case of Hobbes, instrumental reasons for virtues may be incorporated in the most skeptic theory. I believe this suggests that instrumental reasons for virtues have not been ignored by liberal writers: The virtues needed to secure liberal institutions have not generally been conceived of as in tension with liberal principles and aspirations. In order to justify this claim I will examine the virtues of cooperation and tolerance. These virtues are frequently thought of as essential to liberal society. But are they intrinsic virtues? I will argue that the disposition to cooperate with others and to be tolerant may be conceived of as virtues—but only as instrumental virtues. The critique that liberalism ignores intrinsic virtues is consequently left unchallenged.

The Virtues of Cooperation

Yet liberals are frequently accused of ignoring *all* virtues—even those endorsed by Hobbes. The complaint that individualist life-styles have corrosive effects on the institutions of liberal democracy is a common one. The argument is that liberal-democratic institutions will not survive in a society where people consistently place personal and immediate satisfaction before collective goods and commitments. A democratic and liberal society needs virtuous citizens who attend to civic virtues such as cooperation, compromise and tolerance. A liberal theory that fails to recognize the instrumental importance of virtues will, as a consequence, fail to recognize the values that allow liberal institutions to thrive.

Traditionally, these claims have been at the heart of the conservative ideal of virtue.[9] Now the importance of cooperative virtues is emphasized by political scientists who claim allegiance to the republican tradition of political thought. Studies performed by Robert Putnam and Quentin Skinner arrive at the same result; that liberal society ultimately depends on the existence of virtuous citizens and that liberals generally fail to recognize this.

Putnam argues that where there is no faith in the fruitfulness of democratic cooperation people tend to seek more immediate benefits from politics. Where everyone thinks so it will be prudent not to compromise and to place personal advantages ahead of collective goods regardless of the costs to others. Political life as well as the economy will not work smoothly where such attitudes prevail. That is why, according to Putnam, civicness is essential to effective democratic government.[10]

The civic citizen Putnam is thinking of is no altruist, caring for others and not caring for himself. "No mortal can," Putnam assertively claims, "renounce the powerful motivation of self-interest." While the citizen need not identify with the interests of other people as much as with his own interests (that is, he need not be impartial) civic citizens ought to be "sensitive" to the interests of fellow-citizens.[11] To be civic is to be prepared not to pursue personal benefits at the expense of others. In cooperative situations the citizen is thus prepared to contribute as much as anyone else, as long as this attitude is reciprocated.[12] The civic citizen does not cheat—or, at least, he does not cheat when no one else does.

Skinner's critique of liberalism is reminiscent of Putnam's. The pursuit of virtue must be accepted by the liberal state or, Skinner argues, the aim of securing individual liberty will be jeopardized. In order to vindicate this claim Skinner makes two assumptions. It is assumed, firstly, that individual freedom is a legitimate aim and, secondly, that the successful realization of this aim presupposes the existence of a free state. It is assumed, that is, that unless citizens devote some attention to what the government does they will risk the integrity of the government and the state. Citizens need to be virtuous in order to materialize the public good of vigilance that comes with political activity and interest.

Hence a liberal should acknowledge that the pursuit of virtue is necessary for the maintenance of a free society. Liberal institutions cannot be sustained without citizens who feel obliged to do what it takes to maintain their independence. Thus Skinner writes that "freedom depends on our willingness to cultivate the civic virtues."[13] Living freely, or the "*vivero libero*," presupposes certain virtues. Free institutions require that citizens "devote [themselves] *wholeheartedly* to a life of public service."[14] Skinner believes this demonstrates why the liberal understanding of freedom is inadequate. The liberal view is that individual freedom is more important than virtue and that, consequently, virtuous acts can only be the contingent outcome of free choice. This view is now contrasted with the claim that certain virtues must be accepted as *necessary* for freedom of choice to be realized.

The ideas presented by Skinner and Putnam share the feature of charging liberalism with a failure to acknowledge the instrumental value of virtues. The problem, as defined by them, is that liberalism licenses self-interested behavior that is detrimental to liberal and democratic institutions.[15] Self-interest must be moderated by attachment to the common good: civic virtue is needed in order to improve the functioning of democratic institutions and in order to secure individual liberty.[16]

Now the ideas presented by Putnam and Skinner are not entirely new. It has been noted that the claim that virtues are necessary in order to secure the institutions of freedom is characteristic for the republican tradition of thought. Generally, republican writers have conceived their thesis as that of reminding democrats and liberals about the preconditions of freedom. Threats to the republic, whether of external or internal origins, have been their concern.[17]

However, the existence of an interesting conflict between republican and liberal ideas is not evident. In fact, many liberal writers seem to accept the need for cooperative virtues and a degree of "civility."[18] This seems to be the case, for instance, when we consider the ideal of the liberal state found in the work of John Rawls. The idea of a just, liberal society "includes," Rawls argues, an account of the "virtues of fair social cooperation."[19] Rawls also stresses the need for the virtue of compromise and being prepared to meet others "halfway."[20]

The presence in Rawls's work of the virtues of cooperation has been noted by others. Rawls is committed, it is argued, to the view that virtues are "necessities for liberal citizens."[21] However, I believe we should qualify Rawls's concern with virtue as a concern with *instrumental* virtues only. Rawls is not saying that cooperative virtues are valuable in themselves; that the disposition to cooperate and compromise is a mark of a good human being. Rawls does say, however, that these virtues "constitute a very great public good, part of society's capital."[22] The notion of "capital" conveys the image of virtues as useful assets. This reasoning is familiar and evokes Putnam's characterization of virtue as equal to or emanating from a society's "social capital." Virtues are assets needed in order to achieve certain collective ends. In the case of Rawls the end is that of a constitutional democracy: The virtues of political cooperation "make a constitutional regime *possible*."[23]

The instrumental flavor of Rawls's conception of virtue is evident and further illustrated by the way Rawls justifies these virtues. Citizens should, granted that they think rationally, realize that they want to live in a society where people are disposed to cooperate. The citizen should acknowledge, Rawls claims, that it is "rational for members of a well-ordered society to want [virtues] in one another."[24] That Rawls is right is easily demonstrated. It is rational for everyone to prefer in other people a preference for cooperation to a preference for maximizing personal benefits that include a disposition to cheating. Each is better off by preferring cooperation to cheating when all people adopt this preference.[25]

The function as well as the justification of virtue is, in Rawls's work, described in instrumental terms. Nowhere does Rawls recognize the intrinsic value of virtues, and everywhere Rawls emphasizes the need for and rationality of accepting the virtues of cooperation.[26]

Rawls shares with Hobbes an instrumental perspective on virtue. As a consequence, the critique by writers like Skinner and Putnam, that liberals do not recognize the dependence of liberty on virtue, seems unfounded. The charge of the republican and the conservative appears to be unjustified with respect to these pivotal theories of the liberal state. Of course, this is not to say that all liberals take into account the value of instrumental virtues. But if the rationale for including at least some account of the virtues of cooperation and compromise is evident, the conclusion must be that liberals *should* recognize them. In that sense, the republican critique might serve as a reminder to the liberal. The claim, that even the liberal state needs virtues for instrumental reasons, does not in other words constitute a very interesting challenge; it does not challenge liberal values or principles. The fact that Hobbes and Rawls devote only a few sentences to make clear the role of virtues testifies to the fact that this issue is rather uncontroversial.

I believe the relevance of the distinction between instrumental and intrinsic reasons for virtues is clear. In what follows I will examine the notion of *tolerance* in order to further support the idea that the liberal perspective on virtue is predominantly instrumental in kind.

Is Tolerance a Virtue?

Whether tolerance is a virtue or not is a crucial test for the claim that liberals tend to ignore intrinsic virtues. If tolerance is an intrinsic virtue then, surely, the objection that liberalism ignores all virtues is misconceived. If, on the other hand, tolerance is not a virtue in this sense we will be more confident in our hypothesis.

All this presupposes, for sure, that the idea of toleration is characteristic of liberalism. I think that cannot be doubted. The idea of a tolerant society, where citizens do not persecute each other for the sake of their religious, cultural or ethnic affiliation, is a liberal one, if not exclusively so. Historically, the notion of toleration is in fact so strongly connected with that of liberalism that it is possible to say that the latter emanated out of the former. The religious conflicts that eventually paved the way for toleration also provided a basis for the ideas of freedom of speech and other rights that were later identified with the liberal ideology.[27]

But is the attitude of tolerance a virtue? Rawls and others thought so. "Liberalism includes," according to Rawls, an account of "the virtue of tolerance."[28] The reason for considering tolerance a virtue might seem obvious: surely it is a good thing that people do not persecute each other. Although the value of tolerance is easily seen, the appropriateness of describing it as an intrinsic virtue has been disputed.[29] In order to adjudicate on this matter we need to know more about the reasons for tolerance; what the motives and reasons are that justify a tolerant attitude.

Schematically, I believe it is helpful to distinguish between three kinds of attitudes that might underpin tolerance. Tolerant behavior may be the result of, firstly, a feeling that differences must be accepted for some independent reason or, secondly, a sense of indifference to differences or, thirdly, a conviction that differences are good and ought to be endorsed. Thus, *acceptance, indifference* or *endorsement* may underpin the practice of toleration.[30] Although the behavior that may be the result of these attitudes could be identical, we should hesitate to conclude that these attitudes are equally appropriate in all circumstances. The extent to which people will find tolerance a good thing may in other words depend on what kind of tolerance is at stake.

The most apparent difficulty concerns toleration of racial differences. That people tolerate differences in skin color is definitely good and, yet, many people will be disappointed to hear you say that you merely "accept" such differences.[31] In general, black people do not want to be accepted despite the color of their skin. What they want is that the color of their skin be ignored or, perhaps, endorsed as something good. In relation to racial differences mere acceptance would be considered as a second best: We wish that Nazis were more tolerant and yet it would be better if Nazis renounced their racial prejudices altogether. A Nazi indifferent to racial differences would be preferable to a Nazi tolerant of racial differences.

Cases like these illustrate the tendency to conceive of tolerance as a "negative virtue."[32] The virtue of tolerance is needed only when things are not as they should be. As a consequence, tolerance in the sense of acceptance is not necessarily a virtue to encourage. Indifference or perhaps even ignorance about the relevance of certain differences would sometimes be preferable. But could it not be the case, then, that indifference is a virtue? After all, the world might be a much less violent place if everyone were less caring and attentive to the opinions or tastes of others. That may well be so, though it does not demonstrate that indifference should be equaled with the virtue of tolerance. In the first place, it does seem difficult to accept that being ignorant of a phenomenon or just lacking interest in it should be considered to be a valuable attitude. In fact, to be indifferent is precisely *not* to have an attitude about a certain issue; there is consequently no attitude to call virtuous. As Bernard Williams pointed out, "if you do not care all that much what anyone believes, you do not need the attitude of toleration, any more than you do with regard to other people's taste for food."[33] All we are entitled to say is, I believe, that indifference is a virtue in the metaphorical sense of being something that we approve of. However, indifference is no virtue if by that we speak of a particular attitude or character trait, as I think we should. Thus it is hard to say that indifference could ever be the same as the *virtue* of tolerance.

A more appropriate attitude than that of being indifferent to difference is, in many circumstances, that of endorsing them. That people are of a different persuasion or religious affiliation is, in this view, neither just accepted, nor ignored with a sense of indifference. Tolerance as an attitude of endorsement embraces and encourages people to be different. The fact that society entails divergent or even conflicting views is considered as something good and desirable.

Common as this attitude may be among liberals it is difficult to see it as concerned with tolerance. After all, a person who feels sympathy for a cultural feature or a number of religious creeds is not really tolerating them. We do not tolerate what we like. I do not, for example, tolerate the whims of my wife: I like them because they're hers. Similarly, I do not tolerate the expressions of oriental culture in my city: I enjoy them. This is a conceptual and not a normative point. Toleration is restraint in face of what is disliked or disapproved of.[34]

So that which to many is the most attractive form of toleration—tolerance as endorsement—should not be described as a form of tolerance at all. People who endorse cultural, political or religious differences are making society more tolerant in the sense of "making room for others." Yet, since these people are not tolerating but endorsing, we cannot say that they exhibit the virtue of tolerance.[35]

Indifference and endorsement having been ruled out as virtues of tolerance we must consider the idea of tolerance as acceptance. Though acceptance is perhaps only a second-best in relation to racial differences this does not prove that acceptance is never a virtue.

Presumably, it is a good thing that people with divergent religious views accept that others might be of a different persuasion and that they should not be burnt at the stake because of it. In that case, mere acceptance is certainly a virtue.

One problem that has been noted is that acceptance presupposes dislike and that, consequently, a person who dislikes a lot has the potential of being more tolerant than a person that does not dislike much at all. Thus, one way to increase the latitude of tolerance is to consider more things objectionable without interfering with them.[36] What this suggests is that maximizing toleration is not necessarily a good thing: We should not make indifferent people more aware of things they dislike only in order to applaud their tolerance! However paradoxical this may sound, I do not believe it is sufficient to demonstrate that acceptance should never be encouraged. It does not prove, for example, that taking a tolerant attitude when you already disapprove of some behavior or opinion is not something to encourage and appraise. Tolerance as acceptance is consequently capable of being a good. That is not the issue. The question should be, rather, what *kind* of good it is. Finding an answer to this question prompts us to investigate the reasons for being tolerant in this sense.

Basically, there are two reasons for *accepting* differences one does not approve of (as opposed to being indifferent to them or endorsing them). One reason is that the alternative seems to be worse for oneself. This is toleration by self-interest. A different reason is that tolerance seems called for by the principles one has already conceded. This is toleration by principle.

Tolerance as an attitude based on self-interest is probably a common phenomenon. In situations where deep conflicts of religious or political nature prevail the alternative to an attitude of mutual tolerance may be violent and, indeed, "intolerable." Accepting tolerance out of concern for one's interests in and desire for survival may certainly be laudable. Yet are we prepared to say that the attitude which produces this outcome is itself virtuous? Are you exhibiting virtue when you refrain from cracking down on what you dislike merely for fear of the consequences of doing so?[37] I think tolerance does not, when founded on self-interested calculus, deserve to be called a virtue. Or, perhaps it suffices to say that tolerance when based entirely on self-interest is just an instrumental virtue. It is a virtue in the sense that it allows us to achieve something good: a state of civil peace. However, it is not a virtue in the sense of being a trait of character that we consider admirable.[38]

The last, and most important, version of tolerance as acceptance is based not on self-interest but on principles. In this case we imagine that a person decides to be tolerant because he or she is committed to certain principles that demand this reaction. When tolerance is extended in a society this would, consequently, indicate that people accept fair and liberal principles. Virtue is, in this view, short for "acting on correct moral principles." I believe the notion of tolerance by principle is the strongest candidate for the title "the intrinsic virtue of tolerance." Nevertheless, there are features of such a notion of tolerance that suggest that this conclusion is not adequate.

To begin with, we should note that the idea of tolerance by principle can be given two distinct interpretations. According to the first, a person tolerates another when he or she accepts that people have rights that should not be interfered with. In the second interpretation, a person tolerates another when he or she accepts principles that he or she believes condemn interfering with that person. The distinction might not be obvious. In both cases tolerance is associated with moral principles—after all, even rights depend for their validity on certain fundamental principles. However, the difference is that only the first conception of tolerance describes it exclusively in terms of rights. From this standpoint tolerance means accepting the rights people have (or should have) and acting in accordance with them. In the second view, by contrast, the concept of rights is not used in order to explain tolerance. Instead, it characterizes tolerance as acting on a principle that demands respect and acceptance for others and their differences. The importance of keeping these accounts separate will become clear in the subsequent analysis. However, it should be remembered that the question at stake here is not how to best characterize the notion of tolerance. The question of relevance to us is whether tolerance can, on any account, be represented as an intrinsic virtue.

The idea that tolerance is a matter of respect for rights is a common one. According to the SNS Democracy Audit, tolerance is identified with the "duty to respect the rights of others."[39] Similarly, the philosopher David Richards argues that toleration essentially constitutes the view that "unreasonable abridgements of human rights" should be condemned.[40] Whether people approve of the opinions or behavior of others or not, they should recognize that people have rights that require acceptance and tolerance. Accordingly, the greater the number of other people's rights you accept, the more tolerant you are. I shall take the reasonableness of this view for granted: I will assume that there is a sense in which toleration can be said to increase, once people respect each other's rights to a higher degree. The question of concern here is whether this also implies an increase in *virtue*.[41] Should we characterize a person's respect for the rights of another person as a matter of virtue? I doubt this and I will present two claims to support this contention.

Initially we may note that respecting the rights of another appears to be merely a question of what is *done*. An agent, the state for instance, is said to respect the right to free speech by not interfering with what is said or written in a given society. Similarly, the right to education is respected to the extent that a certain amount of resources is provided. In both cases, the extent to which a particular right is respected can be determined simply by observing the behavior of the relevant agent. Now, it has been argued that mere conformity with principles or ideals cannot in itself be regarded as virtuous. To act so that someone's rights are respected may be a good thing. Yet in order for us to say this act was also virtuous we would like to know something about the motives or intentions. There must be, or so it may be argued, some morally worthy motive in order for us to speak about virtue.[42]

But perhaps the motive acted on is simply the desire to respect the rights of others. In that case, there certainly is a morally worthy motive. Does this fact justify the conclusion that tolerance, as respect for rights, is indeed an intrinsic virtue? I believe it does *not*, and the reason for this is explicated below.

People who have rights owe something to each other. A person who has a right is entitled to your respect for that right. Respecting a person's rights is in that sense a response to the claims that, however implicit, that person has on you. This is to say, using the terminology of Kant, that rights are perfect obligations: rights correspond to duties.[43] The right of A to do X implies that B has a duty to let A do X. Thus, A can claim that B respects his or her doing X. Virtues are not like rights in this respect. Being virtuous is acting out of good motives. But motives cannot be owed by others. People are not entitled to the existence of certain kinds of motives and there is not, consequently, a right to the virtuousness of others. At best, virtues are imperfect obligations, duties we owe to ourselves but not to others.

Why this must be so is easy to see. Though it is possible to claim that another person respects your rights by not interfering with what you are doing, or by providing you with some good, it is senseless to claim that another person is respecting your rights by adopting a certain attitude towards you. It's what is *done* that matters when we speak about rights.

The conclusion of this excursion is that one person cannot have the right to another person's virtuousness. This is why benevolence, sincerity, solidarity, love, and other virtues, should not be perceived as rights. Thus, if tolerance is modeled on the principle that people have a right to be tolerated, tolerance is not a virtue. Acting so as to not interfere with the rights of others is certainly a good thing. Yet, respecting others' rights is to respond to a claim, and this is why such respect should not be considered a virtue.

However, the notion of tolerance by principle is not exhausted by the idea of tolerance as respect for people's rights. There are principles that do not refer to or involve the concept of rights and that might, arguably, present a more convincing case for the virtue of toleration. People may for example believe that the principle of equal respect implies that they should adopt a tolerant attitude. Thus, the prospect of a moral principle being at the heart of toleration probes the question whether acting on principle can provide the basis of virtue. As has been noted, many liberal writers think it is. Many liberals have argued that virtue is to act out of a sense of what is right and just.[44] In our time, this notion finds its most sophisticated expression in Rawls's theory. "The virtues," Rawls argues, are sentiments that give us a desire to "act from the corresponding moral principles."[45] To be virtuous is consequently to act from a conviction that something is required by your moral principles. Now what is that like?

Acting on principle is to act self-reflectively with the intention of satisfying the demands of some normative principle. In the case of toleration, this means that when you face a person you dislike you try to find out what it means to treat him as an equal despite the dislike you have. Acting out of concern for equality means being engaged in interpreting what is required by a commitment to that principle. That is, you use the principle to assess the appropriateness of various responses to given situations. In our case the principle of equality would inform you about how and when to be tolerant. Tolerance by principle thereby resembles what Horton finds to be essential to *any* conception of toleration; "toleration must attend to questions about what is reasonable to object to, as well as about which of those things that are objectionable should be tolerated and which should not."[46]

Now, I suggest that this activity, where principles are used to judge the extent to which a certain attitude is appropriate, cannot be called virtuous in the intrinsic sense. The reason is that such an account would allow for virtues being only conditionally good. When virtues are seen as attitudes dependent on principles (e.g., that tolerance depends on the principle of equal respect for persons) the goodness of virtue exists only when it adequately corresponds to them. For instance, you may hesitate to be generous in relation to a racist because you feel he should feel the costs of his commitments. Your principles thus debar you from being virtuous. If virtue is understood as acting on principle then, of course, generosity is no virtue.

But is this account of generosity appropriate? An alternative and, to my mind, more appropriate view is to say that generosity is always a good even when it is trumped by the demands of some principle. Thus, when you choose to act according to your principles you are not annihilating the goodness of the virtues you might have acted on instead. Generosity is a good in relation to a racist even though you might wish that people were less generous towards them. In other words, that being virtuous is good does not mean that it is the best thing to be. Conversely, that virtues are not always appropriate does not mean that they are no good at all.

If some virtues are valuable as ends and not as means they must remain so even when our principles tell us not to be virtuous. That some people do not act out of the right principles, and therefore are virtuous when we think they should not, must not hide from our sight the fact that these acts are still virtuous. Generosity, honesty, or solidarity might occasionally be stupid, imprudent or even immoral. But to be virtuous at the wrong time and in the wrong place is not the same as not being virtuous. As observed by John Atwell, "that it is bad that [these virtues] are used in bad ways does not entail that [the virtues] *have become bad.*"[47]

Preserving the goodness of virtue in this way would not be possible from the perspective of virtues by principle. If tolerance is derived from a principle of equality you will, in some cases, not be tolerant because you believe equality requires some other reaction from you. When you witness people getting abused you might come to the conclusion that your commitment to equality prescribes opposition rather than tolerance. You will not say then that being tolerant would still have been good. In that case, then, there is no conflict between the demands of toleration, on one hand, and the demands of equality on the other. This is so because tolerance, when modeled on the basis of the principle of equality, *is* appropriate only when required by the principles of equality. If equality demands something else, then this situation would not be one in which tolerance would have been a good.

To sum up: toleration based on either indifference or endorsement should not be considered as a virtue of tolerance. This is accounted for by the fact that indifference is not really a *virtue* and endorsement is not really *tolerance*. I also examined the much more complex notion of tolerance as acceptance. Here, I distinguished between acceptance based on self-interest and acceptance based on conviction or principle. I have argued that selfish acceptance of differences will, at best, justify tolerance as an instrumental virtue. It would be odd to regard tolerance as admirable when it is adopted merely out of fear or of prudence: tolerance for prudential reasons is not virtuous, it's just prudent.

The second version of acceptance—tolerance by principle—undoubtedly represents a more attractive picture of the basis for toleration. Yet there are two points to consider before this notion can be accepted as an example of the virtue of tolerance. To begin with, I have endeavored to demonstrate that tolerance, when based on respect for rights, should be regarded as a duty rather than a virtue. Respecting the rights of others means responding to a claim. But there cannot be a claim to another person's virtue and, therefore, respect for rights is no virtue in more than a metaphorical sense.

A more decisive objection is that tolerance by principle seems to conflict with an ineliminable aspect of the notion of intrinsic virtues—their unconditionality.[48] That intrinsic virtues are unconditionally good does not mean that they are always appropriate or right. Being virtuous might conflict with your interests or the principles you subscribe to. Now my claim is that this possibility, that virtues should not always prevail, must not be confused with the view that virtues are not always good. Virtues are attitudes or motives that we find good in their own right. If this is true, there can be no virtues by principle.

How does this conclusion pertain to tolerance? My belief is that tolerance by principle does not fit the idea of intrinsic virtue. This is so because I do believe that it is frequently correct to think of tolerance as depending on certain principles. Tolerance is a virtue only in relation to the principles we believe in, and this implies that tolerance is not good in all cases. A further implication is, in my view, that tolerance is not an intrinsic virtue.

I have had two reasons for examining whether tolerance is a virtue or not. First, I wanted to respond to the potential charge against this work that liberalism is *obviously* embracing a set of virtues. In arguing against understanding tolerance as a virtue I believe one important claim to that effect has been responded to. Secondly, I believed that engaging from the outset in a discussion about the meaning of "virtue" would shed some light on, and perhaps also make more precise, the issue at stake in this study. However, my ambition has not been to explore all potential virtues in liberal thought. The aim of this analysis has been to prepare the ground for the subsequent investigation of a number of particularly liberal theories. Thus, the virtue of justice, arguably the most important liberal virtue, will be examined in more detail in chapters three and four.

The Question Reconsidered

I contend that instrumental reasons for virtue prevail in liberal writings and that, by implication, the claim that liberals ignore virtues is not correct at that level of abstraction. The interesting issue concerns how and why liberals endorse virtues, not whether they do if at all.

The two questions identified in the first chapter should consequently be qualified. I maintained that the purpose of this investigation is to establish whether, firstly, there are liberal virtues and, secondly, whether there are conclusive liberal arguments against the idea of a politics of intrinsic virtue. Now an examination of these questions will have to take into account two sets of distinctions. One set is the one elaborated on in this chapter; the distinction between instrumental and intrinsic accounts of virtue. The other set is the one explored in the previous chapter; the distinction between political and ethical liberal theories. It follows that my task cannot simply be to examine the extent to which political and ethical liberalism includes or rejects virtues. Rather, I need to examine the extent to which these liberalisms include or reject *intrinsic* virtues. Does a liberal state that is justified in political terms invoke conceptions of intrinsic virtue? Does a liberal state that is justified in political terms give conclusive arguments to the effect that a politics of virtue should be rejected? How does ethical liberalism fare in these respects? These are the questions which the present inquiry will attempt to answer.

Notes

1.   An influential statement of this view is found in MacIntyre, 1985, esp chapters 2, 6, 16–17. So-called "republican" critics of liberalism generally follow this route too. Their claim is that liberalism and republicanism constitute distinct historical traditions; the one concerned exclusively with rights (liberalism) and the other with the common good and virtue (republicanism). Influential statements of this view are found in Peacock, 1981, and Skinner, 1990.
2.   For recent accounts, see Berkowitz, 1999, and Spragens, 1995. See also Höög, 1999, *passim*. The most disputed figure in the liberal tradition is perhaps Immanuel Kant, not the least due to his importance for contemporary liberal theorists. That Kant, despite what MacIntyre and others insist, did adopt a doctrine of virtue, has been forcefully argued in O'Neill, 1989, chapter eight; Louden, 1997 a; Berkowitz, 1999, chapter three.
3.   E.g., Flathman, 1996, pp 45ff; Galston, 1988, pp 1280ff, and Macedo, 1990, chapters one and seven.
4.   Thomas Hobbes quoted in Hampton, 1989 b, p 56. See also Berkowitz, 1999, chapter 2.
5.   Consequently Hobbes (1985, p 217) defines virtue as our "conclusions ... concerning what conduceth to the conservation and defence."
6.   The distinction between intrinsic and instrumental conceptions of virtue is made by Galston (1988, pp 1279ff) and in Galston, 1992, pp 3–6.
7.   Of course, the fact that something is regarded as valuable in itself is compatible with it being valued for instrumental reasons. We may admire honest people *both* because we know they are good for the economy at large and because we believe that honesty is a mark of a good person. My point, however, is that liberals, for reasons set forth in this section, tend to recognize only the instrumental qualities of virtues.
8.   Russell Hardin dismisses the idea of "intrinsic" values as absurd and contends that values are always "conditional" and therefore instrumental. Hardin, 1995, p 66. However, Hardin's point rests on a failure to distinguish the idea that some things are valuable *for* their own sake from the idea that some things are valuable *in* themselves. The latter view, that some things have value in themselves, involves the claim that things may be valuable independently of what anyone thinks (independently, ultimately, of the existence of human beings). This is indeed a controversial claim. But the former view involves no such assumption. An object (a person, a car, or a virtue) may be valued for itself rather than as a means to some other end, and this is not the same as saying that the value of this object derives from itself. For these distinctions see, Korsgaard, 1983, pp 170ff.

9.   I believe the modern conservative attitude to virtue is aptly expressed by James Q
       Wilson when he writes that the government needs to "induce people to act virtu-
       ously . . . if large improvements are to be made in those matters we consider
       problems: schooling, welfare, crime, and public finance." Wilson, 1995, p 22.
10.   Robert Putnam, 1993, *passim.*
11.   Putnam, 1993, p 88.
12.   Putnam, 1993, p 111. In game-theoretic terms this is to say that everyone prefers an
       outcome where everyone cooperates even to being a free rider. That attitude may
       transform a prisoner's dilemma, where cheating is a dominant strategy, to an assur-
       ance game where choosing the cooperative strategy is dominant, provided that this
       behavior is reciprocated. The assurance game is analyzed in relation to republican
       claims in Dagger, 1997, pp 108–116. However, as has been pointed out by Robert
       Bates, an assurance game does not necessarily resolve the collective action problem,
       since deciding *what* cooperative solution to choose may itself constitute a prisoner's
       dilemma or a coordination problem where there is no solution which is both stable
       and optimal. Civic citizens predisposed to cooperation may, that is, prefer coopera-
       tive solutions that promote their interests to others. Bates, 1988, pp 393ff.
13.   Skinner, 1990, p 295.
14.   Quentin Skinner, 1992, p 217 (emphasis added). Also Skinner 1990, p 294.
15.   In Skinner's view civic virtue consists in having a willingness to "serve one's
       community in a military capacity" and to willingly undertake "supervision and
       participation in the political process." Skinner, 1992, p 219 and 1990, p 303.
16.   For an extended discussion of the notion "civic virtue" see Oldfield, 1990, pp 146f.
17   The idea that republicanism is concerned with internal and external threats to the
       "republic" is found in Dunn, 1990 [1984], p 71. For the idea that republicanism is
       characterized by its concern with *securing* liberty, in contrast to liberalism's focus
       on liberty simpliciter, see Pettit, 1994, p 191. It is noteworthy that Skinner now
       prefers the term "neo-roman" to "republican" since, as these observations would
       suggest, the aim of securing liberty are in fact compatible with constitutional mon-
       archy. See Skinner, 1998, pp 11 fn 31 and 55 fn 176.
18.   Allen Patten argues that there is no interesting conflict between Skinner's ideas and
       liberal principles and values. Patten, 1996, p 36.
19.   John Rawls, 1993, p 194.
20.   Rawls, 1993, p 163.
21.   Berkowitz, 1999, p 25.
22.   Rawls, 1993, p 157.
23.   Rawls, 1993, p 157.
24.   Rawls, 1971, p 436.
25.   Again, in game-theoretic terms, this is simply to say that the assurance game would
       be preferred to the prisoner's dilemma.
26.   The salience in Rawls's work of the instrumental perspective is well illustrated by
       the following quote: "Since the ideals connected with the political virtues are . . .
       forms of judgement and conduct essential to sustain fair social cooperation over
       time, those ideals and virtues are compatible with political liberalism" (Rawls 1993,
       p 194).
27.   Arblaster, 1984, chapter five and p 124. See also Rawls 1993, p xxiv.
28.   Rawls, 1993, p 194.
29.   E.g., Tara Smith, 1997, p 36.
30.   The distinctions used here are inspired by those presented by Michael Walzer.
       However, whereas Walzer deals with *five* different attitudes relating to tolerance—
       acceptance for the sake of peace, acceptance for the sake of respect for rights,

38   The Liberal State and the Politics of Virtue

acceptance for the sake of respect for others, indifference and endorsement—I believe the first three are essentially of the same kind. The reason for this is that respect for the sake of peace, rights, or of others, all trades on independent reasons for tolerance. This is not the case, by contrast, with indifference that obviously does not trade on any reason at all. Endorsement is more peculiar in that it *is* based on a reason and yet, as I shall argue, this reason is not really an instance of tolerance. Walzer, 1997, pp 10–11.

31. A convincing case for the inappropriateness of speaking about tolerance in the context of racial differences is found in Mendus, 1989, pp 15f.

32. Arblaster, 1984, p 70.

33. Williams, 1996, p 20.

34. The definition of toleration as non-interference with conduct that is disapproved of is the common one. However, Nicholson (1985, pp 160f) presents a different view according to which the inclinations and feelings of the tolerator are regarded as morally irrelevant. At least when considering ordinary language Nicholson might be deemed right: people usually do describe even sympathetic attitudes as "tolerant."

35. This is to accept Walzer's (1997, p 11) view that endorsement is not really tolerance: "How can I be said to tolerate what I in fact endorse?"

36. Horton, 1996, p 34.

37. I do not mean to suggest that motives of self-interest could never figure in the description of virtuous acts. All I am suggesting is that self-interest cannot be what constitutes their virtuousness. More than one motive can, following Robert Audi, be the basis of virtue if one is prepared—as I believe one should be—to reject the Kantian view that good will alone is virtuous. See Robert Audi, 1995, pp 452ff.

38. See also Susan Mendus's conclusion that tolerance by self-interest "cannot be advocated as a moral virtue." Mendus, 1988, p 9. The conclusion that tolerance based on self-interest is not a virtue is controversial in the sense that it implies a rejection of utilitarian conceptions of virtue. This is so because a basic premise of most utilitarian theories is that intentions or motives cannot have intrinsic value. Thus, Henry Sidgwick—perhaps the most important utilitarian writer—writes that "the presence or absence of any or other of them [i.e., motives] is not implied in our attribution of virtue." What is required for virtue is "merely a settled resolve to will a certain kind of external effects." Thus, from a utilitarian standpoint, self-interested tolerance could certainly be virtuous. Sidgwick, 1981 [1907], p 224.

39. Bo Rothstein (ed), 1995, p 79. The SNS Democratic Audit of Sweden carried out an extensive investigation of tolerance thus defined in Sweden. The result was in many ways disappointing; the average Swede did not feel committed to some of the rights held by immigrants and other minorities.

40. David Richards, 1996, pp 127, 141.

41. My point will be that there cannot be a right to virtue and that, consequently, the virtue of tolerance cannot consist in the respect for rights. Smith (1997, p 3) provides a different argument for the same conclusion. Tolerance, Smith argues, presupposes that you have the moral authority to choose freely whether to accept a difference or not. Now, respecting a person's rights you do not have that choice: respecting someone's rights is your duty and not something you merely choose to do. In contrast to Smith, I believe a person that defers from interfering with what is disliked out of respect for rights could plausibly be called tolerant (but not virtuous).

42. The distinction between the morally right act and acting out of morally appropriate conviction is referred to by O'Neill (1989, p 153) in her attempt to rebut MacIntyre's claim that Kant did not incorporate an account of virtue in his theory of ethics.

43. For a discussion of perfect and imperfect obligations and their relation to the notion of virtue see O'Neill, 1996, *passim.*
44. See MacIntyre's (1981, pp 232f) observation that contemporary liberal writers tend to reduce virtuous behavior to rule-following.
45. Rawls, 1971, p 192.
46. Horton, 1996, p 37.
47. Atwell, 1986, p 15 (emphasis in original).
48. This is not to accept the mistaken view that there are unconditional values irrespectively of the circumstances. Intrinsic virtues are valued *for* their own sake, but they need not—as made clear in footnote 8 above—be valuable *in* themselves. Clearly, the fact that a virtue is regarded as unconditionally good is not to say that it will remain so even when most people cease to regard it as such.

3

The Liberal Way of Life:
Dworkin on Virtue

Liberals are frequently thought to be suspicious of virtues. But it is sometimes argued that liberals themselves endorse certain intrinsic virtues. Liberals do not merely recognize the instrumental value of virtues but want to impose their specific ideals of the good life on the citizens of liberal democracies. Is this true? In this chapter I will examine the political theory of Ronald Dworkin, and I will try to answer this question in relation to the ideas expounded in his work.

Liberalism, Dworkin argues, rejects the idea of politics as "soulcraft"—it rejects the idea that the government should foster a sense of what is valuable in life in its citizens. To mould the souls and the characters of citizens is not the task of the government; "manners" are not the "business of the state," as Dworkin puts it.[1]

Yet Dworkin does not deny the ethical importance of virtues and intrinsic values. The fact that political institutions must not try to impose or inculcate some set of intrinsic values upon another does not, in other words, mean that access to some set of such values is not essential to life. "Much of our life is based on the idea that objects or events can be valuable in themselves," writes Dworkin.[2] He thereby recognizes the significance of intrinsic values and, we may assume, of intrinsic virtues.

The two positions endorsed by Dworkin, one affirming the importance of intrinsic virtues to our lives, the other denying political institutions the authority to impose such values, may of course be regarded as in tension with each other. That some value is of great significance to us could be considered as a reason for the government to support it. The importance of virtues might be regarded as similar to the importance we attach to values such as security or health and surely, in those cases, the government has a reason to help us secure those values. But as far as virtues are concerned their importance does not, in the liberal view, provide a reason for securing them. Instead, the fact that people care a lot for virtues is a reason why governments should *not* pursue those values.

According to Dworkin the liberal doctrine claims that what matters is not only that we live a good life but also that each individual defines which life is good for him or her. The point of life is not only that it is good but that it is chosen and defined individually. Finding out which kind of life is good for you is the "challenge" that is the point of life according to Dworkin's interpretation of the individualistic message.[3] If this is liberalism's idea of the good life it is easy to see why liberals believe the government has a duty to let people choose their own lives. The government must not impose virtues because that would make it impossible for people to successfully respond to their challenges in life.

So Dworkin recognizes the *ethical* importance of virtues at the same time as he denies that virtues should be credited with *political* importance. The cogency of this position will be assessed in later chapters. Instead we must here try to decide whether this description of Dworkin's position is itself a correct one. Is it, in other words, true that Dworkin attaches no political importance to intrinsic virtues? There is at least one reason why we should doubt this. In fact, Dworkin's defense of the idea of a neutral state rests on the belief that some virtues are better than others. The idea of a neutral state does seem to depend on the view that life is a "challenge" and that it is of intrinsic value that citizens define individually what this challenge consists in. But is not this idea of life as a challenge itself a conception of virtue?

This chapter is devoted exclusively to interpretative analysis. My aim is not, then, to examine the arguments for or against the neutral state. Chapters seven and eight will be concerned with *that*. The question I want to answer here is whether Dworkin's political ideal is in fact independent of liberal conceptions of intrinsic virtue.

Liberal Virtues: Mill and Dworkin

Undoubtedly, Dworkin regards certain ways of life as superior to others. It is argued that, for example, an artist does respond adequately to the challenges of life when his paintings are the result of his own strivings and excellence, but that an artist does not respond to the challenges of life when he allows his hand to be pushed across the canvas by someone else. In both cases the outcome, the art produced, may be of equal standard. Yet, only the artist who has himself defined and struggled with his art is improving his life.[4]

Thus, the important thing for a person in order to lead a good life is not only that he or she produces or does something that is of value, but that whatever is done or produced is performed by that person. This simple point has important implications when it comes to judging the success of one person's life. We cannot, in this Dworkinian view, tell whether a life is good or bad merely by looking at the qualities of a person or by observing the results achieved by him or her. Since performance is what ultimately makes a life successful we must also take into account the intentions and beliefs of that person. Only when a person embraces the ideals that he or she is living according to, will life be a performance in the ethical sense.[5] A man that dislikes art is not improving his life merely because he inherits a group of fine pictures. It simply does not improve *his* life if *we* regard such art as enriching or stimulating.

The ethic of liberalism does, Dworkin thinks, encompass the idea that living well is to live through one's individual beliefs and ideals: nothing can be of value to a life unless it is endorsed by the person whose life it is. What we need to know now is whether this ideal is an example of a liberal virtue. Is the idea that life must be a performance part of a liberal conception of the good life? At first we may think that this idea is too flimsy a basis for a political morality and that it could not, therefore, be conceived of as a virtue. If all that is needed in order to be a liberal is that life is regarded as a performance, aren't we all liberals? Is not such a liberalism a trivial doctrine?

That, however, would be a premature conclusion. Certainly it is a general feature of liberalism that it allows for many different ways of life. And yet, though it is true that *many* different lives could be liberal, it need not follow that *any* life could be liberal. People without a sense of having the power to make choices and to reflect upon them cannot perform their lives. People whose lives are dominated by others may, for instance, lack the capacity to lead a liberal life in Dworkin's sense. Consequently, the fact that liberalism may be "ecumenical", as Dworkin writes, does not necessarily exclude the possibility of a liberal way of life.[6] This is why we must return to the initial question and ask whether performance is not in fact a virtue and an expression of a truly liberal ideal of the good life.

At this point it might be helpful to compare Dworkin's ideas with other candidates for virtue that have been of importance to the liberal tradition. One such idea is the notion of individuality, which bears much resemblance to Dworkin's ideas. According to one view individuality is the idea of life as an art. The beauty of life is not what is accomplished but the artwork itself. The "doer" matters more than the results.[7] This view resembles Dworkin's description of life as a "creative activity" and a challenge.[8] But it is also related to what is perhaps the most influential account of individuality, the one explored by John Stuart Mill. Since Mill elaborated further on this idea, it may be helpful to compare his idea of individuality to Dworkin's ideas of performance. This would be especially interesting since Dworkin admitted that he has been influenced by Mill. Dworkin agrees with what he takes to be Mill's position, namely, that neither society nor the state has the right to decide the personality of its members.[9] Thus, while there might be a parallel between Mill's and Dworkin's ideas of individuality, it is also the case that both effectively reject the idea of the government molding the character and virtues of the citizenry.

Turning to Mill's work we find in *On Liberty* a description of an ideal character. The desires and impulses that we have must be "our own" and they should also be governed by a "strong will." Only then, Mill thought, can we develop the "energetic character" that individuality requires.[10] Thus Mill associated individuality with "strength." Mill lamented the prevalence of "weak" feelings and wished that people would one day have stronger desires and wills.

Whereas it may be difficult to grasp the point of having strong feelings there is a less literal interpretation of this view. That the individual should have an "energetic" and "strong" character could in fact be understood as a way of emphasizing the values of originality or independence. Thus, the claims about intensity are perhaps better understood as concerned with distinctiveness of character. As is well known, Mill thought that one essential requirement of individuality is that we form our *own* opinions and desires. When we take this as essential to individuality we can understand the idea of "strength" as a metaphor for the idea of independence. We need strength to resist the pressure of public opinion and prejudice; only then can we be individuals, in the Millian sense, with originality and independence. We should cultivate what is individual and not succumb to habit and custom. In fact, it appeared to Mill as desirable that people become more eccentric; that each individual distinguish him- or herself more sharply from the "mass."[11]

Mill's ideal of individuality has several affinities with the ideas defended by Dworkin. In his considerations on individuality as a form of originality we can distinguish between the belief that thinking independently is valuable, and the belief that the outcome of such thinking may be valuable due to its original character. Thus, not only the process of forming our convictions in an independent way is valued. Mill also thought that the substance of those convictions is valuable due to their originality. Each individual has a specific character and it is desirable that it can be articulated in full. Human nature, Mill wrote, "is a tree, which requires to grow and develop itself ... according to the tendency of the inward forces which make it a living thing."[12] There is thus a "force," or a "tendency," that is unique to each individual, and Mill believed that we should strive to express or articulate that part. I will argue that both ideas, the one concerning the end or substance of individuality, the other the ways to achieve it (independence), can also be found in the writings of Dworkin.

As we have seen, to conceive one's life as a performance implies that we live from the convictions and beliefs that we have. In order for some value or activity to be valuable people have to *endorse* it. According to Dworkin this implies that people are not successfully living their lives when they conform to "the fiat of other people."[13] To be led in one's acts by anything but one's personal convictions is to lack what Dworkin calls "ethical integrity." To act out of conviction is to have integrity because it allows us to perceive ourselves as authors of our lives, and this corresponds exactly to the idea of performance.

The value of integrity in life is generally accepted according to Dworkin. Generally we do, for example, admire those who do it "their way," whether or not we share their ends or convictions. Generally too we regret those instances where people forfeit their ideals due to pressure from others.[14] These common reactions not only demonstrate that integrity is of value to us but also make the procedural nature of that value evident. As Dworkin points out, a life with integrity presupposes some substantive convictions; but it does not define what these convictions are.[15]

In these respects Dworkin appears to advocate an ideal close to that found in Mill's writings. To both, independence in the forming of our opinions and in the direction of our actions is of great value. However, their writings on individuality seem to share features on a deeper level too.

Dworkin embraces the more specific idea that it is valuable that people express their genuine and particular characters. We can detect traces of that assumption in his effort to explicate further the notion of performance. As we know now, Dworkin defends the view that a precondition for an experience improving the life of an individual is that he or she endorses an ideal according to which this experience is part of the good life. Now Dworkin makes the further claim that the endorsement itself must be genuine.[16] Thus, though people's beliefs and opinions will be genuine (or achieve integrity in Dworkin's terminology) to the extent to which they are endorsed, there must be something further that makes the *endorsement* genuine. The need for some such further guarantee is in a sense obvious. A person who thinks that he or she is an egalitarian, a devoted Catholic, or a golf fan is not—merely by believing it—a true egalitarian, Catholic or golf fan. To believe that one is committed to an idea is surely a prerequisite for endorsing that idea. But it is not a sufficient condition. For one thing, people sometimes discover that what they used to believe was in fact at variance with their deeper convictions. They will then realize that what they used to believe does not correspond to what they believe is a more authentic self. The former, inauthentic, belief is then rejected. This idea, that we are sometimes wrong about who we think we are, is in fact fundamental to ordinary life. Things said or done when you speak spontaneously, when you are tired, distracted, fuddled by drink, or just stupefied by something that has happened, may sometimes be explained as inauthentic. Soberly reflecting on the situation, people occasionally realize that their earlier reaction was premature or wrong.

The conclusion must be that a standard of genuine endorsements is needed. We admire people when they do it "their way." But the reason why is not merely that we respect independence of thought and action. After all, people are sometimes blamed for being too independent or being independent in the wrong way. What we hope for when people do it "their way" is that they do what is right for them: we hope they have chosen the course of action that best corresponds to what they "are." In fact, we assume that there are genuine and non-genuine ways of doing "it."

Now, Dworkin's theory accounts for this intuition. There is a standard for when an endorsement is genuine that depends on the assumption that individuals have unique characters that may be expressed and manifested.[17] Life is genuine only when there is a match between the deeper self and the beliefs or values that people have. Consequently, Dworkin argues that the value of integrity rests on the idea that it is valuable that we have "the capacity to express our character."[18] What matters is that we shape our lives according to our distinctive personalities: "each of us should live in a way that is appropriate to who and what he or she is."[19]

Affirming the value of genuine endorsements is reminiscent of what John Gray described as Mill's concern with authenticity. As observed by Gray and others, Mill cared for more than the virtues of self-direction and independence. It mattered a lot to Mill that people acted not only on their own but also that what they acted on was truly theirs.[20] The emphasis Mill gives to "original character" corresponds neatly to Dworkin's idea of the importance of "personality." These remarks seem to reinforce the impression that Dworkin's idea of performance has important affinities with Mill's notion of individuality.

Two Versions of the Liberal Way of Life

Is the idea of individuality a virtue that exemplifies a liberal conception of the good life? Some think not. George Kateb denies the existence of any liberal notion of the good life and argues, instead, that individualistic life is simply a life "that is not bad." When individuals are recognized as such they are freed from the yoke of "inferiority, contempt, invisibility" that follows from any imposed identity of a caste, class or ethnic group. Freed from these evils the individual achieves "a sense of life" in Kateb's words. This is not the same as *the* good life. The life of the individual is, Kateb paradoxically claims, a "good" which "is not *the* good life."[21]

The ambiguous standing of individuality might be due to the particular interpretation Kateb accepts. To him, individuality means having independence and to be in charge of one's own life. As we saw, both Mill and Dworkin go further than that. To them individuality is also to have originality or to express the personality that is specific to each individual. But are these, more specific ideas of individuality enough to establish a liberal idea of the good life?

An important aspect of both Mill's and Dworkin's ideas of individuality is that it is compatible with many different experiences and values. When each individual attends only to his or her own original feelings and opinions, there is no particular attitude or belief that is better than the other. The idea of authenticity is incompatible with the idea that there is a specific content of the good life: anything could make people authentic. Perhaps some person, faithful to the ideal of Mill or Dworkin, will eventually end up with a highly religious or even dogmatic character. To be authentic, to achieve integrity with one's convictions, may lead one person towards Christianity and another towards atheism. Nothing in the idea of individuality denies this possibility.

> The challenge model of ethics does not discriminate among substantive ethical convictions. People who think the good life lies in religious devotion and others who think it requires unconventional sexual variety may all treat their convictions as opinions about the most skilful performance of living.[22]

Thus individuality may be described as a second-order ideal in that it concerns the *way* we maintain our convictions and desires. In contrast to a first-order ideal, which would specify some particular conviction or act as valuable, a second-order ideal specifies as valuable only ways of believing or doing things. No particular belief or desire is superior in itself according to a second-order ideal.[23] But can second-order ideals be virtues? We can safely argue, at least, that the occurrence in a theory of discriminations between good and bad desires of the *first-order* is sufficient in order to ascribe to it the existence of virtues. Should we also argue that the existence of first-order ideals, defining some particular motives or beliefs as valuable, is necessary for the existence of virtues?

The opinions of scholars who have studied Mill's relation to virtues seem to be that second-order ideals can be virtues too. Ideally, Mill believed that people should have the capacity to give a rational account of their choices and convictions.[24] There is, in other words, a normative standard of character that tells us that it is a good thing to reflect on what we do and who we are. To be directed by reason, to be reflective in every aspect of life, is thus the chief virtue in Mill's liberalism. Yet, it is easy to see that the requirement to be reflective does not imply that some particular belief or desire is more valuable than another. Anything goes as long as it is reflected upon. Being reflective is thus a second-order ideal too.

Of course, it may be that scholars actually do not refer to the same idea that I have argued for above. After all, the idea of reflection has not loomed large in the ideal I have tried to establish as Mill's. But the impression that reason has no place in my interpretation of Mill is false.

By individuality Mill meant two things, I argued: that we form our own opinions (independence) and that we regard those opinions as expressive of our true and specific nature (authenticity). Now I believe a certain emphasis on the role of reason is implied by these notions. The idea that people should think *for* themselves, and that they should try to identify their authentic selves, plausibly requires the use of reason. People need to be reflective when life is up to themselves. When no one else tells you what to do or what to think you have no choice but making the decisions yourself. Deciding then becomes a matter of reflecting on what you really want rather than succumbing to custom, expectations, or social norms. The need for reflection is strengthened by the fact that you will want to make the right decision. The decision should be compatible with your commitments and ideals. The decisions you make should, in other words, be authentic.

We must conclude then that there is no conflict between reflection and individuality. The idea of individuality encourages the virtue of reflection. Individuality allows for reflection and, in fact, requires a degree of reflection.[25]

The similarities between Mill and Dworkin thus seem to be important. Dworkin, just as Mill, regards reflection and individuality as inseparable. To be independent, to respond to the challenge of life, we need to be able to reflect on and critically assess our beliefs, wants and desires.[26] Can we safely conclude then that Dworkin and Mill defend only what I call virtues of the second-order? Do Mill and Dworkin eschew virtues other than those of independence, authenticity and reflection? Before we can be confident in that conclusion we need to know in greater detail how Mill argued and applied the ideal of liberal individuality. Instructive in that respect are Mill's arguments for sexual equality.

Justice and Virtue: What Mill Said

Mill's famous *The Subjection of Women* is commonly read as primarily an argument against the political and legal discrimination of women. Yet the aim of Mill's book can be described somewhat differently; as an attempt to identify the political and legal reforms necessary to make accessible to women the virtues of liberalism.[27] Thus, Mill perceived liberal institutions, including the equal protection of law and equal rights and freedoms, as a means to the cultivation of the liberal virtues. The fact that women are discriminated against, in that they do not enjoy the same legal rights as men, and the fact that women are oppressed by their economically more powerful husbands, are problems of virtue as well as of justice. To Mill, justice and equality were the means of virtue; "the equality of married persons . . . is the only means rendering the daily life of mankind a school in moral cultivation."[28] Only when individuals have a sense of their equal worth and when they can feel secure that others will meet them with respect will they be able to develop their moral and spiritual senses. Oppression thwarts virtue, but Mill also thought that *oppressing* is inimical to the sense of freedom. The liberation of women is thus more than a service to women. It is also a service to the men whose character is "perverted" by their own sense of superiority.[29]

The reason why Mill regards inequality as a barrier to freedom can be explained in relation to his notion of individuality. The feelings of superiority and inferiority that come with unequal relationships are impediments to the articulation of our authentic selves. No room for virtue exists in a character filled up with arrogance or submissiveness. Thus, the feelings that are encouraged by unequal relations to others prevent the cultivation of independence and authenticity. Feelings of certain kinds may consequently suppress the individual in the same way as the yoke of custom or tradition. The individuality of people is thwarted by the arrogance that follows from a false sense of superiority as much as it is thwarted by imposed codes of conduct.

The connection between unequal relations and a loss of originality is explicit in Mill's writings. Not until women are respected as equals will they, Mill argues, have the opportunity to develop their individuality in full. Distinctiveness of character is a virtue that will be encouraged by increasing equality of status.[30]

Justice and Virtue: What Dworkin Cannot Say

A consequence of the close relationship between individuality and equality accepted by Mill is that no life could be truly good in an unjust society. The good life requires justice. This idea is actually one defended by Dworkin too. "Everyone is insulted by a political and economical system dedicated to inequality," Dworkin argues.[31] Hence not even those who have something to gain from an injustice can live a really profitable life when relations with others are unjust.[32] This is so because justice is a "parameter," as Dworkin calls it, of a life well lived. A "parameter" is a feature that is inseparable from what we take a good life to be; that is, if justice is a parameter to a good life, it is not a mere barrier or obstacle that we could do without, but a component of that life.[33] But why is justice a parameter of living well? Why is it that Dworkin believes that, for example, men could not live well at the same time as women are oppressed, or that rich people cannot attain a really good life when at the same time the poor are treated unjustly? We know why Mill believed that injustices were detrimental to the good life. Mill associated injustices with specific sentiments that served as obstacles to individuality and a good life.

One possible way to account for the fact that Dworkin regards justice as inseparable from the good life is the idea that people are endowed with a "sense of justice." Thus, Dworkin writes that "a life well lived [must] respect our sense of justice."[34] Everyone has certain intuitions about justice and these intuitions, or "senses" as Dworkin calls them, must be respected in order for our lives to be good. Assuming that everyone has this sense of justice we can appreciate the idea that not even the most happy or authentic person lives a good life if he or she is, at the same time, profiting from unjust relations to others.

But the appeal to a sense of justice is awkward in light of the other ideas accepted by Dworkin. A fundamental idea is that the success of a life cannot depend on some value or aspect that is not recognized by the individual. This is implied by the idea of endorsement. In order for Dworkin to say that justice is important to the good life, it must be true that this is what people think. That people think that justice is important to the good life is an empirical claim however. As such it is, of course, not necessarily true for everyone. Thus, it cannot be the case that unjust relations are *always* detrimental to the good life. This is so because only *if* people believe that, i.e., that injustice makes their lives bad, can we legitimately hold that they cannot at the same time profit from unjust relations and live good lives. This, however, is merely a truism. Obviously people are not living good lives when they believe that some of their features are bad! Explaining the relation between justice and the good life in such terms is not very illuminating.

Another, and arguably better, way of accounting for the importance of justice to the good life is to point out the social effects of injustices. Surely there are demoralizing effects on a society whose economic or even political institutions are biased or discriminating. Dworkin in fact argues that injustices will distort social relations. Rich people will not, for instance, be able to establish such relations with the poor that a good life would require.[35] To live well has a social dimension according to Dworkin.[36] Since injustice distorts such relations we have another reason, quite independent of the idea of life as a challenge, why injustice "insults everyone" in society. People indifferent to the distortion of social relations that are due to injustices will live a worse life then they could have.

Even this version of the empirical argument seems to run into difficulties however. The obvious problem is that it seems to depend on normative rather than descriptive assumptions about which social relations are proper for people. Take the relation between the extremely rich and the extremely poor. Surely their relations will be very peculiar and perhaps also difficult to maintain. The poor might be excessively submissive and filled with resentment. Correspondingly, the rich might be excessively arrogant and filled with contempt. These feelings will undoubtedly affect the relations they have and make friendship and love more difficult. Yet, we cannot say that the rich and the poor do not have *relations*. They do. The crux is, rather, that we disapprove of them, that we find them deplorable. This is a normative point and it presupposes an ideal of which social relations are good. But Dworkin cannot justify his vision of the good life on normative assumptions of this kind; Dworkin must not assume an ideal of social relations. How could some relations be considered to be better than others when, in the liberal view, individuals are supposed to define their own challenges of life? According to the liberal view, any ideal is valuable only on condition that it has been endorsed by the individual. A specific conception of social relations will, consequently, be valuable to people only on condition that they have endorsed it—and what is endorsed will naturally vary between individuals. No *one* ideal of social relations is therefore likely to be established as the right one.

Justice and Virtue: What Dworkin Can Say

A more plausible way to account for Dworkin's ideas is to explain the relation between the good life and justice as theoretical rather than empirical. Now, I believe this is what Dworkin actually does. Dworkin claims that when we accept life as a challenge we will unavoidably realize that some set of resources is needed in order to meet the challenge we identify for ourselves. The life of a tennis player, a monk or a scientist requires certain economic resources without which these lives could not be realized. Access to certain resources is a prerequisite for any kind of life. This means, also, that it is necessary for everyone to face the question of what amount of resources is just for each to have.[37] Questions of justice cannot be separated from questions of what makes life good and virtuous.

Yet this does not demonstrate that injustices are always detrimental to the lives of people. Perhaps injustices—just like other difficulties in life—are part of what individuals must deal with in order for their lives to evolve. This is in fact suggested by a recent writer. In this view, the individual grows even out of the struggle for justice.

> People grow in a society where they are faced with difficult and unjust challenges. These injustices cannot be handed over to the Welfare State. We cannot demand that injustices will never happen, because life is not just.[38]

The basic idea behind this objection is that a good life can only be the result of individual endeavors. People grow more when they overcome difficulties on their own than they would had these difficulties been removed by someone else (e.g., the state): "Quality and satisfaction in life cannot be given from one person to another. These are things individuals can achieve only on their own."[39] A life without problems, without battles to fight, and with no difficulties to overcome, could never be a good life.[40] Therefore, injustices should not be described as inimical to the good life; they are part of what makes the good life possible.

That the good life requires individual efforts and responsibility is in fact an important feature of Dworkin's ideal. Life is a challenge and success in life depends on the extent to which the individual manages to "perform" it. The performance is, in turn, measured in relation to the challenges that are seen as important by the individual. Dworkin would consequently agree that a government that decides to remove obstacles and limitations in people's lives does not necessarily improve their lives in an ethical sense. To give everyone what they want would be nice. Yet simply having one's dreams fulfilled will, in a sense, make life less attractive and meaningful than if these dreams had been realized by individual effort.

There is a point in this observation and, yet, justice is not something that should merely be dreamed of. Injustices are not like the so many other obstacles in life that we may consider to be part of what makes life good. There is a point in saying that people that forgo consumption for some time in order to afford a house have, because they made an effort, achieved something. Had the house been given to them, the achievement simply would not have had the same ethical importance. However, there is no point in saying that people, when paid so little that they must starve in order to feed their children, are achieving something valuable merely because they make an effort on their own. To make an effort or to take responsibility is frequently a good thing. But efforts that are forced upon you by the injustices of the economic or political system cannot be part of what makes your life good.

To perform life, to make it something, is what life is all about from the liberal standpoint. However, it is essential that individuals can make their lives respond to the challenges they define for themselves.[41] Injustices erect barriers that are not challenges in this sense. Injustices—a discriminative legal system, a lack of means of living, or an exploitative relation with your employer or husband—does not call for achievements or performances. They are barriers to the good life, not part of the barriers people need to cope with in order to make life their own achievement. In terms of authenticity we could say that injustices make life inauthentic by depriving individuals of the power to define their own challenges. Children who are prevented from attending school because of injustices in legal or economic institutions are not merely having a different challenge in their lives. In fact, they are not given the opportunity to define a challenge for themselves at all. To the extent that people suffer from injustices they will not be able to realize the full potential of their individuality.

To sum up, Dworkin does not assume the existence of a mysterious "sense of justice" or a normative ideal of what social relations should be like. Dworkin merely assumes that the idea of an authentic life is incoherent without reference to an idea of social or distributive justice. There is in other words a theoretical relation between justice and the good life that seems to depend on two considerations. The first is that since material resources are implicit in any life, everyone needs to deliberate about the proper and just amount of resources they are entitled to. Thinking about what makes life good inevitably provokes questions concerning justice. The second point is that there is a close connection between the idea of an authentic life, where individuals define their challenges, and the ideal of a just society. The good life presupposes that individuals achieve something on their own, and that they tackle the barriers and difficulties they are confronted with individually. Yet, injustices are not part of the challenges that make life authentic and worth living.

Individuality and Virtue: Mill's Distinction

Though Dworkin's ideal of the good life does not seem to include any first-order virtues, Mill's may. A liberal ideal on the first-order, according to which some beliefs and desires are less and other more worthy, is more explicit in the writings of Mill. This is well illustrated by returning to Mill's writings on the inequality of sexes.

The problem of the inequality between the sexes can be stated, from a Millian point of view, in a more radical way than earlier. Inequality is not merely a barrier to the authenticity and individuality of men and women as Mill certainly believed. Mill also believed that inequality is a barrier to nobler and higher pleasures. Women should not only be allowed to be free and authentic. Women should also be allowed to enjoy the higher pleasures of the world. These pleasures are accessible only to free and authentic individuals. Only beings with individuality have the appropriate "energy" of character. As we know, Mill believed that a free and authentic human being would achieve "nerve and spring" to the faculties of mind.[42] Now this increased intensity to the mind makes the intellect attentive to "larger and higher objects." Women, when freed, will thus develop nobler feelings.[43]

Nowhere does Mill state clearly what the idea of a more active mind refers to, or the nature of the higher objects that will present themselves to such minds. Yet, similar distinctions between various qualities of mental experience are to be found in other writings. In *On Liberty*, Mill declares that individuality will inspire "high thoughts and elevated feelings."[44]

By invoking the notion of "higher" objects and feelings Mill seems to suggest that a person with individuality can attain some good that is distinct from that of his own individuality and originality; there is a different value that is "higher." But the meaning of these passages is somewhat unclear. Is Mill saying that to develop individuality is *the same* as enjoying higher objects, or is he saying that there are some *other* objects that people with individuality may enjoy?

Actually, Mill's point seems to correspond more to the latter suggestion. As is made clear elsewhere, certain activities are worthier than others by virtue of their "nobleness." An individual who has developed his or her various faculties of mind prefers activities that will stimulate these faculties. In the choice between the full satisfaction of some lower pleasures, and the merely partial satisfaction of some of the higher, a person with individuality will choose the latter—despite the fact that it entails a lesser amount of pleasure.[45] Thus, there is a "kind" of pleasure that people will prefer.

What kind of claim is this? Gray notes the use of a descriptive language and argues that Mill in effect only made predictions about what people *would* prefer *if* they made use of their various faculties. On that account Mill is not filling individuality with a normative content. Mill is not making a normative statement when, for example, he writes that it is "better being a human being dissatisfied than a pig satisfied."[46] That claim is merely an empirical observation about what developed people do believe.[47]

The reading Gray suggests is supported by Berger's findings. Mill's ideas of higher pleasures, Berger argues, hinges on a distinction between the "higher faculties" of human beings, and the feelings of pleasure and pain allowed by these faculties.[48] The only sense in which some pleasure may be higher than another is that it depends upon the faculties that are higher; i.e., that belong to us "by virtue of being human."[49] Thus, those pleasures associated with the mind are

higher than those associated with the body, not because those pleasures themselves are more worthy but because they make use of the
faculties that are higher. As in the case of Gray, though in a somewhat
different manner, Berger consequently understands the idea of higher
pleasures as a descriptive claim. Mill does not define some pleasures as
more valuable than others. Mill is simply pointing out what faculties
are used whenever we enjoy pleasures of a certain kind.

Now, I do not fully agree with Gray's and Berger's reading according to which Mill's distinction between "higher" and "lower" is
purely descriptive. In fact, it seems to me that this reading would be
incompatible with some of Mill's statements. It is true that Mill sometimes uses descriptive language. He writes, for instance, that "few
humans would consent to be changed into any of the lower animals."[50] This claim definitely appears to be descriptive and not normative. However, my suspicion is that Mill also intended to make a
normative point and that he wanted to present a liberal conception
of the good life.

One indication that Mill had such intentions is the way he sum-
marizes the discussion on higher and lower pleasures. The fact that
informed persons will prefer higher to lower pleasures is, Mill argues, a "verdict" from which "there can be no appeal."[51] I think that
in order to make sense of these words it is reasonable to assume that
by the "verdict" he refers to the normative and not the descriptive
claim. It is almost pointless to say that the "verdict" of what people
prefer is what is preferred. It is not trivial, however, to say that the
verdict of which pleasure is *preferable* is what people prefer.

The opinion of informed and experienced individuals thus defines what is of superior value. That this is how Mill should be understood is also indicated by the opening sentence of the whole discussion. It is there stated that the task is to explain what is "meant"
by the idea that some pleasures are more valuable than others.[52] The
purpose of the examples given is thus to defend an idea of what is
valuable. But if these examples are descriptive they do not explain.
The example of some people preferring some pleasures to others
cannot explain what is meant by the idea that some of these choices
represent "higher" pleasures. Only if the reference to what people
prefer is understood normatively will it elucidate what Mill intended
to demonstrate, that is, why some pleasures are more valuable than
others.[53]

It seems to me that Berger ignores the normative character of Mill's assertion that some faculties of the mind are more "human" than others. Arguably, which skills that deserve to be called human, and which that do not, is a normative and not a descriptive issue. Only from the point of view of a normative ideal could some aspects of the human being be described as "the distinctive endowment of a human-being."[54] In fact, Berger does appear to observe that Mill includes only *some* faculties as distinctively human.[55] In Mill's view only those faculties of the mind that are engaged in intellectual activities could properly be called human.

Thus, Mill believed that there are some pleasures which are better than others. We can know which those pleasures are by observing the behavior and the opinions of experienced people with a well-developed individuality. Mill defends this way of reasoning by posing the following rhetorical question: "What is there to decide whether a particular pleasure is worth purchasing at the cost of a particular pain, except the feelings and judgement of the experienced?"[56] If we allow that the good life is defined by the choices of these individuals, the conflict between individualism and the idea of standards of pleasures can be avoided. There are standards of good and bad desires and, yet, the desires of the individual are authoritative: the standards prescribe as higher those pleasures that the well-informed individual would not wish to change for another. Mill thus suggests a solution to a classical liberal dilemma: how to reconcile the idea of individuality with the observation that some activities that individuals may undertake are more desirable, or more valuable, than others.[57]

The charge often directed towards liberals is that the primacy of individuality makes all activities, whether cultural or carnal, equally good. This, of course, was something Mill feared. What if individuality did not lead to the cultivation of mind or the development of our moral senses? What if the authentic individual discovered that he or she was more interested in orgies of shopping and sex than in the refinement of his or her intellectual abilities?

Mill resolved this tension by making the definition of "higher" pleasure (i.e., those stemming from intellectual activities) dependent on the choices of persons with individuality. Consequently, a person with individuality chooses what is good to choose. There is, then, no conflict between individuality and standards of good character.

Yet Mill did not deny that a person with individuality *could* choose to pursue only "lower" pleasures. Individuality and standards of good character are still two distinct phenomena. At any rate, the question of how to live up to the ideal is different from the question of what the ideal is. Ideally, the choices made by true individuals define what a good character would be like. The ideal of good character is thus procedurally defined and not possible to specify in substantive terms.

This peculiar aspect of Millian liberalism should not conceal from our sight the fact that it includes a first-order ideal of virtue. At the heart of Mill's writings is an idea of which pleasures are good and bad. Mill's ideal consequently includes a first-order distinction since it specifies some desires or beliefs as necessarily more valuable than others. As I have tried to demonstrate, the second-order idea which Mill defended, the notion of individuality, is related to this first-order ideal in a complex, but coherent, way.[58] Thus, Gray's revised assessment of Mill's theory seems more correct. Gray now asserts that Mill embraced a set of substantive claims about the content of human well-being.[59] Richard Bellamy's characterization of Mill as a defender of a perfectionist idea of autonomy seems to be appropriate. According to Bellamy, Mill advocated the idea that deciding for oneself is valuable—not in itself—but by virtue of its effects on the character of the individual.[60] Yet, both Gray and Bellamy believe that there is a tension in Mill's work between the ideal of independence and the ideal of virtue. They do not appreciate that Mill effectively suggested a solution to this tension.

Dworkin's Virtues

It is high time to shift our attention back to Dworkin's work. Does *his* ideal, that of life as a challenge, include any first-order virtues? The answer to that question will depend on whether Dworkin makes qualitative distinctions, as Mill does, to the effect that some pleasures, motives, or desires are regarded as intrinsically superior to others.

Now, Dworkin could not accept Mill's reasoning at this point. In fact, it is clear that Dworkin does not embrace a theory of which first-order desires are valuable. From Dworkin's perspective, any first-order ideal of virtue would seem to be incompatible with the idea of life as a challenge. People successfully lead their lives in his view when *they* respond to the circumstances in which they find themselves. The challenge of life must be identified individually and not by liberal theory.[61]

Yet, the idea of individuality has implications for which second-order beliefs are desirable in a liberal democracy. First, it is of great value that people do in fact identify their challenges individually. However, this idea, we know now, includes the further idea that people should be reflective and that they should aspire to realize their authentic selves.

These liberal virtues are second-order conceptions: they do not identify which beliefs or desires that are valuable but they tell us how to proceed when choosing them. In any case, these second-order beliefs must be regarded as desirable in the liberal citizen since they constitute the basis for liberal institutions. That is, liberal institutions are not justified merely because they are abstractly right or true, they are justified because they correspond to an arguably attractive ideal of the good life.

Yet Dworkin denies that the idea of life as a challenge constitutes a particular conception of the good life. The liberal ethic is not just another ideal of the good life according to Dworkin, but an account of ethics itself. Thus, the idea of life as a challenge, the idea that integrity and independence are crucial aspects of life, does not merely represent the liberal way of doing things but the ethical way![62] By describing his position not as a conception of the good life, but as a conception of ethics, Dworkin apparently aspires to avoid being classified as "sectarian" or as a defender of just another political ideal. However, the fact that Dworkin believes that he has provided a general account of ethics and not a specific idea of the good life cannot itself be a conclusive reason to accept it as such. But which reasons are valid in this context? The conclusion of this chapter is, in any case, that the theory elaborated on by Dworkin includes a catalogue of the virtues of liberalism.

Notes

1.   Ronald Dworkin, 1978, p 18.
2.   Ronald Dworkin, 1993, p 69.
3.   Ronald Dworkin, 1990, pp 67f and 75ff.
4.   This example is discussed in Dworkin, 1990, p 77.
5.   Dworkin, 1990, p 77.
6.   Dworkin, 1990, p 58.
7.   See George Kateb, 1989, p 187.
8.   Ronald Dworkin 1993, p 84. It should be noted, however, that Dworkin explicitly rejects the romantic notion of life as an artistic, creative, performance in the aestethical sense (Dworkin, 1990, p 64, fn 39).

9.   Ronald Dworkin, 1977, p 263f.
10. John Stuart Mill, 1977 [1859], p 264.
11. Mill, 1977, p 269.
12. Mill, 1977, p 263.
13. Dworkin, 1990, p 80.
14. Dworkin 1993, p 205.
15. Dworkin, 1993, p 205.
16. Dworkin, 1990, p 79.
17. For the importance of this idea in liberal thought in general, see Lukes, 1973, chap 10.
18. Dworkin, 1993, p 224.
19. Ronald Dworkin, 1996 a, p 43.
20. John Gray, 1996 a [1983], pp 73, 79, and Nancy Rosenblum, 1987, pp 134f. The potential conflict between independence and authenticity is discussed by Gray (1996a, p 89).
21. Kateb, 1989, p 188f (emphasis added).
22. Dworkin, 1990, p 111.
23. See Harry Frankfurt, 1971. A helpful discussion on the implication of second-order ideals is also found in Barry, 1995 a, pp 128–133.
24. H S Jones, 1992, pp 288, 299. See also Clor, 1985, pp 10, 21.
25. Fred Berger suggests, in a similar fashion, that reflection is a result of *and* a condition for individuality. Berger, 1984, p. 335, fn33. Perhaps Dworkin nevertheless puts less emphasis than Mill on the role of Reason for the good life. "A good life need not be an especially reflective one; most of the best lives are lived rather than studied." (Dworkin, 1993, pp 239f.) It is also clear that Dworkin rejects "autonomy" as an ideal for liberalism. See Dworkin 1983 a, p 47, fn 1. But cf Dworkin, 1977, p 292.
27. See also Jones, 1992, p 305.
28. John Stuart Mill, 1985 [1869], p 259. See also Jones, 1992, pp 305ff.
29. Mill, 1985, p 298. Mill also believed that unequal relations between the sexes encouraged a love for power. The dangers that follow from the love of power were emphasized in the writings of Bertrand Russell (and Russell did recognize Mill as a source of inspiration on these issues). E.g., Bertrand Russell, 1938.
30. Thus Mill argued (1985, pp 288ff) that women's loss of originality was a direct consequence of the pervading sexual inequality.
31. Dworkin, 1990, p 103.
32. Dworkin does not say, however, that unjust relations always distort a good life. Perhaps domination is exactly what makes the life of the psychopath or the sadist successful and authentic. Consequently, Dworkin (1990, p 75) accepts that there will always be exceptions though they are "statistically insignificant."
33. Dworkin, 1990, pp 66ff.
34. Dworkin, 1990, p 73.
35. Dworkin, 1990, p 74.
36. Dworkin, 1990, p 103.
37. Dworkin, 1990, pp 71f.
38. Dick Erixon, 1999, p 56 (my translation): "I ett samhälle där medborgarna kämpar med svåra och orättvisa motgångar växer människor. Det går inte att överlåta dessa orättvisor på välfärdsstaten och kräva att den skall se till att orättvisor inte uppstår. Livet är inte rättvist."
39. Erixon, 1999, p 52 (my translation): "Livskvalitet och tillfredsställelse är inget som någon kan ge bort eller ta emot. Det är kvaliteter som varje individ bara kan tillföra själv."

40. See, for instance, Charles Murray, 1998, pp 32f.
41. Dworkin, 1990, p 72.
42. Mill, 1985, p 313.
43. Mill, 1985, p 313.
44. Mill, 1977, p 266.
45. John Stuart Mill, 1969 [1861], pp 211–213. Rawls (1971, p 210 and 426) notes the similarity between Mill's ideas and his own "Aristotelian principle" which says that people will prefer the activity that is more complex because it makes use of "a larger repertoire of more intricate and subtle discriminations."
46. Mill, 1969, p 212.
47. Gray, 1996 a, p 72, 88.
48. Berger, 1984, p 236.
49. Berger, 1984, p 236.
50. Mill, 1969, p 211.
51. Mill, 1969, p 213.
52. Mill, 1969, p 211.
53. I thus agree with Vinit Haksar's claim that Mill developed a kind of "choice theory of value." Haksar, 1979, pp 203 and 206ff.
54. Mill quoted in Berger (1984, p 236).
55. Holmes describes this as Mill's "hidden teleological premise" since it implicitly defines some human capacities as "more human." Stephen Holmes, 1989, p 138. Though Holmes's conclusion seems right, I suggest that Mill did not merely *assume* or *assert* that some faculties are higher than others but that he endeavored to demonstrate this by defining "higher pleasures" as those preferred by people with individuality.
56. Mill, 1969, p 213. Cf Rawls (1971, p 432) who regards it as a "deep psychological fact" that people tend to prefer the more sophisticated activity when given the opportunity to choose. See also Haksar, 1979, pp 195f.
57. Note that I do not regard it as my task to evaluate the extent to which Mill was philosophically successful in this endeavor. For a good survey of the inconsistencies found in Mill's work, see John Plamenatz, 1992 [1963], pp 260ff.
58. George Sabine claims that proposing distinctions between higher and lower pleasures is a "contradiction in terms" since it amounts to "demanding a standard for the measurement of a standard." But certainly *that* is not contradictory. Just as the meter was defined by the platinum item kept since 1799 by the French Academy in Paris, the standard of individuality may require some standard by which that is measured. See George Sabine, 1973 [1961], pp 640f.
59. John Gray, 1996 b, p 140.
60. Richard Bellamy, 1992, p 26.
61. Dworkin, 1990, p 66.
62. Thus Dworkin (1990, p 113) argues that "the challenge model captures intuitions that almost everyone has about ethics." Yet, on the same page, Dworkin writes that his theory expresses the creed of the "liberal community." Arguably, not both statements could be simultaneously true unless "almost everyone" is a member of "the liberal community"—which seems most unlikely.

4

The Liberal Citizen: Rawls on Virtue

Does liberalism include an account of intrinsic virtues? Is the liberal state justified by reference to a doctrine of the good life? I have argued that Dworkin's liberalism includes a set of second-order virtues: these virtues specify how people ought to make choices about their lives, not what choices they ought to make. I now turn to the theory of John Rawls, where we shall find a very different approach to liberalism. Rawls explicitly denies that liberalism includes an account of which virtues or lives are good. The citizen in liberal democracies need not accept one or the other conception of the good life in order to realize that liberal institutions are legitimate. The liberal state does not express an opinion about "what is of value in human life as well as ideals of personal virtue and character."[1] There is a necessary distinction, Rawls believes, between political and ethical issues. The legitimacy of political systems is a political matter whereas the goodness of virtues is a matter of ethics, and these questions should be kept separate.

Now, the aim of this chapter is not to assess the validity of this position, but to interpret it. The question asked in this chapter is how Rawls's position ought to be described, not if the position ought to be accepted. The question, in other words, is whether it is true that Rawls's liberal theory does not refer to intrinsic virtues.

One important reason for pursuing an investigation of Rawls's ideas in relation to intrinsic virtues is that, although Rawls asserts that he does not affirm any specific conception of such virtues, many writers claim that he does. In particular, Rawls is ascribed the view that the liberal state depends ultimately on the virtues of justice and autonomy. Stephen Macedo and Richard Flathman defend the idea that Rawls endorses an ideal of the virtue of justice.[2] More emphatically, writers like William Galston, Ronald Beiner and Richard Dagger have argued that Rawls is committed to the virtues associated with moral autonomy and self-control.[3] Some of these writers are critical of Rawls for exactly this reason. They repudiate the ideal of autonomy and do not find it attractive as an ideal for a liberal society (Beiner and Galston). Others are sympathetic to Rawls for the same reason. They believe liberal politics should accept moral autonomy as an intrinsic virtue (Dagger). In either case, these assessments of Rawls's work, where it is interpreted as advocating a number of intrinsic virtues, appear to conflict with Rawls's own words. That is, Rawls insists that he has not included an account of intrinsic virtues in liberalism. This fact, together with the fact that Rawls occasionally refers to the value of certain virtues, gives us good reason to investigate his work further.

Despite these appearances, and despite the views expounded by these commentators, my belief is that Rawls's liberalism is not committed to any virtues or conception of the good life. The liberal ideal, as spelled out by Rawls, does not refer to the intrinsic value of any traits of character. Since this claim happens to be controversial, and the aim of this chapter is to defend it. In doing that my aim is not merely to restate Rawls's own picture of his theory. The fact that the liberal ideal, as found in Rawls's work, is agnostic with regard to intrinsic virtue is not to say that it is symmetric between different ways of life. As I shall argue, liberalism may be ethically neutral and yet it is *asymmetrical* in a certain sense. The implication of this notion is explored in the last part of this chapter.

The Fraternal Society and the Virtue of Fraternity

There is one virtue referred to by Rawls: the virtue of fraternity. Rawls claims that fraternity is expressed by the principles of social justice that are at the heart of liberalism. The virtues of "civic friendship" are, according to Rawls, implied by the idea that society ought to be arranged so that wealth is distributed to the needy. Thus, since liberalism emphasizes the need for social justice it provides an "interpretation of the principle of fraternity."[4]

The fraternal element of liberal justice is further illustrated by the fact that the relation between the citizens in a just society is, according to Rawls, analogous to the relations between the members of a family. In a family, each member is expected to forego maximizing individual benefits unless they know this is to the benefit of all. Decisions concerning the allocation of expenditures and the distribution of incomes ought to be sensitive to the interests of all members of the family. By analogy, the liberal principle of justice prescribes as a condition for growth and wealth-maximization that it is for the benefit of the worst off.[5] Citizens in a liberal society will in this sense treat each other as "brothers" and "sisters."

It would be wrong to characterize Rawls's account of fraternity as instrumental. Fraternity is an aspect of social justice, and surely Rawls believes that social justice is an essential aspect of the liberal ideal. Justice is not accepted merely for instrumental purposes. The obligation to share society's wealth is not accepted merely because it is necessary in order to secure public order or stability. Justice, in Rawls's view, is a necessary implication of liberal values. Does this mean then that fraternity is an example of a genuine liberal virtue?

I believe the answer to this question is negative. There is a problem with Rawls's definition of fraternity. Following David Miller, I believe we should say that solidarity and fraternity presuppose the intention to care for others.[6] Arguably, when people act in ways that just happen to benefit others, we do not say that they are, for that reason, virtuous out of solidarity. Consumers in Western Europe do not, for instance, exhibit solidarity with the poor farmers of South East Asia merely because they happen to import their rice. Likewise, paying taxes is no sign of solidarity unless they are paid deliberately with the aim of improving the life of fellow-citizens.

If we accept Miller's point, Rawls gets into trouble. To Rawls, it is enough that the consequences are for the benefit of the poor in order for all citizens to be credited with virtue and solidarity. Rawls seems to believe that living in a just society is a sufficient condition for exhibiting the virtue of fraternity. In other words, people's intentions or attitudes are considered irrelevant. But this cannot be right. The virtue of fraternity pertains to people because of their intentions, and the liberal state can therefore show solidarity or be fraternal in a metaphorical sense only.

The conclusion is that Rawls does not endorse the virtue of fraternity. Although Rawls approvingly refers to it, this should not be taken to indicate that fraternity is acknowledged as an intrinsic virtue. Rawls's liberal state, consequently, is not committed to any particular "ideal of personal virtue and character."

Implicit Virtues

Rawls's explicit reference to virtue has now been examined. Yet a theory generally conveys values or commitments in subtler ways too. Premises and assumptions may reveal commitments that are not explicitly recognized as such. This means that the possibility that Rawls's liberal theory includes an account of virtue remains. Is there an ideal of the good life hidden in the foundations of liberal theory?

This suspicion is one nurtured by William Galston. Galston's complaint about Rawls is not that he is too ignorant or negligent about virtues. Rather, the main defect of Rawls's theory, according to Galston, is that it includes too many liberal virtues. Galston's claim is in effect that Rawls wants to impose a doubtful ideal of the good life on citizens.

> The problem with Rawls's revised Kantian doctrine is not that it abstracts completely from conceptions of character but, rather, that *it prescribes, as valid for all, a single, substantive, eminently debatable ideal of moral personality.*[7]

Galston's claims are of course surprising in light of my previous conclusion. Galston evidently believes that Rawls, on a more general level, embraces a particular ideal of personality and of virtue. Patently, we cannot assess Galston's statement merely by investigating the explicit references to virtue in Rawls's work. As we know now, these references either convey a purely instrumental view of virtue (the virtues of cooperation) or do not amount to a conception of virtue at all (fraternity, toleration).[8] So, we have to penetrate the surface, the explicit statements concerning virtue in Rawls's work, and begin to examine the basic ideas of Rawlsian liberalism.

The fundamental idea of liberalism is, in Rawls's view, that society ought to be arranged according to principles everyone can accept as reasonable. Liberal principles are, in turn, reasonable because only they are impartial. Liberalism pretends to avoid partiality, but how is that achieved? The response delivered by Rawls seems to be that liberalism avoids partiality because its principles do not depend on anyone's particular moral, ethical or religious convictions (egoistic, Christian, Marxist, etc.). Furthermore, liberal principles do not express the interests of any particular persons (owners of capital, consumers, farmers etc).

So, as to avoid partiality in any of these senses Rawls believes the citizen should reason as from behind a "veil of ignorance." When citizens consider the shape of a just society they should disregard their particular ideas of the good life and ignore whatever social and economic position they might have. These constraints prevent our considerations about justice from being influenced by ideas or interests that would otherwise have made them partial. The veil of ignorance secures the impartiality of political norms and institutions by eliminating potential biases in our reasoning about them.

A potential problem in this model is that it may be abstracting too much from actual facts and circumstances. Is it possible to make choices or to discuss the meaning of justice while being totally ignorant of one's beliefs and ideals? Though Rawls uses the metaphor of a cloth (the *veil* of ignorance) that restricts our knowledge, it may be more appropriate to describe the proposal as an undressing of the subject. Rawls is not giving people more to wear: the thin veil of ignorance is, after all, substituted for people's ordinary clothes. One objection to Rawls's proposal is, then, that people generally need a lot of clothes in order to function normally. That is, in case people are not allowed to use their actual beliefs when making choices about justice they would need some new set of beliefs. *Some* beliefs or ideals are simply needed in order for any idea of justice to appear from behind the veil![9]

Rawls is not unaware of this problem, of course. Another premise of his theory, therefore, is that people have certain fundamental interests. It is assumed that, when thinking about justice, people know that they will want to realize whatever ideal of the good life they may have. Citizens should assume, in other words, that they want to live some kind of good life. They also know that people in general will want to live *different* kinds of life. Accepting these assumptions the citizen should acknowledge that it is rational to choose principles that accord equal political freedoms to all and that do not depend on anyone's particular conception of the good life.

Michael Gorr has pointed out that this assumption is not really that innocuous. Rawls assumes that everyone has an interest in pursuing the good life. But that assumption represents the deeper belief that political institutions should express a person's "nature as a free and equal rational being."[10] Gorr's observation seems to be correct; Rawls argues that the principles of justice are designed to "realize this self."[11] In other words, liberalism favors one conception of the "self" before others.

Could it be that it is these remarks about the self that make Galston suspect that there is a "hidden" ideal of man lurking beneath the surface of Rawls's theory? Surely, to assume that people are by nature free, equal and rational is to affirm a normative conception of man.

However, this conception is found in Rawls's early work. In contrast to Gorr, Galston is concerned with Rawls's more recent writings. In these writings Rawls is explicitly concerned with avoiding ambiguities and misinterpretations about the status of liberal ideas. The ambition of the later Rawls is explicitly to "remove inconsistencies" of the kind identified by Gorr.[12] Yet Galston believes that even Rawls's recent writings convey a conception of a moral person. This conception includes ideas about which personal capacities are valuable from a liberal perspective and, consequently, an account of which virtues are good.[13]

Galston's suspicions seem justified, since Rawls now argues that liberalism includes an idea of which "moral powers" citizens should have. The first is that people need to have a capacity for a "sense of justice." The second is that people need to have a capacity to "form, revise, and rationally pursue a conception of the good."[14] These ideas represent an account of the capacities citizens should have: they should be naturally inclined towards justice and they should have the desire to pursue and revise a conception of the good life. Now, Galston claims that these assumptions are controversial. A liberal state justified with reference to these ideas will in fact adopt a "moral goal."[15] Rawlsian liberalism therefore gives voice to a liberal ideal of man.

Is this true? Does Rawls's theory express an ideal of the good life simply by assuming the existence of two moral powers? Galston believes it does, and there is some plausibility to this conclusion. Rawls's theory specifies an ideal of the liberal citizen. Thus, to the extent that this ideal is accepted by the liberal state, it will seem natural to encourage and support the virtues specified by it. In fact, the ideal of the liberal citizen is, in Rawls's work, part of the basic set of beliefs that justifies liberal institutions. In other words, the idea of liberal justice entails a liberal conception of man. This intimate relation between a theory of justice and a conception of the good life is in fact recognized by Rawls.

> [A]ny conception of justice expresses a conception of the person . . . To accept the principles that represent a conception of justice is at the same time to accept an ideal of the person; and in acting from these principles we realise such an ideal.[16]

As Rawls writes, "acting" from a certain ideal of justice is to "realize" a specific ideal of the person. Accepting liberal principles is then to accept a particular idea of what is important in life. Rawlsian liberalism is a political ideal designed to realize a particular doctrine of the good life. Galston's interpretation definitely seems to be justified.

The Virtue of Justice

Whereas we have hitherto found some support for Galston's conclusion it is my belief that we should hesitate to accept it. First, we have not examined Rawls's own reasons for invoking the two moral powers. It would definitely be unfair to Rawls if we were to base our judgement of his ideas solely on the interpretation provided by Galston. Secondly, there is a textual contradiction that Galston appears to leave unsolved. This contradiction consists in the fact that Rawls introduces the notion of the two moral powers, not in spite of but in order to support a liberal theory uncommitted to intrinsic virtues. Now the fact that Rawls believes that he does not endorse a conception of the good must be accounted for in some way. In other words, we need to investigate further the notion of the two moral powers and the purpose they are intended to serve.

As we already know, the first power assumes that the citizen has a sense of justice. Thus Rawls assumes that citizens have a desire to act in accordance with principles they believe to be just.[17] The objection raised by Galston is that there is no reason to regard the virtue of justice as more important than other virtues. A disposition to act justly is not necessarily more important than a disposition to act courageously: "it is by no means clear why a sense of justice should be emphasized whereas courage and a variety of social virtues are excluded from Rawls's model conception."[18] By giving priority to the virtue of justice Rawls is, Galston claims, surreptitiously giving priority to a certain model of man: certain virtues are encouraged at the expense of others. This point is supported by Flathman's observation that Rawls's theory "enmeshes" society in a scheme that serves "justice and other virtues."[19]

But I think Galston and Flathman are both over- and understating the importance of a sense of justice. The importance of the virtue of justice is overstated because Rawls does not, I take it, propound justice as a moral virtue at all. Rawls's emphasis on the sense of justice—or the virtue of justice—should be understood as instrumentally motivated. In fact, the importance of the virtue of justice is understated for exactly the same reason: the instrumental character of the virtue of justice is not sufficiently appreciated. In sum, my point is that the sense of justice is essential to liberal society, but not because this virtue has intrinsic value or because it is itself part of the liberal ideal, but simply because citizens need some virtues in order to remain faithful to their considered intuitions and beliefs about what is just. The purpose of the sense of justice is to guarantee that justice agreed on will also be justice complied with.

The problem addressed by Rawls is that the citizen, in ordinary life, may not find that respecting the principles of justice is rational in each particular circumstance. The principles identified as just for all may later be found to be in conflict with things which would best promote the individual's needs and interests. So, to protect ourselves from the incentive of violating the principles of justice we assume that everyone is provided with a sense of justice.

The relevance of this idea can be illustrated in relation to Rawls's idea of redistributive justice. Rawls argues that when you do not know how successful your life will be, you will find it reasonable that society supports the poor and needy.[20] After all, anyone could have been born poor or disabled. However, assuming that your life turned out to be economically successful, you may no longer find public support for the needy all that reasonable. When you are wealthy you may no longer see the rationality in sharing your wealth with the poor and the unfortunate. Now, the sense of justice helps the rich, in that case, to remember the premises of the social contract. The sense of justice makes citizens faithful to the initial agreement: everyone deserves support from society because no one knows what his or her life will be like.[21]

How should we characterize the instrumental role played by the sense of justice? In fact, I believe there are two essentially different ways of analyzing it. The sense of justice could be understood as a device that secures either collective *or* individual rationality. In both views the sense of justice is having an instrumental role in that it secures compliance with the principles of justice. However, these views differ as to *what* citizens are to comply with. When compliance with just institutions is described as a problem of collective action you are assuming that justice would be advantageous if everyone complied. That assumption is not implied when, on the other hand, the problem of compliance is described in terms of individual rationality. I will now explicate this point further.

In explaining how a sense of justice may fit the patterns of collective rationality we may use the distinction between rationality in the context of *regulation* and rationality in the context of *action*.[22] A certain principle may, while considered as a principle for regulation, be considered as the most reasonable for society as a whole. In Rawls's work the context of regulation is modeled by the idea that citizens should agree on a scheme of justice from behind the veil of ignorance. However, what appears as rational for *all* from the perspective of social justice may not appear as rational for *each* from his or her personal standpoint. Rawls explicitly alludes to this problem.

> [F]rom the standpoint of the original position, the principles of justice are rational . . .
> yet in everyday life an individual can sometimes win even greater benefits for himself
> by taking advantage of the cooperative efforts of others.[23]

This is to say that what is rational in the context of regulation need not be rational in the context of action.[24] It may in other words be rational for each citizen not to comply with the requirements of justice. The solution to this difficulty is to invoke the idea of a sense of justice; "to insure stability people must have a sense of justice."[25] The virtue of justice ensures that individuals will not take advantage of their fellow citizens and that they will, as a consequence, keep the agreements made about what is just.[26] Hence, the purpose of the virtue of justice is to secure collective rationality. It secures rationality by allowing individuals to do what they wanted to do (achieve justice). It secures this collectively by excluding the incentive for each person to take advantage of others.

One peculiarity with this view is that it pictures just institutions as advantageous—the problem is just that even those who do not cooperate may enjoy these advantages. This is the case, for example, with the thief who enjoys his or her stolen property and thereby benefits from the norms of respect for property. Thieves consequently take advantage of an institution (the right to property) they do not support. In any case, the point here is that the institution of justice is, in this view, described merely as more or less beneficial: justice is good only because it benefits everybody more than injustice.

Now, in his early work Rawls probably did perceive justice as a matter of benefits.[27] By contrast, the elder Rawls explicitly rejects the idea that rationality alone ought to guide citizens' choice about justice.[28] The purpose of just institutions is, instead, to realize "the values of liberty and equality."[29] Now if justice is not a matter of what is advantageous, non-compliance with just institutions can no longer be described simply as a matter of taking advantage of others. That is, the notion of collective rationality no longer fits the picture. Justice cannot be a matter of collective rationality because we cannot coherently accept both the view that "everyone needs to be virtuous so that we can continue to live in a society that maximizes our benefits" and the view that "the purpose of a just society is to realize the values of liberty and equality." These statements conflict because the first presupposes that which the second denies. The logic of the virtue of justice is different from that which pertains to the virtue of cooperation. As I argued in chapter two, Rawls and others endorse the idea that, in a liberal society, the virtues of cooperation are of immense instrumental value. They are valued because they enable a collective good that rational and self-interested individuals might not be able to realize. By contrast, justice is not a virtue that secures collective rationality.

In sum, the instrumental character of the virtue of justice remains, but it should be described in terms of individual rather than collective rationality. Individuals who aim at realizing certain values, such as equality and liberty, might occasionally have an incentive to act in conflict with these ends. The virtue of justice secures rationality by preventing individuals from being seduced by more powerful, but less important, preferences. The case of the rich refusing to pay taxes to support the poor is still relevant. The rich, just like thieves, might need a sense of justice to remind them of the requirements of living together under fair conditions with others. But the need for a sense of justice is not to be explained in terms of collective rationality. Rather, the rich need to be reminded about the fact that all citizens are equals and that they would *all* agree to distribute wealth to the poor (the sense of justice, then, does not tell the rich that they will necessarily benefit from keeping the poor along). Similarly, thieves need to be reminded that they too would consider private property as just when agreed to among equals (the sense of justice, then, does not tell the thieves that they will benefit from the institution of private property). The sense of justice is instrumental to the values already accepted as valid by individuals. This interpretation seems to be congenial to Rawls's view that "citizens have a sense of justice and so they generally comply with society's basic institutions, which *they regard as just*."[30] The sense of justice allows citizens to realize the society they believe to be just—not the society they believe to be advantageous.[31] Thus, I believe we can safely conclude that, for Rawls, the virtue of justice has only an instrumental role in liberal society. Galston mistakenly attributes to Rawls the view that the virtue of justice is ethically more important than other virtues.

The Virtue of Choice

The second moral power refers to the idea that the citizen has the capacity to form, revise and pursue an idea of the good life. Obviously, this capacity does not favor any *particular* conception of the good life. There is an obvious difference between prescribing a single conception of the good as valid for everyone, and prescribing a capacity to choose a conception of the good. The whole point of this (second) moral power is to guarantee that political institutions are arranged in a way that preserves the possibility for each individual to choose his or her *own* way of life. According to Rawls, this is a "second-order interest" we all have.[32] In Rawls's own words, the capacity to form and revise and pursue an idea of the good should simply be seen as a guarantee that the just society will permit us to promote our aims "*whatever these are.*"[33] Rawls evidently accepts a position similar to that of Dworkin's. What matters, from a liberal point of view, is not which virtues are chosen but how they are chosen. Can this view be accused of being biased?

However, even the idea that each individual ought to choose his own good is distinctively liberal. The capacity to choose your own way of life and to critically examine these goals and values is a typical liberal virtue. A number of writers argue that this idea amounts to an ideal of autonomy.

As a second-order virtue, the idea of autonomy might be less oppressive than most first-order virtues. After all, autonomy preserves the opportunity of choice. However, this does not change the fact that autonomy is a specific conception of the good life. The idea of autonomous man is a specific liberal idea of life that, as Ronald Beiner points out, is endorsed not only by Rawls but by many liberals:

> The liberal way of life, upheld by a particular dispensation, a particular ethos, is one where the liberal self draws its constitutive identity from its capacity to choose autono-

mously how and where it will work, who it will marry, where it will live, how and where it will seek means of leisure, where it will drive in its car; in short, who it will be.[34]

The idea that all citizens should form, revise and pursue a conception of the good might, as intimated by Beiner, not be as easy for everyone to swallow. Though expressed in the form of a *moral* power it would, if Beiner is right, be more accurately described as a *liberal* power.[35] Once again we are confronted with a potential contradiction in Rawls's work. Despite the fact that Rawls explicitly denies that his principles rest on any ideal of man, it now seems that he does in fact advocate an ideal of autonomous man.

For example, while discussing the role of the second moral power, Rawls explicitly asserts that this idea is *not* accepted merely for instrumental reasons. The idea of a power to form, revise and pursue a conception of the good "is not a means to but is an essential part of a determinate conception of the good."[36] The notion of autonomy is not, in other words, a mere heuristic device but an "essential part of" an ethical ideal. Thus, the liberal ideal of the state appears to rest on a theory of the virtue of autonomy.

According to this interpretation Rawls affirms a particular way of life: the autonomous life. To Beiner and Galston this fact demonstrates why Rawls's project should be rejected. They find the liberal ideal too narrow and would like to see other virtues publicly affirmed and recognized. On the other hand, there are commentators that consider the virtue of autonomy as a distinct virtue of Rawlsian liberalism. Writers like Richard Dagger and Stephen Macedo see in Rawls's work a combination of the best parts of the liberal tradition. They see Rawls's principles as expressing a well-balanced combination of a commitment to liberty and a sincere concern for virtue.[37]

Liberalism: Neutral but Asymmetric

We are now faced with the conclusion that Rawls defends a substantive ideal of autonomy. In this account, the idea that people can form and revise a conception of the good is regarded as of intrinsic value. But one problem remains. It consists in the fact that Rawls explicitly rejects the idea of autonomy as fundamental to liberal society: "the ideal of autonomy [is] *incompatible* with the political liberalism of justice as fairness."[38] Rawls does not believe, then, that his ideas and principles express the idea that it is intrinsically good that people are autonomous beings. A liberal state should not encourage, or be justified in terms of, the idea that a self-chosen life is a superior life. In other words, the reading of Rawls that is favored by writers like Galston, Beiner and Dagger is in conflict with Rawls's own self-understanding. Thus I believe we should take Rawls's own words more seriously. Moreover, I believe Rawls's own statements could be defended and that there are compelling reasons to conclude that Rawls is not advocating the idea that autonomy is a superior virtue.

A defense along these lines will rely heavily on revising the *status* of Rawls's assumptions. Instead of understanding the power to form, revise and pursue a conception of the good as an substantive ideal its role should be understood as purely *formal*. The virtue of autonomy is, in a peculiar sense, instrumental and not presented as a conception of the liberal way of life. I will now defend this claim.

As we have seen, Rawls asserts that the capacity to form, revise and pursue a conception of the good life is "not merely a means" but also "a part of" a conception of the good. This seems to suggest that a formal interpretation is not very plausible. We should observe that Rawls says that the idea of autonomy is *also* to be understood as a means:

> [T]he capacity for a conception of the good can be part of, as well as a means to, someone's determinate conception of the good.[39]

But how can this be? What does it mean to say that autonomy is both a means and an end, both a formal and a substantive idea? Let us begin by examining in what sense the capacity for a conception of the good could be conceived of as a "means."

To begin with, we have to realize that accepting that there is a capacity to choose and revise our conception of the good, does not imply that this capacity need to be exercised. Recognizing that everyone has the *power* to autonomy is not the same as recognizing an obligation to *be* autonomous. This distinction should clarify the limited nature of Rawls's idea.

I further believe that this distinction provides the basis for a reply to Beiner. In Beiner's view, the idea of liberal autonomy imposes choice and rational reflection as an ideal for all citizens. Now this interpretation appears less plausible. What Rawls attempts to do is to present a view that people with any conceivable identity or ideal could accept. The point of assuming a capacity to choose any life you like is not that you *must* choose but that you *could* choose:

institutions that recognize the potential of autonomy allow people to have different identities.[40] The capacity to form, revise and choose a conception of the good expresses the idea that people will make different choices and lead different lives, but that this fact is compatible with them accepting liberal institutions. You can be anyone, even a non-liberal, and yet find liberal principles acceptable. By doing that you need not recognize that choice and reflection are very important to your life.[41] In sum, the point of Rawls's notion of autonomy is not that everyone should strive for self-reflection and self-control but that everyone has the right to be what they are or want to be. This is the sense in which the second moral power is a formal and not a substantive ideal of the good life.

Now, since citizens are free to be anyone, they are obviously free to be liberals too. Some citizens may choose to pursue the ideal of the rational and autonomous person. But this is just one choice of many that are open to them. Because citizens are assumed to be autonomous, they can choose to reject the ideal of autonomy. This ideal is as compatible with Rawls's ideal as any other.

So much being granted, we have a clue to understanding Rawls's claim that the capacity to form and revise a conception of the good *can* be a part of a "determinate conception of the good." Though this quote may seem to contradict the formal interpretation, by taking this capacity to be a moral ideal, this is not really the case. This is accounted for by the fact that Rawls's theory is not *symmetrical* between those who chose an autonomous life and those who do not. Rawls's ideal of the liberal state will mean different things to liberals and to non-liberals, though they may all be able to accept it.

To religious or otherwise non-liberal persons, the capacity to form, revise and pursue a conception of the good means that they can be who they are. This implication is of course valid for the liberal person who believes in the good of autonomy too. However—and this is where the asymmetry is found—if you believe in autonomy you may perceive Rawls's second moral power as an affirmation of your particular conception of the good. Autonomous people are not merely allowed to be who they are. Their identity of autonomous choosers of ends is in fact affirmed by the liberal state (when it is justified in a Rawlsian fashion).

Liberals, but not traditionalists that is, will receive recognition of their particular identities simply by virtue of living in a society that recognizes each individual's right to be who he or she wants to be. The paradox of the second moral power, the fact that Rawls believes it to be both formal and substantive, reflects the asymmetrical standing of liberal and non-liberal citizens in a liberal society. Every autonomous choice of a life-style is good in the eyes of the liberal, whether the choice is itself a choice for a liberal way of life or not. But the same is not true for the non-liberal. To him or her there is no value in the fact that people make autonomous choices unless this choice is in fact a choice for the *correct* life-style.[42] These differences show us that the capacity to form, revise and pursue a conception of the good will have both formal and substantive values for a liberal. The autonomous life-style is enabled as well as encouraged, whereas the non-autonomous life-style will merely be enabled. To them, liberal institutions and values will be of purely instrumental, or formal, value.

Yet, the formal value of autonomy is all Rawls wants to establish. As a formal value it fits with the overall ambition of Rawls's theory. A liberal theory of justice does not provide an answer to the question of the meaning of life. A liberal theory of justice should provide viable and just options for political life.

> [J]ustice as fairness does not seek to cultivate the distinctive virtues and values of the liberalisms of autonomy and individuality, or indeed of any other comprehensive doctrine.[43]

The ideas invoked in the justification of political institutions shall therefore be considered as valid exclusively in relation to this political end. The assumption that people have two moral powers should be accepted as valid for political life, not for ordinary life. The scope of liberalism is consequently restricted. This is the implication of Rawls's notion of *political* liberalism.[44]

When the political purpose of liberalism is appreciated it becomes easy to see why Galston's, Beiner's and Dagger's interpretations are mistaken. As an example we may take the reasoning found in the work of Richard Dagger. Like many others he believes that Rawls defends the ideal of moral autonomy. Dagger concludes that, "[Rawls's] attachment to autonomy is plain."[45] To vindicate this conclusion Dagger quotes Rawls as saying that "the exercise of the two moral powers is experienced as a good."[46] On Dagger's reading this reference shows that Rawls perceives the autonomous life as desirable in itself.

Nevertheless, Dagger's interpretation is unwarranted. Once we realize that the moral powers are valued "politically" it should be easy to see that they should be "experienced as good" only in this context. It is only when people enter the role of the citizen, when they discuss the constitutional basis of their society, that they need to accept that everyone has the capacity to choose a conception of the good. The citizen need not be autonomous, nor need he or she strive to become autonomous. Rawls's liberal theory does not prescribe the "exercise" of the moral powers as generally good or desirable. These powers are just, as Rawls points out, part of people's "essential nature of *citizens*."[47]

Rawls's Virtues

The conclusion of this chapter is that Rawls's theory does not include an account of intrinsic virtue.[48] This conclusion is supported by an analysis of Rawls's work with regard to both explicit statements about virtue and implicit ideas. In the first instance, it could be established that Rawlsian liberalism does not encompass the virtues of solidarity or fraternity in but a metaphorical sense. The virtue of fraternity Rawls claims to support is not supported at all.

Secondly, I have examined the assumptions at the foundation of Rawls's liberal theory. The notion of "moral powers" found there has frequently been interpreted as expressing an ideal of virtue. However, I have endeavored to make clear that these "powers" are defended for either instrumental or political reasons. The virtue of justice is an instrumental virtue: it makes people act in accordance with their considered judgements about justice. The virtue of autonomy is not adequately characterized as instrumental, because it is not supposed to be acted on at all. The liberal state does not express a preference for autonomous lives over others. However, the liberal state recognizes the capacity of autonomous choices of life-styles. The virtue of autonomy is political: it is not a virtue to be supported, encouraged or acted on. In sum, the Rawls theory does not express a commitment to a liberal ideal of man and does not, consequently, include ideals of intrinsic virtues. In contrast to Ronald Dworkin, Rawls does not believe that liberalism rests on any set of ethical beliefs. There are no second-order virtues recognized by Rawlsian liberalism: no traits of character that are considered as intrinsically valuable.

However, by defending Rawls's own interpretation of his theory another criticism is found warranted. This is the criticism leveled by certain writers that liberalism does not recognize the relevance of intrinsic virtues. The claim that liberals deny a political role to intrinsic virtues appears to be justified in respect to Rawls. Whether this denial is justified, in the case of Rawls, is a question that remains to be answered. Subsequent chapters will deal with this matter. The arguments of Rawls will be assessed in chapter five and, especially, in chapter eight.

Notes

1. Rawls, 1993, pp 13 and 175. Also, Rawls, 1971, p 25.
2. Flathman, 1995, pp 47f; Macedo, 1990, p 256.
3. See Ronald Beiner, 1992; Richard Dagger, 1997; William Galston, 1991. The attribution to Rawls of an ideal of the autonomous person is also found in Vinit Haksar (1979, p 199), and Michael Sandel, 1982, pp 106f, 176f, and *passim*. However, Haksar's and Sandel's assessments rest exclusively on Rawls's early writings and are for that reason less relevant.
4. Rawls, 1971, p 105.
5. Rawls's famous principle of distributive justice states that social and economic inequalities are justified *only* when more beneficial to the worst-off than any alternative distribution. Rawls, 1993, pp 5f, 291; Cf Rawls, 1971, pp 60f, 83. It may be noted that Rawls, in his recent writings, puts somewhat less emphasis on matters of distributive justice. Rawls (1993, p 229) no longer believes that distributive justice is a "constitutional essentiality."
6. David Miller, 1977, p 487.
7. Galston, 1991, p 129, (emphasis added).
8. The virtues of cooperation and tolerance were analyzed in chapter two.
9. It is against this disrobing of the subject that Michael Sandel has forcefully objected. Sandel (1982, p 119) argues that a self without commitments and allegiances (an "unencumbered self") would not be able to "choose normative principles at all" and that a self without identity is utterly inconceivable.
10. See Michael Gorr, 1991, p 21. See also Rawls, 1971, p 255, 561.
11. Rawls, 1971, p 255.
12. Rawls, 1993, p xvi. Rawls does not specifically point out which inconsistencies he refers to though they are characterized as concerned with the "comprehensiveness" of his earlier work. Brian Barry denies that Rawls's early work is "comprehensive," in the sense of including conceptions of the good life. Interestingly Barry seems to charge Rawls with misunderstanding his own theory. Barry, 1995 b, p 877.
13. Galston, 1991, p 120.
14. Rawls, 1993, p 19.
15. Galston, 1991, p 121.
16. Rawls, 1979 [1975], p 6.
17. Rawls, 1993, p 19.
18. Galston, 1991, p 122.
19. Flathman, 1995, p 47. See also Macedo (1990, p 256) for a similar but more sympathetic interpretation.

20.   Remember that Rawls's second principle of justice states that "social and economic inequalities . . . are to be to the greatest benefit of the least advantaged members of society." See Rawls, 1993, pp 5f.

21.   It has been objected that the realization of Rawlsian justice requires an *ethos of justice* that "guides choice within the rules [of just institutions], and not merely direct agents to obey them." Gerald Cohen, 1997, p 10. Yet, as I understand the notion of a sense of justice it requires that citizens have *whatever* dispositions which are necessary in order for social justice to materialize itself. The sense of justice will, if necessary, include an "ethos of justice."

22.   William Riker & Peter Ordeshook, 1973, pp 277–280.

23.   Rawls, 1971, p 497.

24.   "[T]here is no reason to suppose that the answers to questions of action and regulation must be consistent. " Riker & Ordeshook, 1973, p 278.

25.   Rawls, 1971, p 497.

26.   Rawls´s argument is, following this interpretation, analogous to Rousseau's (as often cited as misused) assertion that the citizen might have to be "forced to be free." The point is that it may be rational to allow the use of force upon free-riders, including oneself potentially, in order to secure collective rationality. When you are forced to comply with principles you have freely accepted you are in fact "forced to be free." See also Jörgen Hermansson, 1997, and Walter G Runciman & Amartaya Sen, 1965, pp 556, 559f. Cf footnote 31 below.

27.   Brian Barry powerfully argues that the early Rawls is committed to the idea of justice as "mutual advantage." Barry, 1989, *passim*.

28.   Rawls, 1993, pp 48ff.

29.   Rawls, 1993, p 5.

30.   Rawls, 1993, p 35, 141 (emphasis added).

31.   This view challenges the established analogy between Rawls and Rousseau (see fn 26 above) according to which the virtue of justice helps us to secure collective rationality. Rather, the virtue of justice "forces" citizens to be free because it "helps me to be the sort of person I want to be" (Plamenatz, 1992, p 173). Using Sen's terminology, we may say that acting in accordance with the idea of justice is to prefer one ordering of preferences (where equality and liberty is the aim) to another (where maximizing self-interest is the aim). See Amartaya Sen, 1974, pp 63f.

32.   Rawls, 1993, p 107.

33.   Rawls, 1971, p 143 (emphasis added).

34.   Beiner, 1992, pp 32, 42. For explicit connections between the ideal of autonomy and Rawls, see Beiner (1992, pp 42f).

35.   Richard Bellamy and Vinit Haksar draw similar conclusions from their analysis of Rawls's work. Thus Bellamy argues that "the significance Rawls gives to the two moral powers . . . will only make sense within a comprehensive liberal view." Richard Bellamy, 1996, p 86. Similarly, Haksar (1979, p 199) concludes that "we can only make his [Rawls's] argument work if he allows autonomy as an intrinsic good . . . admitting perfectionism as a political principle."

36.   Rawls, 1993, p 314.

37.   Dagger, 1997, pp 190f; Macedo, 1990, pp 255f.

38.   Rawls, 1993, p 99 (emphasis added).

39.   Rawls, 1993, p 315.

40.   Rainer Forst, 1992, pp 298f.

41.   "Of course, many persons may not examine their acquired beliefs and ends but take them on faith, or be satisfied that they are matters of custom and tradition. They are not to be criticized for this . . . " Rawls, 1993, p 314.

42.   This is not to say, of course, that every non-liberal will find other people's choice of a liberal identity as of *negative* value. The traditionalist (and, possibly, some liberals too) may be completely indifferent to how others choose to live. However, in contrast to the liberal the traditionalist will not find *positive* value merely in the *way* choices are made.

43.   Rawls, 1993, p 200.

44.   Rawls, 1993, *passim*. See also Mulhall & Swift, 199, pp 12, 175, 207.

45.   Dagger, 1997, p 190.

46.   Dagger, 1997, p 190, 192.

47.   Rawls, 1993, p 203 (emphasis added). Cf. Beiner's (1992, pp 42f) conclusion that Rawls, by making "much of the ideal of designing for ourselves a 'rational plan of life'" is thereby committed to the value of autonomy. See also Sandel (1982, p 176) who ascribes to Rawls the idea that citizens must regard their "values and choices [as] the products of choice." Direct references to Sandel's claim are found in John Rawls, 1992 [1985], p 204, fn 21, and in Rawls, 1993, p 27, fn 29. But cf Rawls, 1971, pp 407–411.

48.   In this respect I agree with Brian Barry's characterization of Rawls's theory as not being "ideal-regarding," a theory that does not prescribe as valid for all a specific ideal of the good life. Barry, 1990 [1965], pp xlv–xliv. Cf Rawls, 1971, pp 326f.

5

Rights and Virtues: In Conflict?

Will a state that promotes some particular virtues necessarily violate the rights of individuals? A number of liberals have been inclined to answer in the affirmative. They believe that whenever the aim is to improve the character of citizens the state is given an excuse to "bully, oppress and torture" them.[1] From the perspective of a liberal commitment to the institution of individual rights, the idea of a politics of virtue will appear as a dreadful alternative. However, my aim in this chapter is to demonstrate that there is no necessary conflict between the idea of a state that encourages virtue and a commitment to individual rights.

What I want to stress, in effect, is the possibility of a liberalism less hostile to virtues that is, at the same time, firmly committed to the protection of individual rights. The basic idea is that a state that recognizes virtues need not violate individual rights, although it is commonly believed that it will. The aim of this chapter is in this sense rather negative: I will not defend a particular theory of rights, or a theory of virtue. My aim is to examine the rationale for the view that rights and virtues could not be protected simultaneously by the state.

Yet the alleged conflict between rights and virtues is nurtured not only by liberals but also by the conservatives' claim that rights encourage vicious and selfish characters. In this view, the more the state attends to the protection of individual rights the less virtuous people are likely to be. Thus, there are two versions of the claim that virtues and rights conflict. I believe they are captured by the following statements:

1. A state protecting individual rights will not successfully promote virtue.

2. A state promoting virtue will not successfully protect individual rights.

Notwithstanding appearances to the contrary, these claims are not identical. The first claim (that the protection of rights impairs virtue) could be true even if the second (that the pursuit of virtue harms rights) were not. To reject the second claim is to say that rights may be adequately protected even when the state pursues certain virtues. However, this is not to say that virtue prospers under these circumstances. Perhaps the protection of rights inhibits the pursuit of virtue? In that case the first point is still valid although the second is not. In sum, in order to establish the general compatibility of rights and virtues we will have to examine both claims.

Virtue and the Protection of Rights

One argument for the incompatibility of virtuous behavior and the protection of rights runs as follows. The institution of rights encourages certain attitudes and behavior. Where rights exist, the relations people have tend to be antagonistic and conflicting. Do not trespass: I have a right to this property! Do not touch me: I have a right to physical integrity! In this view, the behavior and the attitudes that come with rights are detrimental to the institutions that foster many valuable virtues. Rights separate people from each other. Claims of rights tend to break up ties of friendship and intimacy that otherwise provide a home for love and virtue.

The destructive consequences of rights are visible in countries where rights have made "relationships generally more adversarial" according to one writer.[2] Most alarming are the effects of rights on intimate relations, where we generally believe that generosity and solidarity should prevail. To the extent to which we find those virtues valuable we must, consequently, abandon some of the rights we have. Liberalism's emphasis on individual rights is detrimental to the growth of virtue.

Against this view it has been pointed out that the relation between rights and virtues is one of mutual dependence. Rather than suppressing virtuous action, the institution of rights secures the basis for such action.[3] Unless individuals have rights that protect them from abuse and oppression they will be unable to do good to each other and exhibit virtues of generosity and love. Thus, claims of rights are not the enemy of virtuous relations but provide a condition for them.

The two perspectives referred to above suggest two conflicting views concerning the relation between rights and virtues. According to the first, rights tend to bring people against each other and thereby reduce the opportunity for virtuous action. According to the second, rights provide the secure and necessary framework for virtue. As they stand, these views seem to contradict each other. However, I believe that the arguments referred above are not in conflict, though often presented in terms that encourage this interpretation. In this section I will show why this is so by analyzing a recent debate about the place of justice and virtue in the family.

The Family: Virtuous or Just?[4]

In both liberal theory and practice, the introduction of notions of justice and equal rights in the context of the family is a latecomer. Whereas the relation between parent and child or between wife and husband was for a long time regarded as beyond the sphere of rights, there is a growing tendency to include these relations as well. Rights are no longer the privilege of the public sphere, as shields against the power of state or the market. Rights also regulate how the members of the family should treat each other.

Now, the relations between the citizen and the state, or the relations between consumers on the market, are obviously different from the relations that prevail within families. One apparent difference is that the relations in a family usually are more intimate and affective: There are emotional bonds that tie family members together that do not seem to have any correlative in the public sphere. Michael Sandel has taken this fact as demonstrating the irrelevance of rights in this sphere. For instance, while claims of justice are frequent in political and economical contexts they seldom appear in the family. Sandel believes this absence of right-claims is only natural given the characteristics of family-relations. Claims of justice, Sandel writes, "are seldom invoked [in the family], not because injustice is rampant but because their appeal is pre-empted by a spirit of generosity in which I am rarely inclined to claim my share."[5] Thus, Sandel believes that generosity and virtue replace justice and rights in the family. Where everyone shares with the others and where kindness and intimacy prevails there simply is no need to claim possessions, redistribution or distance. Although somewhat idealized, it must be noted that this assertion is descriptive. Sandel's claim about the generosity that pertains in the family states what *is* and not what *ought* to be. Yet, Sandel believes that this alleged fact has normative implications.

Assuming that families are naturally inclined towards virtuous behavior Sandel invites us to consider whether introducing ideas of justice and rights in this context is necessarily desirable. If the family is not generally unjust, as Sandel argues, and if the members in the family typically are generous towards each other, why should the principles of justice apply?

Well, someone might answer that it is desirable, even for virtuous families, to introduce principles of justice that guarantee every member a share of the family's wealth. A fair share, secured by a conception of justice, is not a bad thing. But to this argument Sandel objects that justice may in fact be bad. Introducing notions of rights and justice will affect people's dispositions and attitudes and may make them less generous. Sandel believes that claims of rights encourage conflictual attitudes. We may need some examples to illustrate this idea. For example, where I know I have the right to a certain amount of the total wealth of my family I may become less inclined to give any of it away. Where rights dominate the scene people will ask themselves, "Is this all I am entitled to?" and "Am I required to give some of it away?" In contrast, where generosity is the norm the question of what you *must* give to me or what I *must* give to you simply is not the relevant one. We show generosity to those we love by giving spontaneously, not by acting out of duty. Feeling obliged to give does not show intimacy. If this picture is true, if justice means that what Sandel calls a "judicious temper" replaces generosity and affection, the conclusion may in the end be that introducing rights in the family is a mistake.[6]

Susan Moller Okin rejects Sandel's analysis of rights and justice in the family. In fact she challenges two of Sandel's claims. Okin argues, firstly, that the presence of "standards of justice" will not disrupt the affective bonds within the family.[7] Justice and love can coexist. Okin thereby seems to reject Sandel's idea that a "judicious temper" will destroy the intimacy and generosity that characterizes family relations. To this claim Okin adds a second which contradicts, and does not merely deny, the ideas Sandel stands for. The point is not only that rights do not cause any harm to virtuous institutions, but that rights are in fact necessary in order for virtue to grow and prosper within such institutions.[8] The virtues Sandel speaks about will develop *only* when justice and rights exist. In order for family members to exhibit virtues they need the guarantee for integrity and security that rights and justice can give. According to this view, virtue depends on rights. According to this view, virtuous behavior presupposes a system of rights.

Rights as "Fall Backs"

It is clear that Okin and Sandel believe they represent opposing standpoints. Their attitudes to how virtues and rights are to be integrated with the family appear to be incompatible. However, it is less clear whose claim is the better. Taken separately, their views may seem to be equally justified.

On the one hand, it seems undeniable that Sandel is justified in warning us against the application of strict justice within the family. If the distribution within the family of money, food, or goodies, is made to depend on the right-claims of the members this may harm intimacy and the propensity for generosity. Considering for a moment what a right is lends further support to this claim. This is so because rights are inseparable from the making of claims. This feature of rights is part of what makes them so important in political and economical contexts.⁹ The logic of rights, where the making of claims abounds, explains why they are likely to encourage conflict. Moreover, that conflict is detrimental to affective and intimate relations is clear.

On the other hand, we must grant that Okin's view is also true and important. Okin argues that rights are essential to the practice of virtue. When someone's rights are violated—it may be the right to physical integrity or the right to a fair share of the family's resources—he or she will certainly be less likely to develop a virtuous disposition. To be treated justly by the members of the family is plausibly a condition for developing virtues such as generosity.

Thus, we are faced with two views that seem equally plausible and, yet, these views are incompatible. Or, are they really? I believe, in fact, that there are several issues at stake here, not one. Disentangling these different issues will reveal that the dispute between Okin and Sandel is chimerical and that they can, therefore, both be right.

Let us first look at ways of analyzing the basic terms of the dispute. In discussing the place of rights in marriage, Jeremy Waldron distinguishes between rights as "fall-backs" and rights as "constant restraints."¹⁰ The idea is that a right may be understood either as a shield we use exclusively when relations break down or as a device that always constrains and regulates the way partners treat each other. Waldron does not pursue this idea much further. In any case, it appears to be relevant to the issue discussed here.

For instance, while the right not to be physically abused can be seen as a constant restraint on how parents should treat their children some other right may be more like a fall-back. Take the right to a fair share of the family's wealth. Arguably, it is unjust for wealthy parents to withhold their wealth and let their children subsist on a bare minimum level. It is possible, in other words, that parents treat their children unjustly in relation to a conception of social justice. Still, many people would hesitate to subject family relations to ideals of distributive justice. Using the terms introduced by Waldron, justice may be a fall-back rather than a constant right. Justice in the family is important when things go seriously wrong but does not define norms for how members should treat each other when things go well.

Waldron's distinction appears to be helpful in order to understand the issue at stake between Okin and Sandel. It would seem that what Sandel objects to is the idea of rights as constant constraints. He believes that a continuous and consistent protection of rights in the family will disrupt the affective bonds that is the basis for virtue. In contrast, Okin's claim can be understood as an insistence on the importance of rights as fall-backs. She need not necessarily deny that a *constant* protection of rights can be harmful. What matters is that there are rights that protect family members when relations break down. Therefore, for Okin the essential point is that rights as fall-backs exist. Now, if Sandel speaks about rights in the sense of constant constraints and if Okin speaks about rights in the sense of fall-backs there is no longer a conflict between them. Sandel can accept Okin's claim, namely that there should be rights when relations break down. Okin can accept Sandel's claim, namely that rights should not be insisted upon in normal functioning relations. The idea of rights as fall-backs is then a correlative to Sandel's idea that justice is a mere "remedial virtue," something we appeal to when life is not as it should be.[11]

Rights: Language or Fact?

Yet the problem is not so easily resolved. We may wonder, firstly, whether Okin is really prepared to accept that rights are relevant merely when relations break down. The point of departure for Okin's critique of Rawls is, after all, that the contemporary institution of the family is *not* just. Rather, the way responsibilities, recourses and roles are distributed within the family is according to Okin "a relic of caste and feudal societies."[12] Thus, rights and justice must be immediately relevant. The institution of the family is and has always been "astray."

Secondly it does not seem that Waldron's distinction fully catches the basis for Sandel's complaint. Sandel's critique is aimed primarily at the "judicious temper" that he fears will imbue family relations. Sandel is concerned with the "motivations" and "dispositions" that characterize family relations. When we come to think of it, this question does not concern what rights people have. The question of which dispositions are appropriate is in principle distinct from the question of whether rights establish constant or occasional constraints. In fact, it should be possible for Sandel to accept that there are rights within families and that principles of justice are relevant. Why must he even restrict the validity of rights to fall-backs? What should matter, from Sandel's perspective, is not which rights there *are* but which rights we *claim*. A person may plausibly have a great deal of rights in relation to those whom he or she loves most. That does not, by itself, affect the intimate relations of that person. However, relations are affected when we begin to claim these rights as rights. But then it is the language of rights that causes a problem and not the fact that people have rights.[13] There is, as has been pointed out in relation to the rights of children, a difference between possessing a right and claiming a right.[14] A person need not claim all the rights he or she possesses.

By interpreting Sandel's anxiety as concerned more with the language of rights, and less with the existence of rights, the gap between him and Okin can be narrowed. It is clear that Okin does not speak about the uses of language. What matters to her is that people respect each others' rights. But in order for that to happen there is not necessarily a need for more claims of rights. If there is some truth in Sandel's warnings about the detrimental effects of right-claims, justice may be more effectively realized by *not* presenting it as a claim. Perhaps discussion, common deliberation, or the introduction by the state of some form of incentives, is more conducive to justice between wives and husbands or between parent and child.

It is not self-evident that to claim a right is the best way to secure respect for that right. So, Okin could well accept Sandel's point without abandoning her aim that rights and justice ought to be secured within the family. Similarly, Sandel could accept Okin's aim without withdrawing his idea that the language of rights is generally inappropriate in affective relationships. Thus, the distinction between possessing and claiming rights tends to resolve the conflict.

However, the reconstruction of the debate I propose does have substantive implications for our understanding of Sandel's position. Once we accept Sandel's complaint as concerned with the rights vocabulary rather than with the existence of rights, we must reconsider his view that justice is a "fall-back" and a mere "remedial virtue." In this view, rights and justice within the family are secondary to virtues. Yet, we know now that this assertion harbors a certain ambiguity. Justice may in fact be secondary in two different ways, corresponding to the distinction between possessing and claiming a right. By describing justice as "remedial" we may mean that it is less important that justice and rights *exist* than which virtues and dispositions that do. But there is a different way of understanding the "remedial" character of justice. The idea might be that it is less important that *claims* of justice are made than that the principles of justice are satisfied. The idea that justice is secondary may in other words refer either to the existence of justice or to the claims of justice. Sandel appears not to perceive the difference. Unfortunately this mistake encourages a reading whereby the existence of justice and rights is treated as less important than the existence of virtue. That position is rightly criticized by Okin. Nothing could plausibly be more important than securing the rights to physical integrity, life and welfare. The virtue of generosity, cherished by Sandel, is no substitute for the right not to be physically abused.

However, my point is that a subtler reading of Sandel eventually makes the objections raised by Okin superfluous. The sense in which justice and rights are secondary to the question of which virtues and dispositions we have, is that which concerns the language and claims we make. The idea is that it matters a lot, especially in intimate relations, which vocabulary we use. Words like "right" and "claim" may have disruptive effects. This is not to say that institutions of rights and justice should not exist. All this means is that it is more important that rights *are* respected and that justice *is* made than that the claims of rights and justice are *heard*.[15]

The Importance of Language

In this section I have dwelt on the idea that a politics of virtue is in conflict with the protection of certain claims of rights. My analysis of the controversy between Michael Sandel and Susan Moller Okin is intended to illustrate some of its aspects. As I discovered, the dispute is due to a failure to distinguish between the different modes of rights. In this context it is necessary to separate claims concerning the language of rights and claims concerning the existence of rights. Once we appreciate this distinction I believe we are in a position to reconcile the perspectives of Sandel and Okin. To the extent to which this result is generalizable we may conclude that the growth of virtue, even within intimate relations, is not thwarted or distorted by the existence of systems of rights and justice however extensive. What matters in order for virtue to prosper is not which rights we have but the use that we make of them. In order to preserve intimate relations it may sometimes be prudent to restrict the use of right-claims. However, this observation does not warrant the further conclusion that a concern with virtue is in conflict with the institution of rights.

The Fear of Virtues

At least since the French Revolution, many liberal writers have argued that a politics of virtue leads to encroachment on individual rights. This claim is backed up with examples from history. "The Reign of Terror" during the French Revolution, the "Red Terror" following the Russian Revolution, and even the atrocious regime of Nazi-Germany, are all taken to illustrate the violent excesses of virtue. In crystallized form, the American libertarian Ayn Rand expresses the idea that the politics of virtue implies terror:

> If a man believes that the good is intrinsic in certain actions, he will not hesitate to force people to perform them . . . It is the intrinsic theory of values that produces a Robespierre, a Lenin, a Stalin, or a Hitler.[16]

Rand argues, in effect, that belief in intrinsic virtues produces violence and terror. She blames the "intrinsic theory of values" for the atrocities committed by Hitler and others. It is noteworthy that such a claim attributes moral responsibility to a theory and not to the men and women who enforced it. Yet the argument is not without its historical precedents. In Talmon's influential work on totalitarianism, Robespierre is quoted as declaring that terror is the natural consequence of virtue; "La terreur n'est autre chose que la justice prompte, sévère, inflexible; elle est donc une émanation de la vertu."[17] Virtues and terror, in other words, are inseparable.

Quotes like this may convey the revolutionary spirit of Robespierre and his time. Yet there is a difference between creating a "sense" of certain events and creating a good argument. What is the justification of the claim that the belief in intrinsic virtue "produces" terror and violence? I believe it is helpful to distinguish between *historical* and *conceptual* evidence for this view. Either, the claim is a statement of empirical facts or, the claim is about conceptual relations between virtue and other notions. According to the first view, a politics of virtue *produces* coercive or violent acts. According to the second view, a politics of virtue *justifies* terror and rights-violations.

There is also another, slightly different way of stating the difference between these arguments. The question discussed in this chapter is whether the idea that the state pursues virtue is inevitably in conflict with the protection of individual rights. But this question is highly ambiguous because there are two importantly different ways in which the state may fail to respect the rights of individuals.

In the terminology of Judith Thomson, a right is *infringed* whenever the state fails to comply with a right. By contrast, a right is *violated* not only when the state fails to comply with a right but also when the state should not have failed to comply with that right.[18] Thus, when the failure to comply with a right is described as an infringement, the question whether there were good reasons or not for that failure remains open. That a right is infringed upon is merely to say that the right-claims of someone were not in fact respected. For example, when a car hits you your right to physical integrity is infringed on, whether or not the driver was in fact justified in hitting you. It may be the case that the infringement was quite justified. Perhaps hitting you with the car was the only way to prevent you from hitting a couple of children playing on the road. However, in case no such justification can be found the hit will be a violation of your rights. A violation occurs only when a failure to respect a right is considered as illegitimate and unjustified. When we say that a right is violated we are not merely reporting but evaluating a fact. In other words, violations are the same as unjustified infringements.

Here, the distinction between infringement and violation corresponds to the distinction between the historical and the empirical argument. The historical argument is that the politics of virtue infringes rights. The historical claim is about facts, not whether they are justified or not. The conceptual argument goes further than that. It says that the politics of virtue violates rights. The politics of virtue will, on the conceptual view, justify and motivate rights-violations. Implicit in the conceptual claim is the conclusion that these rights should not have been violated.

The Historical Argument

Historical evidence for the destructiveness of virtue is frequently referred to. In general the argument is that many violent regimes in fact celebrated the need for virtue or pursued a politics of virtue. The argument is, in other words, that there is a strong empirical correlation between a belief in virtue and the infringement of rights.

Yet, in order to have faith in the historical claim, we would need to know whether the regimes that celebrate virtue are indeed more violent than those that do not. After all, it may well be that *all* moral and political ideas are risky. Joseph Raz has pointed out that not only virtues and ideas of the good life have been used as a pretext for terror. Accordingly, there are generally good reasons to be cautious about the powers granted to the state. Yet, it is difficult to prove that ideas of virtue are so risky that governments should never promote them.[19]

Such points indicate some of the weaknesses of the historical argument. The problem is perhaps also a question of generalization. Can we legitimately claim that the wrongs committed in the name of virtue in 1789 and 1917 provide an argument against official support for virtues in 2000? Well, the current practice in Taliban controlled Afghanistan might make us inclined to answer in the affirmative. The armed patrols of Kabul, preserving the population's "virtue" and protecting them from "vice," show us that the historical argument is still relevant. But if there is reason to believe that a politics of virtue generally leads to terror there must also be a general theory that accounts for this. Why, more exactly, does the pursuit of virtue have such sinister consequences?

One possible answer is to be found in the seemingly intrusive character of any attempt to foster virtues. To make a person virtuous is, after all, to interfere with a person's life. This is the basic idea in Robert Nozick's general critique of state interventions. Whether the intention is to improve the living conditions of citizens or to encourage virtue, such actions are likely to infringe the rights of individuals. Nozick argues that this occurs whenever the state tries to make society conform to *a pattern*. But what is a pattern? It is a distribution that follows what Nozick calls "a natural dimension." A natural dimension, in turn, is a feature that varies naturally between individuals and/or across time. So, to distribute a good according to "moral merit," "need" or "usefulness to society" is to pursue a patterned principle.

The idea of patterned principles is, in Nozick's work, primarily designed to dismantle the alleged corrosive effects of attempts to create distributive justice. Nozick argues that anyone that believes that justice means "to each according to ... ..." is predisposed to a patterned theory.[20] But as is intimated by Nozick's example, the rejection of patterned theories does not only concern theories of social and distributive justice. Since the politics of virtue represents an attempt to distribute some amount of public resources according to one "natural dimension," i.e., the likelihood that an activity or institution promotes virtue, it too must be rejected. The politics of virtue may, just like theories of distributive justice, be presented as an attempt to impose a pattern on society. And, unsurprisingly, that is what makes such policies wrong in Nozick's view.

Since the main target of Nozick's critique of patterns is Rawls's theory of social justice, it is somewhat surprising that Rawls should recently have articulated some closely related ideas. Using a different terminology, Rawls points at the inherent danger of a state committed to the maintenance of "comprehensive doctrines." Rawls writes that "a continued shared understanding on one comprehensive religious, philosophical, or moral doctrine can be maintained only by the oppressive use of state power."[21] Rawls's claim is that the government is unlikely to maintain one specific doctrine for a consequent period of time without taking recourse to violence and oppression. The maintenance of Catholic faith through the Middle Ages is taken to illustrate this thesis. Though society changed and developed the state tried to maintain strict adherence to the doctrine of

Catholicism. The inevitable consequence of such a policy was a high degree of oppression. The Inquisition "was no accident" Rawls concludes.[22] In sum, the rights of individuals are likely to be infringed whenever the state endeavors to maintain a certain doctrine over time.

Despite the fact that Rawls does not share Nozick's political ends—Rawls argues in favor of distributive justice and Nozick argues against it—they appear to have one basic assumption in common. Both believe that there is a "natural" distribution of values or resources that varies, in an equally natural way, over time. Any attempt to maintain a specific distribution of them will therefore require interference with processes otherwise spontaneous and free. Both Nozick and Rawls in other words emphasize the complexity and dynamics of society. They argue that, because of this complexity, the state is unlikely to be successful in any attempt to mould society according to some ideal. Or, to put it in another way, if the state is successful this can only be the result of extensive use of coercion and violence. Thus, Nozick argues that "the general point . . . is that no . . . principle of justice can be continuously realized without continuous interference with people's lives."[23]

One difference between Nozick and Rawls is, of course, that while Nozick speaks about natural dimensions of *any* sort Rawls only refers to the doctrines or belief-systems people have. Hence, Rawls is saying that variations in beliefs, but not in wealth or property, should be protected from interference by the state.

However, that the theory of patterns provides a convincing argument against the pursuit of virtue is not self-evident. Nozick's claim is that policies of redistribution or of virtue, where the aim is to pursue a certain pattern, will require "continuous interference with people's lives." Now, we must ask what the alternative to a politics of pattern may be.

Nozick, presumably, believes that the opposite of a patterned political system is one in which no interference with people's lives occurs. In other words, the alternative advocated should be a politics of "non-interference." Now, can the state ever be non-interfering? Wouldn't even a libertarian state have to use force in order to maintain its own legal, political and economic systems? Certainly a state that accepts Nozick's definition of justice, according to which justice means freedom of acquisition, will require "continuous" corrections. Just entitlements might be disrupted, as Nozick points out, by people that "steal from," "defraud" or even "enslave" others.[24] Whenever that happens, a state committed to the protection of justice will have to interfere in order to protect the original distribution. In order to maintain just entitlements, there must exist in other words a system that can justify interference and the use of violence. The exclusion of patterns cannot, consequently, be motivated solely on the grounds that this will *avoid* interference. The non-interference thesis does not hold.

The same point is of course valid against Rawls too. Just as Nozick's system justifies violence in order to maintain itself, Rawls's ideal of social justice will require constant corrections. Interference is required whenever wealth and property become unevenly distributed as a result of unfair processes. The existing system of rights will have to be protected by the threat that force and violence will be used if necessary.

Yet, is it not true that the preservation of property rights will necessarily imply *less* interference with people's lives than any patterned theory would? Surely, to prevent damage to life and property will require less violence than any attempt to make people virtuous. However, this assertion is rather controversial. In fact, it brings us back to where we started: the belief that ideas of virtue are necessarily more violent than other ideas (such as the protection of rights). I concur with Raz in believing that there is no general reason to conclude that this is so.

There is no reason, for instance, to believe that a libertarian regime that ignores distributive and social justice will not be highly repressive. The regime of Pinochet is a case in point. The exact aim of the junta was to protect property and wealth. However, these rights were protected only at the price of immense human suffering in terms of torture and death. Similarly, a libertarian regime that ignores social and redistributive issues may, unintentionally, find itself unable to cope with social pressure for change without using repression and coercion. When huge social and economic differences persist in a country (which people wrongly, according to the libertarian theory, may find unjust) the consequence is likely to be popular pressure for change. Then, when the masses oppose the system and call for social reform the libertarian regime may have to use force in order to restore order. In fact, "have to" is no mere hypothesis but a statement about what the state has a duty to do in terms of libertarian morality. Not repressing attempts to implement social justice would in fact be failing to preserve just entitlements (property rights). The libertarian state will, in other words, have a duty to interfere violently with people's lives in order to preserve existing holdings of property and wealth.[25]

A more specific reason to doubt the correctness of the less interference thesis in relation to Nozick's ideas, is the observation that he *prescribes* a great deal of immediate interference with people's present holdings and property. Nozick in fact argues that the entitlement system of justice, which gives prominence to the protection of property rights, will require a "rectification" of the present distribution of wealth.[26] Since the present distribution of wealth is to a considerable extent based on the cumulative effects of historic grievances (colonialization, confiscation, insufficient compensation for labor, etc.) the need for redistribution and compensation is immense. Nozick, plausibly, believes that a consistent protection of property rights must assume that the property people have at present is not due to past injustices. Yet, apparently, to implement this idea would mean justifying a lot of interference. The truth of the "less interference thesis is therefore doubtful.

A final objection to be leveled against Nozick is that his own theory cannot avoid making use of patterns. Nozick's point is, remember, that a pattern is a certain distribution of something that normally varies according to some natural dimension. The claim is that a state exclusively concerned with the protection of just entitlements, the rights to life and property, is not pursuing any patterns. Any distribution of merit, wealth etc, is a possible outcome and the state must not interfere in bringing any specific distribution (or pattern) about. Yet, as pointed out by Will Kymlicka, Nozick in fact defends one specific pattern: the Lockean proviso.[27] There is no right to acquire and to monopolize a resource that is necessary to the life of others or such a right exists only where there is "enough and as good left over." This proviso, named after John Locke, will in fact require the libertarian state to pursue a certain pattern. This is so because not every distribution of wealth and property is consistent with the Lockean proviso. Goods, wealth and property cannot, consequently, vary freely along natural dimensions.[28] Even the libertarian state is bound to pursue a certain pattern.

One question arising from this discussion is whether patterns can *ever* be avoided. Another question is whether avoiding patterns is necessarily desirable. Though it may be true that Nozick is inconsistently affirming the Lockean proviso, it is not necessarily true that the best response for him is to abandon the proviso rather than to abandon his insistence that no patterns may be pursued. In sum, the aim and the purpose of interference may be more important than the amount of interference. Perhaps the libertarian state becomes more just, more legitimate, when the Lockean proviso is accepted. In that case, it is not the amount of violence or interference that matters most. What matters is *why* the state uses coercion.

The amount of violence needed in order to sustain a particular ideal will undoubtedly affect the burden of proof. If a political system that fosters virtue interferes more with people's lives than a libertarian system, then perhaps the former system will require a more extensive justification. The amount of violence, coercion and interference is relevant after all. But there is, I contend, no reason to believe that the exclusion of patterned theories necessarily makes the state less interfering or violent. To demonstrate that virtue, or any other pattern, implies excessive use of coercion would require further empirical evidence—which does not, so far, exist.[29]

And yet, making people virtuous does seem to require a lot of interference in their lives. How can the rights of individuals be secured when the state pursues excellence, virtue and goodness? This question points at the possibility of virtues being conceptually related to the infringement of rights. The problem with regimes that promote virtues is not that they are *likely* to infringe rights. The problem is rather that the idea of virtue in fact *justifies* acts of violence and terror. The conceptual claim is consequently stronger. Instead of infringements we are now, using Thomson's terminology, speaking of violations. However, the thrust of my argument will be that the conceptual argument is only conditionally valid. The propensity for conceptions of virtue to justify violations of rights exists only when certain assumptions are made and believed to be true. My claim will then be that these assumptions need not be accepted and that, consequently, the critique does not hold good.

The Conceptual Argument

The reason why the politics of virtue lead to misery, Hegel thought, is that it is impossible to demonstrate virtuousness. If being virtuous means having a "clean conscience," then no one else but the individual can know whether he or she is in fact virtuous. A clean conscience cannot be observed from the outside and there is, therefore, a permanent reason to doubt any pretence of virtuousness. Thus, the inescapable consequence of a society where virtue is the highest good will be suspicion and paranoia. Hegel went so far as to say that "death" is inevitable where virtue reigns.[30]

In contrast to the historical argument, this point is conceptual. Zeal for virtue causes terror, according to this view, because virtuousness is impossible *per definition* to demonstrate.[31] Hegel's observation about the inherent dangers of virtue represents one version of the conceptual argument. Liberal writings convey other versions.

Generally, the point is that an extensive use of violence might be justified where the need for virtue is regarded as a political aim. The belief that people may be better than they are, that they can be more virtuous, is therefore dangerous. A belief like that makes us indifferent to the sufferings of existing people, since it nurtures the illusion that we have the power to create people that are more virtuous. Isaiah Berlin defended this dystopic view of virtue. He thought that the belief in a better self justifies tyranny and torture.

> Once I take this view, I am in a position to ignore the actual wishes of men or societies, to bully, oppress, torture them in the name, and on behalf, of their "real" selves.[32]

Berlin argued that the notion of virtue introduces a split in our image of the self; the real self is set against a possible better self. The rulers may use this gap, Berlin feared, to neglect the actual wants and feelings of people.[33] When rulers say they want to promote a higher good they are given an excuse for eliminating what actually is.[34] But the split between a real and an ideal not only threatens people as they are. In Rawls's view, the belief in intrinsic values may also be used to justify the violation of the rights of some people in order to produce this good for others.

> Whenever a society sets out to maximize the sum of intrinsic value . . . it is liable to find that the denial of liberty for some is justified in the name of this single end. The liberties of equal citizenship are insecure when founded upon teleological principles.[35]

There is nothing in the idea of a politics of virtue, Rawls seems to say, that tells us why it is wrong to produce more virtuous people even at the expense of the rights, or lives, of some other people. Again, the idea is that virtues are conceptually related to the violation of rights. The point is that one good idea (that the good should be promoted) will justify a bad idea (that the rights of individuals may be violated). The idea that society ought to "maximize the sum of intrinsic value" excuses the denial of some people's liberties according to Rawls.

There are, in sum, three versions of the conceptual argument against virtue. The first claim, the one Hegel makes, is that virtue leads to terror because virtuousness cannot be proved. The second claim is that the pursuit of virtue might make us ignore people's actual wants and desires. This claim is Berlin's. This *intra*-personal problem is contrasted by the third claim, presented by Rawls, that concerns an *inter*-personal problem. Rawls warns us that the maximization of virtue may turn out to justify the violation of some people's rights in order to make other people more virtuous.

The inter- and intra-personal problems envisaged by Berlin and Rawls have important features in common. They both believe that rights violations cannot be justified merely for the sake of creating more virtue or goodness. Rights can never be *compensated* for, they argue. But the implications of this claim need to be appreciated carefully. As noted by Derek Parfit there are two aspects of the claim that what is bad cannot be compensated for.[36] In fact, Berlin's and Rawls's point consists of two claims: that no individual rights must ever be violated, *and* that rights can never be compensated for.

The meaning of the first claim is obvious: a right must not be violated even when potential benefits from doing that are important. Using Thomson's terminology, this means regarding any infringement of a right as a violation of it. Infringing rights can never be justified.[37]

The second claim, that rights cannot be compensated for, is a different one. It is directed towards the assumption that a moral harm done to one person can be redeemed if only enough good is given to someone else. This idea is rightly criticized. Shooting one person in order to save five others does not mean reducing or compensating the harm to the first person.

Still, rejecting the idea of compensation is not to accept that rights can never be violated. It is no contradiction in terms to agree that harm to one individual cannot be compensated for and, at the same time, claim that it is sometimes legitimate to violate some person's rights in order to produce some good. There is no contradiction here since even if compensation is impossible, overriding the rights of someone may nevertheless be the best alternative. This is illustrated by the example discussed above. It may be right to shoot one person in order to save five others even though the good consequences of doing that does not compensate for the evil caused to the person that is killed. That consequences are better is not the same as saying that consequences compensate. The issue is not, in other words, whether the violation of rights can be compensated for. Plausibly they cannot. The issue is whether violating rights can ever be justified.

Now, liberals claim that virtues do justify the violation of rights. Why is that? A clue is found in the fact that liberal objections to utilitarianism typically are regarded as valid in relation to theories of virtue too. Rawls explicitly makes the parallel.

> The situation resembles that of classical utilitarianism . . . the sum of value might be best increased by very unequal rights and opportunities favoring a few. Doing this is not unjust on the perfectionist view provided that it is necessary to produce a greater sum of human excellence.[38]

Rawls uses the term "perfectionism" to describe the position that virtue ought to be the end of politics. The idea that unites utilitarianism and perfectionism is, according to Rawls, that it is desirable to increase the sum of certain values. In the utilitarian view, value might be defined in terms of preference satisfaction, utility or pleasure.[39] Defenders of virtue, in contrast, define value in terms of good character or virtuous acting. However, in both cases it is assumed that political decisions should be made with one single value in mind and that they should maximize this value.

The problem with this view, from a liberal perspective, is that every right becomes susceptible to balancing.[40] A utilitarian might accept the existence of individual rights. However, the weight accorded to any right will depend on the extent to which it is conducive to the maximization of utility. Similarly, where there is one single conception of the good life, the value attached to rights is always considered with this ideal of the good in mind. On these accounts, individual rights are always justified with reference to a dominant value such as utility or virtue.

By contrast, where rights are "taken seriously" the value of a right cannot be balanced out by some other value. In the liberal view, to have a right *is* to possess a claim that one's interests are not balanced against some other values or interests.[41]

Thus the objectionable feature of utilitarianism and conceptions of virtue consists in their propensity to make rights a question of balance. But is this allegation fair? It should be noted that the force of the critique hinges importantly on the *analogy* between utilitarian theories and theories of virtue. To the extent that the analogy holds good the critique may well be justified. However, to the extent that the analogy does not hold good the objections will lose much of their force. And, in point of fact, I do *not* think that the analogy does hold good.[42] My belief is that the similarities that Rawls ascribes to utilitarianism and the theory of virtue do not apply. I do not think that a defender of virtue need subscribe to the view that political decisions should always be made with the idea of maximizing virtue in mind. Though perhaps inseparable from utilitarianism the ideas of dominance and maximization are not necessarily (or even plausibly) associated with any conception of virtue. I shall now explain why.

The First Analogy: Dominance

Utilitarianism makes utility or happiness the dominant value of society. By "dominant" I mean here that one particular conception of the good is considered valid in all spheres of society. In the case of utilitarianism this good is usually specified as welfare.[43] Decisions concerning health, happiness, sex, or moral rightness, should all be made with the aim of increasing welfare. Arguably, it is sometimes the feature of dominance that makes utilitarianism objectionable in the eyes of the liberal. If all decisions should, ultimately, produce welfare then the individual's rights cannot be given any special status. Rights seem always to be at the mercy of welfare in the utilitarian world.

Do defenders of virtue typically argue that all normative questions should be addressed from the point of view of virtue? Do all decisions need to be made with the promotion of the dominant value of virtue in mind?

It is obvious, firstly, that many defenders of virtue do not identify one single virtue as good. Usually, there are a great number of virtues that are considered as desirable to cultivate. The ecologist may for instance insist that concern for nature and concern for animals are both intrinsic virtues. According to classical tradition, furthermore, the virtues of wisdom, courage, justice and temperance were all regarded as intrinsic, or "cardinal," virtues. These examples could be continued. Which virtues do Marxists and conservatives subscribe to? Whatever the answer, it is implausible to suppose that the answer will refer to only one virtue. The virtues that are good are commonly considered as plural rather than singular.

Yet, the insufficiency of this point is easy to see. Whereas it might be clear that a politics of virtue always includes many virtues, it certainly seems to embrace only one *set* of virtues. Ecologist virtues might be plural. But the ecologist way of life is just one way of life. Hence, we do not avoid the conclusion that there is only one dominant set of values.

Another argument is therefore needed. A distinction has to be made between a dominant moral value on the one hand and a dominant political value on the other. A conception of virtue and the good life may dominate morality. After all, it may be true that the basic moral terms we use are in fact reducible to a singular category of the good life. This may be so, although many writers advocating virtues deny that this is the case.[44] But this issue, concerning the nature of morality, need not concern us here. The issue we are interested in is how to make political decisions. In that regard we need not assume that there is only one value of relevance. A *politics of virtue* need not, that is, be identical to an *ethics of virtue*. In that way, the feature of dominance can be avoided. Considerations of virtue may apply to some political issues (say, cultural policy) whereas considerations of individual rights might be more salient in others (say, criminal law). Advocating the idea that a multiplicity of moral ideas is relevant to political decisions is not the same as committing oneself to a position about the nature of morality or ethics. That certain ethical terms are relevant to decisions of policy can be conceded without taking a stand on one of the fundamental issues of ethical and moral theory.

Utilitarianism typically does not distinguish between these matters. The utilitarian equates moral theory to political theory and thereby treats all political decisions as moral decisions. However, there is no need to accept this view. The ethical foundation need not be the same as the political foundation. Anyone sensible to the multitude of considerations that are relevant in politics will acknowledge that no singular set of concepts should be dominant.[45] And this suggestion can be accepted whether or not ethics is in fact singular or not.

I conclude, in other words, that one important objection to the politics of virtue can be met by modifying its pretensions. Just as it is ridiculous to believe that political questions should be concerned exclusively with utility or rights, so it is ridiculous to believe that virtues should play this dominant role. The thrust of a politics of virtue is the idea that considerations of virtue should sometimes be allowed to influence decisions made by public institutions. The idea of a politics of virtue is a theory about politics and should consequently be distinguished from the notion of an ethics of virtue. Therefore, the observation that an ethics of virtue is singular just like utilitarianism is simply irrelevant.

The Second Analogy: Maximization

Consider the example where the right to a fair trial is ignored for the purpose of delivering unambiguous and deterring convictions to the public. The aim is to promote virtue (of the public) and the rights of only one person (the accused) are ignored. This example illustrates well the similarity between virtues and utilitarian theories. Utility could be substituted for virtue in this example without significantly changing the point.[46]

Should virtue, just like utility, be maximized?[47] If that is so, some of the objections that apply to utilitarianism will apply to virtues too. The fear expressed by liberals is that a duty to maximize a value will justify that burdens are imposed on some people in order to maximize this value to others. Cruelty can be justified as long as it maximizes the good. Berlin expressed this fear in writing that when virtue or utility guides the efforts of society the government is provided with an "excuse" to "bully, oppress or torture" its citizens.

Calculations of this kind cannot be avoided merely by rejecting the idea of dominance. The idea of submitting other values or practices to the supreme end of virtue involves two further ideas that appear to be common to utilitarianism and conceptions of virtue. One idea is that values can be added and summed together. This is a precondition for the utilitarian's idea that all decisions should be conducive to utility or welfare. The moral costs of one act must be comparable with the costs of another act in order to determine what ought to be done. Sen and Williams identify this feature as the idea of sum-ranking.[48] Sum-ranking is a distinct idea to that of dominance (e.g., welfarism): it is imaginable that only one kind of value is recognized (e.g., welfare) but that there is no acceptable way of deciding how to weigh and compare welfare between individuals.[49] To these two ideas utilitarianism typically adds a third: the idea of maximization.

This idea is distinct from both dominance and sum-ranking. The idea that the good should be maximized does not depend on the view that all values can be subsumed and added together into one great calculus. That values are possible to count and add, sum-ranking, is an idea about how to compare values. The idea that values should be maximized is an idea about what to do with them.

Maximizing seems a powerful idea especially due to its close relationship to the idea of rationality. Surely, a rational person prefers more rather then less of what is good.[50] Here I will focus on the idea endorsed by utilitarianism, that it is a moral obligation to maximize what is good. This idea is in fact central to teleological theories of which utilitarianism is one version. The teleological feature is that the right action is that which produces "maximal goodness." Acting morally is, then, to act in a way so that the good is maximized.[51]

Despite the salience of the idea of maximization it is surrounded by mysteries. What is the source of the obligation to maximize? "To *whom* is it a duty?" as Kymlicka rhetorically asks.[52] Does the fact that some value is good imply that we ought to maximize that value? Is it irrational to believe that what is good need not be maximized?

Take the good of food. Everyone agrees that food is good and that it is a moral good that everyone has food. Now, is this a reason to maximize the supply of food? In the abstract this seems an impossible question to answer. How can we know whether the supply of food ought to be maximized before we know how much food people need? Now, the fact that the question lacks an answer in the abstract suggests that there is *no* general duty to maximize the supply of food. There is plausibly a moral duty to help provide food to those who have no food. Yet, such a duty does not really imply that food supplies ought to be maximized. All it implies is that *enough* food is produced. It seems pointless to continue to maximize a good at the point where everyone is satisfied.

Yet, the example of food could be objected to. A utilitarian might say that food is not a "real" good but just an instance of what is a more basic good. Certainly, people cannot have more food than they need, there is no need to maximize beyond that level. That is, the real good at stake is not food but utility. It is because food brings utility to people that we have an obligation to provide people with food. The duty to maximize therefore applies to utility in the first place and to food only to the extent to which this is necessary in order to maximize utility.

Demand being necessarily limited, then, is no objection to the idea of maximization. Utilitarians can accept this but maintain that it applies only to what people happen to want. What is morally important, i.e., utility or welfare, should always be maximized. Nevertheless, there are important objections to the idea of maximizing utility too. Whether total or average sums of utility are maximized the conclusion might be far from attractive. Is a world with only a few people morally better than a world with many, if average utility is slightly higher in the first? Or would it be morally desirable to increase the world's population enormously, even if it meant making people very poor, just because doing that would increase the total sum of utility?[53] A consistent maximizer would have to answer in the affirmative to these questions. A consistent maximizing policy might therefore be of a doubtful merit.

However, a more specific point concerning the maximization of virtue would be more adequate and, in fact, I believe there are arguments to the effect that virtue is especially inappropriate to maximize. My belief is in fact that the idea of maximization is incompatible with the idea of intrinsic virtue. I will give two examples to defend this claim.

First, imagine a number of virtues: courage, friendship and political participation for example. Let us assume that these virtues are all considered to be intrinsic values and part of our conception of the good life. In this view courage, friendship and political activity are valuable in themselves. Now let us assume that there is a duty to maximize what is valuable. To accept that the virtues mentioned here are valuable would then imply that courage, friendship and political activism ought to be maximized. Again, the theory need not recommend us to *aim* at maximization. The theory defines as good our acting in ways that will have the *result* of maximizing virtue and the best way to do that need not be aiming at maximizing: looking for friends is not always the best way to make friends.

There is, nevertheless, something weird about the idea that the best state of affairs is that in which a maximum amount of courage, friendship and political activity exists. Friendship is perhaps a valuable virtue. But it is difficult to see why having ten friends should necessarily be more valuable than having five.[54] It is equally difficult to see why a person that devotes two hours a day to his or her local party is necessarily more praiseworthy than the person who devoted only two hours a week. Obviously, a person that is more active will perform more virtuous acts than a person who is less active. But is that person therefore more virtuous? I do not think the answer is obvious. A good friend, a good citizen or a good adventurer is not necessarily a person who exhibits these virtues more frequently. These virtues are, after all, meant to be part of the good life, and a good life to me might just include a few friends rather than many. The point of the good life is not to contribute to the total sum of virtuousness in the world. This point is aptly summarized in Kymlicka's question, "to whom is maximizing a duty?"

There is another way of putting this objection. When a value is maximized we are not merely achieving certain results. To maximize something is also to act on calculative reasons. There is a certain amount of deliberation necessary in order to choose the courses of action that will in fact give maximal leverage.

Now, many virtues, for example the virtue of friendship, do seem to be incompatible with deliberate calculation. Arguably, a friend who is calculative will not be considered very trustworthy. Can you trust a friend who is committed, not to you, but to the abstract end of maximizing friendship? Wouldn't you always fear that the relation risked being sacrificed on the altar of maximization?

Perhaps the maximizer of virtue can accept this point. Admittedly, to maximize is self-defeating in order to achieve certain virtues. But a more prudent maximizer will then just refrain from being calculative in such cases. In that way virtue will be more effectively maximized.

However, this consideration misses the point. The point that calculation is incompatible with certain virtues holds good even though the rational maximizer deliberately avoids a maximizing attitude. Christine Swanton has persuasively made this point.[55] The fact is that friendship, if considered a virtue, is not merely incompatible with a calculative attitude: the virtue of friendship is arguably incompatible with calulative behavior. It is not enough to say "alright, now I'm your friend and I won't be calculative any more" when the reason for saying that is to maximize virtue.

In sum, *being* calculative may ruin the achievement of virtue. This is the case when a person is friendly in order to receive benefits or in order to maximize goodness. *Acting* on calculative reasons will also be detrimental to virtue. This is the case when a person decides to become your friend in order to receive benefits or in order to maximize goodness. This, again, is the case when a person decides to be politically active for the sole purpose of maximizing the level of political activity in his or her community. In neither case is maximizing appropriate, despite there being a good that is desirable.

To conclude, there are two reasons why maximizing intrinsic virtues is not a feasible idea. The first has to do with the apparent implausibility of assuming that more virtue is always better. Virtue is supposed to be an ingredient of the good life. But the best life need not be maximally virtuous. Maximizing utility may be reasonable but to maximize friendship, love or courage surely is not. It is not clear that a world where more people rather than less are courageous or in love is for that reason necessarily a better place.

The other reason for being suspicious about the idea of maximizing virtue is the fact that calculation and deliberation are dispositions that do not go easily with certain virtues. The problem does not just concern the case where a person acts virtuously from calculative motives. *That* problem need not bother the maximizer, who is more concerned with maximal results than with maximizing attitudes. The problem in fact concerns the entire idea of introducing calculative reasons into the context of virtue. Choosing the dispositions that best maximize virtue, even if that need not imply a calculative attitude, will ruin many virtues. Being virtuous is to have certain dispositions and motives because they are good and not because they produce more virtue. The difference in relation to utilitarianism is, in this case, perhaps best stated as a difference concerning the ethical significance of motives. The defender of virtue does allow that motives and reasons for action may have intrinsic value. The utilitarian cannot do that.[56]

Rawls's and Berlin's analogy between virtues and utilitarianism consequently fails.[57] The liberal fear is that individual rights will be sacrificed for the sake of virtue. But when it becomes clear that virtue should not be maximized this fear is eventually shown to be unjustified.

The Failure of the Analogy

My idea is that the propensity of a theory of the good to justify violations of individual integrity and rights will diminish once two assumptions are abandoned. The first assumption is that there is one single good only. The second assumption is that the good must be maximized. The presence of both assumptions characterizes classical utilitarianism. An objection to that theory is that it justifies the violation of individual rights by subordinating them to the abstract end of maximizing the good. This is the case when the good of one person is likely to be increased in the future by violating his or her present interests (Berlin's objection). Violations may also occur as a result of a trade-off between the interests of different persons (Rawls's objection). Perhaps, on the aggregate, there is a potential net gain of virtue or utility by violating the rights of some individuals.

By combining the two dimensions discussed here in figure 5.1 it appears that four different positions can be distinguished. The point here is that the idea of a politics of virtue is structurally distinct from that of classical utilitarianism. That is accomplished by changing position on the two issues: by moving from the upper-right box to the lower-left box. The elements of dominance and maximization are abandoned.

Figure 5.1
The Relation between Conceptions of the Good
(e.g., utilitiy or virtue) to the Institution of Rights

		The good is:	
		Non-dominant	*Dominant*
The good should be :	Maximized	Rights are not defined in terms of the good, the good is maximized	Rights are defined in terms of the good, the good is maximized (e.g. classical utilitarianism)
	Not Maximized	Rigths are not defined in terms of the good, the good is not maximized	Rights are defined in terms of the good, the good is not maximized *

*This position corresponds to the modified version of utilitarianism proposed by Kymlicka (1991, chapter 1)

My general argument in this section is that none of the features that have provoked the critique from liberal writers are necessary to a politics that recognizes the relevance of intrinsic virtues. In relation to the *historical* argument I pointed out that a politics of virtue does not necessarily involve more violence than the protection of rights. Any political system justifies coercion and violence to a certain extent. Whether one system should be preferred to another does not primarily hinge on whether it is less or more violent but on the extent to which this violence can be justified morally. Whether coercion is justified or not cannot be answered simply by investigating empirical or historical evidence.

In relation to the *conceptual* argument my focus has been on the assumptions implicit in the liberal critique. I have endeavored to demonstrate that the belief in the danger of a politics of virtue stems from assuming an analogy to utilitarianism. While it is true that there are similarities in the structure of theories of virtue and utilitarianism it is also true that there are important differences. Where virtues are promoted they need not be thought of as the sole end of the political community. Neither must a politics of virtue depend on the idea of maximization. By rejecting assumptions like these, it is possible to avoid balancing virtues and rights against each other in a simplistic way.[58] The promotion of virtue will not, that is, justify the encroachment of the rights of individuals.

The general conclusion of this chapter is that a commitment to rights is not in conflict with the idea of a politics of virtue. A government that decides to pursue certain conceptions of the good need not infringe or violate the rights of its citizens. Although I have not proved that a politics of virtue is necessarily desirable, I have attempted to prove that some of the conflicts that frequently are assumed to exist between virtues and rights are illusory.

Virtues and rights may, consequently, be consistently protected by the state. This fact suggests a further conclusion. Since adherence to rights can be paired with the pursuit of virtue, the common claim that the liberal state is or ought to be neutral to conceptions of the good and to virtues appears as a distinct demand. Giving rights priority does not mean, then, that the idea of a neutral state is accepted. The argument for neutrality must be assessed as a separate claim.[59]

In the following chapters I shall discuss the reasons and beliefs associated with the ideal of a neutral state. This complex and often forceful ideal has exerted much influence on recent liberal arguments. However, I shall argue that the considerations underpinning the idea of neutrality cannot establish a conclusive case for the exclusion of virtues and conceptions of the good life. In this chapter I have assumed that the insistence on rights is justified. I asked whether taking rights for granted would by itself constitute a reason against a politics of virtue. In the chapters that follow I shall not assume the validity of the principle at stake. Thus I do not propose to examine whether the principle of neutrality and the idea of a politics of virtue conflict or not. I shall take that for granted. My aim is rather to examine whether neutrality can be justified in the sense that politics of virtue are excluded from politics. Are there convincing arguments to the effect that the liberal state should be neutral in relation to conceptions of the good and of virtue? That is the question to which I now turn.

Notes

1. Isaiah Berlin, 1984 [1969], p 24. In the Swedish context Ingemar Nordin defends a similarly drastic view. The state in attempting to improve the character of citizens is likely to end up with "murder, physical abuse, theft or enslavement" (my translation). Ingemar Nordin, 1992, p 45.
2. Beiner, 1992, p 94. For this view, see also Mary Ann Glendon, 1991, pp 9 and 14, Ronald Terchek, 1983, p 77ff, and Charles Taylor, 1986, p 57.
3. That rights are the basic condition for virtuous behavior is argued, for example, by Holmes (1993, p 236).
4. See also Beckman (1999), where the liberal conception of the family is explored.
5. Sandel, 1982, p 33.
6. Sandel, 1982, pp 32–33. Incidentally, Sandel's position recalls Robert Nozick's (1974, p 167) critique that justice is "inappropriate . . . as a governing principle within a family."
7. Susan Moller Okin, 1989, p 32. Okin is explicitly addressing Sandel's claim.
8. Okin, 1989, pp 28f, 97–100. The basic point stressed by Okin is that justice in the family is essential for justice in society as a whole. Unequal or oppressive relations between parents, or between parent and child, will prevent the growth of a sense of what is just and fair in other, wider, contexts.
9. That rights are typically claims is persuasively argued in Joel Feinberg, 1966, pp 143f. Note that the sense in which rights are, in this view, "claims" is sociological and not philosophical. It is therefore unrelated to Hofeldh's distinction between claim-rights and liberty-rights. In Feinberg's view, to which I refer, *all* rights are associated with the making of claims. I can claim my right! This primitive sense of claim is not identical to the subtler distinction between rights that imposes duties on others with respect to me (i.e., the duty not to torture me) and rights that protect us from having duties (i. e., the absence of a duty to paint my house in any particular color). While the former are called claim-rights and the latter liberty-rights, they both involve claims in Feinberg's sense, since they enable the making of a specific moral or legal demand on others. On Hofeldh, see Peter Jones, 1994, pp 14–22.

10. Jeremy Waldron, 1988 a, pp 643f.
11. Sandel, 1982, pp 31–32.
12. Okin, 1989, p 22.
13. Sandel never makes this distinction, though it figures in the work of Ronald Beiner and Mary Ann Glendon. They criticize what Beiner (1992, p 95) calls the "language of rights" or what Glendon (1991, p x) identifies as the "rights discourse." They accept as unproblematic however "rights as a philosophical category" (Beiner) and "notions of rights" (Glendon). Their complaint concerns the language of rights, which Beiner finds "ugly." Yet, their position is nonetheless ambiguous, since it is not clear how legal rights fit into their categories. Do legal rights belong to the category of "notions" or the category of "discourse"? Should some legal rights be dispensed with or not?
14. David Archard, 1993, p 90.
15. Whether the language of rights and justice will in fact have distortive effects on intimate relations is partly an empirical question, however. Callan (1997, pp 86f) has argued against Sandel, but without using much empirical evidence either, that raising claims of rights do *not* conflict with the demands of love and intimacy.
16. Ayn Rand quoted in Harry Binswanger, 1986, p 228.
17. See Jaaqov Leib Talmon, 1986 [1952], pp 114f.
18. Judith Jarvis Thomson, 1990, p 122.
19. Joseph Raz, 1986, p 160. See William Connolly's remark that "it is never in itself a sufficient argument against an idea to say that it can be misused. That is true of all important ideas." As Connolly makes clear the important question is therefore to prevent the idea from being misused. William Connolly, 1993 [1974], pp 144f.
20. Robert Nozick, 1974, p 159. The (unpatterned) idea Nozick defends is summarized by him as "from each as they choose, to each as they are chosen" (p 160). This saying is, of course, a parody of the Marxist formula; "from each according to his ability, to each according to his needs." Karl Marx, 1977 [1875], p 569.
21. Rawls, 1993, p 37.
22. Rawls, 1993, p 37.
23. Nozick, 1974, p 163.
24. Nozick, 1974, p 152.
25. A related question discussed by Thomas Scanlon is whether social justice in fact requires "continuous interference with people's lives." Though using the state apparatus for redistributing wealth necessarily involves taxation and, therefore, some interference with people's lives, it does not follow that the state must interfere with all transactions. Nozick claims that "giving" is made suspect in a society where incomes are (however marginally) redistributed by the use of taxes, because any free gift will upset the desirable pattern of equality. Yet, giving is not incompatible with the ideal of social equality. In other words, to give is all right but to keep it all is not. See Thomas Scanlon, 1982 [1976], pp 110ff.
26. Nozick, 1974, pp 152f.
27. Kymlicka, 1990, p 158, fn 10.
28. The case discussed by Nozick in this context is where the monopolizing ownership of natural resources, e.g., the sources of water in a desert, threatens to kill the remaining inhabitants.
29. One exception is perhaps to be found in the work of Ernest Gellner. He argues that, in the case of the Soviet Union, the illiberal outcome was the result of a combination of belief in virtue and zeal for industrialization. Ernest Gellner, 1994, pp 135, 137ff, 179.
30. "Gesinnungsterror" is the term used by Hegel. See Hegel's *Vorlesungen über die Geschichte der Philosophie*, quoted in Steven B Smith, 1989, p 251. In fact, Talmon

(1986, pp 159f) who appears to be unaware of this precedent was to repeat many of Hegel's points in a twentieth-century context.

31. The same point is made by Robert Louden who notes that it is difficult to "infer character by observing conduct" and impossible to "see inside" people in order to observe their character directly. Robert Louden, 1997 b [1984], pp 187ff.

32. Berlin, 1984, p 24. In contrast, Ian Hampsher-Monk argues that Berlin's point is empirical rather than conceptual. Yet, as I understand Berlin his argument is that certain horrifying actions may be justified in terms of virtue. Berlin does not merely say, although he may say that too, that certain (violent) acts are historically correlated with certain ideas (of virtue). Cf Ian Hampsher-Monk, 1995, pp 272, 286 fn 19.

33. Compare this view with Judith Shklar's crisp statement of the liberal creed: "[liberalism] is a government for people as they are, not as they might be." Judith Shklar, 1984, p 235.

34. Thus, Berlin's condemnation of virtue follows from his more general point that "ideals" are inherently dangerous. See, for this view, Isaiah Berlin 1990 [1988].

35. Rawls, 1971, p 211.

36. Derek Parfit, 1984, pp 337f.

37. Thomson 1990, p 122.

38. Rawls, 1971, p 330.

39. While a preference-utilitarian maximizes satisfaction of existing preferences, a hedonist utilitarian maximizes satisfaction of utility in terms of pleasure and pain, and the ideal utilitarian maximizes certain intrinsically good states of mind (that are defined independently of the agent's preferences and of what maximizes pleasure). John Harsanyi, 1982 [1977], p 51.

40. E.g., Raz, 1986, pp 271ff and Thomas Scanlon, 1999, pp 84f.

41. This is a point pressed with particular emphasis by Dworkin (1977, *passim*).

42. That the analogy can be questioned will not appear as surprising to anyone familiar with the fact that utilitarianism has been under frequent attacks from various defenders of virtue. For an assessment of the critique against utilitarianism articulated by the advocates of virtue ethics, see Paul Kelly, 1994. But compare with Trianosky's view that a paradigmatic communitarian such as MacIntyre is in fact a utilitarian. Gregory Trianosky, 1990, p 339.

43. Amartya Sen & Bernard Williams, 1982, pp 3f. Sometimes utilitarianism is characterized for this reason as a *monistic* theory. See David McNaughton, 1988, p 164. But cf James Griffin, 1986, pp 89ff.

44. See Charles Taylor, 1982, p 142 and Thomas Nagel, 1979. Taylor recognizes as separate claims of utility, rights and virtue, whereas Nagel distinguishes between considerations of obligations, rights utility, and virtue.

45. Thus, a person may think that virtues are fundamental to his or her life and, yet, believe that virtues should not dominate political life. Likewise, a person may not feel that virtues are important to his or her life but accept that virtues should matter in politics.

46. The problems associated with utilitarian punishments are classic. The question whether a utilitarian would recommend framing an innocent in order to prevent destructive riot is a typical example discussed in McCloskey, 1963.

47. It should be noted that the question here refers to the idea that the right action is that which maximizes goodness. This is a criterion for rightness and not a criterion for action. All acts need not *aim* at maximizing goodness in order to *be* maximizing in this sense since it may sometimes be the case that not maximizing will maximize better results.

48. Sen & Williams, 1982, p 4.

49.   In fact, the opposite conclusion is defended by James Griffin (1986, pp 89ff) who argues that there are many non-reducible values and yet a "super-scale" on which they can be ranked.

50.   For a helpful overview of the issues connected with maximizing rationality, see Michael Slote, 1989.

51.   I follow Brink, Trianosky and Kymlicka in taking the defining feature of teleological theories to be the idea that the right is "maximum goodness." See Brink, 1989, p 215, Trianosky, 1990, p 338, and Kymlicka, 1991, pp 26ff. There is, however, a further sense of "teleological" stemming from historical or sociological contexts where the idea is that there is a definitive direction to history, to mankind or to the universe. Lundström (1993, p 10) discusses the second version at length.

52.   Kymlicka, 1991, p 28.

53.   These examples are from Derek Parfit's examination of the idea of maximizing. The objection to maximizing *average* utility is the "mere addition paradox"; the absurdity that two people leading excellent lives should be preferred to a thousand other people living lives almost as good as theirs, since that maximizes average utility. The idea of maximizing the *total* sum of utility runs into the "repugnant conclusion" which says that for every population of people living high quality lives there is always a larger population, where people's lives are barely worth living, whose total sum of utility or happiness is larger. Since the total sum of utility should be realized, the latter world should be preferred to the former. Parfit 1984, chapters 17 and 19. For an attempt to meet some of the objections raised by Parfit, see Roger Crisp, 1992, pp 150ff.

54.   See also Griffin, 1986, p 145. Griffin nevertheless makes a strong case for maximizing in the personal context of "making life as good as possible." This conception does not entail the maximization of any particular value, because what makes life maximally good for you is certainly just *some* amount of each value.

55.   Christine Swanton, 1997 [1993], pp 90f.

56.   This conclusion is supported by Taylor's remark that the moot point between virtues and utilitarianism concerns the ethical status of motives. See Charles Taylor, 1993 [1986], pp 348f, and Charles Taylor, 1995 b, pp 135f.

57.   Cf Thomas Hurka, 1993, p 56.

58.   However, I do not think my answer is complete. What about the case, for example, where a major catastrophe is likely to occur unless some, perhaps minor, right of an individual is violated? Yet, in ignoring these extreme issues I am not alone. Nozick (1974, p 30) in fact writes that "the question of whether . . . they [rights] may be violated in order to avoid catastrophic moral horror . . . is one I hope largely to avoid." To protect all rights and to avoid every moral catastrophe may be practically impossible. Perhaps Taylor is right to say that only "a monster of consistency . . . will stick . . . to rights regardless of the consequences." Charles Taylor, 1985, p 201.

59.   This does not mean that rights cannot or have not been used in order to preserve the idea of a neutral state. As Sandel has argued the American constitution, the Bill of Rights and the amendments, have continuously been interpreted as restricting public deliberation and policy with respect to conceptions of the good. Michael Sandel, 1996, chapter 2.

6

Dimensions of Neutrality:
The Neutral State as an Ideal

Recent debate on the foundations of liberalism has to some extent been focused around the idea of the state as ethically neutral. Numerous critics have claimed that the idea of neutrality is a sham and only serves to hide the substantive ethical content of liberalism. In one sense the critique seems now to have been effective. Most recent statements of liberalism explicitly refrain from using the term "neutrality" in order to characterize the ideal of the liberal state.[1] Yet, it would seem as if the basic ambition of contemporary academic liberalism remains the same: the idea that comprehensive ideas, or conceptions of virtue and the good life, must not be admitted to influence the basic principles of political institutions. Therefore I take it that the idea of neutrality is still normatively relevant.

Neutrality may be understood as a normative criterion with which to judge the extent to which political institutions conform to the liberal ideal. According to this view, the government that prohibits abortion by referring to the sacredness of God's creation, or enacts discriminatory laws on grounds of the superiority of one race over another, is illiberal since it fails to be neutral among conceptions of the good. Enacting laws by reference to God or race is wrong, not merely because such laws may do harm to particular individuals, but because they are grounded on illegitimate reasons. The liberal demand of neutrality concerns the *legitimacy* of the state.[2]

However, critics have argued that the idea of neutrality makes the liberal notion of political legitimacy too restrictive. The complaint consists in the observation that neutrality expels not only *bad* justifications from political life. As neutrality excludes *all* reasons that rely on specific ideas of the good life, it will exclude what many citizens regard as *good* reasons too. It would seem, for instance, that state support for specific cultures, support for particular life-styles, support for the survival of ecosystems, or the fostering of virtues within the schools, would be difficult to reconcile with the idea of neutrality. These implications of liberal neutrality are clear from Rawls's work. "[T]he principles of justice do not permit subsidizing universities and institutes, or opera and the theatre, on the grounds that these institutions are intrinsically valuable."[3] A neutral government cannot recognize that a culture, an activity, an aspect of nature or some trait of character, is of intrinsic value and cannot therefore support them for such reasons.

As a challenge to this conception of liberalism communitarian writers have articulated an alternative view. In their account politics must not be separated from questions of the good life. Rather, the liberal state must be "deliberately non-neutral" in order to maintain a society where cultural and moral pluralism thrives. The government should provide support to social forces congenial to the values of liberal pluralism.[4] Consequently, the communitarian view entails the rejection of the idea of neutrality. According to this view, conceptions of the good life may provide a legitimate basis for political action; the state cannot, even should not, be neutral.

But what is it that liberals and communitarians quarrel about; does the disagreement really concern the ideas of the neutral state? Some think this is not the case. They argue that those criticizing liberal principles of neutrality misrepresent them, deliberately or otherwise. Some even claim that the communitarians themselves endorse the idea of neutrality, and that their rejection of that idea is therefore based on a misunderstanding. The meaning of the idea of neutrality is contested and so, consequently, is any account of the implications of this idea.

It is evident that we need to clarify the idea of the neutral state before we can assess it. *What* is supposed to be neutral? Which are the implications of neutrality? In the following I shall argue that there are three different aspects of the idea of a neutral state: aims, justifications, and consequences. I shall also suggest that we should distinguish more carefully between differences in scope of principles of neutrality.

A few writers have previously observed these different aspects of the idea of the neutral state.[5] Yet I do not believe that the importance of these distinctions has been sufficiently appreciated. I believe they can fruitfully be applied to the contemporary debate about the liberal state. The aim is to improve our understanding about the various problems raised by the idea of a neutral state. I shall begin this chapter by referring to recent attempts to explain this issue in order to indicate, at the end, where they are defective and how they ought to be reinterpreted.

Confusions about Neutrality

Is the idea of the neutral state disputed? Communitarian writers claim that the liberal idea of neutral government is suspect. There cannot be an ethically neutral state they claim. However, Simon Caney has recently argued that the same communitarian writers do not in fact reject the idea of neutrality. Caney claims that we may, in the writings of a communitarian writer such as Michael Walzer, find support for the conclusion that neutrality is not in conflict with the communitarian idea of politics. Thus Caney argues that "Walzer defends liberal neutrality."[6] In yet another commentary, Alan Patten asserts that Charles Taylor—who is frequently considered to be a communitarian writer—should not be understood as criticizing liberal neutrality. Instead Taylor should be understood as defending the view that the state should not take a stand on questions of the good life: Taylor is in effect an advocate of the liberal ideal of neutrality.[7]

Now this is not how Taylor perceives his own position vis-à-vis liberal neutrality. Yet, we find again the assertion that communitarians do not really deny what they believe they do. Neutrality is not, according to these commentators, a principle with which communitarians do in fact disagree. The claims of Caney and Patten are relevant to us since they argue that the idea of neutrality is virtually uncontested. The view that the idea of a politics of virtue is in conflict with the notion of neutrality is challenged by the claims advanced by Caney and Patten.

However, my conviction is that Caney and Patten are wrong. I believe that there is indeed an important disagreement about the cogency of the liberal ideal of neutrality. But can I justify this claim? For example, Taylor, in discussing the role of the state within a multicultural society, does recognize the value of a state that does not adhere to any specific religion. The liberal principle of neutrality, he contends, is "very important" in questions of religious faith.[8]

And Walzer argues that it is necessary to separate the church from the state.[9] Thus it seems that the state should be neutral to religion even from a communitarian standpoint. But how can that be? Does not their defense of conceptions of the good imply a break with neutrality altogether?

As I will attempt to demonstrate, the present confusion depends on the fact that we have not so far clarified which theoretical sense liberals give to neutrality. There is not, I shall argue, one sense in which the state may be neutral. Once this is realized we will be able to see why it would be wrong to refer to "neutrality" *simpliciter*. In my view there are *several* distinct disagreements about the idea of the neutral state.

Two Conceptions of the Neutral State

What does the "neutrality" of the neutral state refer to? In a recent work the idea of a neutral state is described as requiring the state to take a "neutral posture" towards different ways of life.[10] Neutrality means, it is argued, that "no particular moral conception should be favored."[11] Apparently, the reference made here is to what the state *does*. The principle of neutrality imposes restrictions on the actions of the state; it must not favor one particular way of life or "moral conception" at the expense of another.

The view defended in this work may be compared to the very influential idea of liberal justice defended by Rawls, according to which it is essential that political institutions be "independent of opposing and conflicting philosophical and religious doctrines."[12] Now I believe that these statements reflect two different accounts of neutrality. In contrast to the first statement, the second is concerned with the *reasons* motivating political institutions. What matters to Rawls is not primarily what the state does, but that the state does not justify its actions by a doctrine of the good life. Neutrality is, in Rawls's account, a norm that restricts the range of legitimate political arguments and reasons.

This points at the possibility of making a distinction between neutrality in the justification of political acts or institutions, and neutrality in their aims. Generally speaking, then, there is a distinction between the grounds for an action and the purpose of it. Thus, when speaking about a neutral state we may either refer to the aims or to the justifications of that state.

This distinction is seldom made. The confusion can be illustrated by a number of examples from writings where the idea of the neutral state is defended. The writers I shall refer conspicuously fail to make clear whether they advocate neutrality of aims or neutrality of justification, or both.

Take first Ronald Dworkin's influential account of neutrality. According to Dworkin, liberalism takes the view that "political decisions must be *independent* of any particular conception of the good life, or of what gives value to life." Later Dworkin argues that the liberal view is that the government must not "*prefer* one conception [of the good] to another."[13] Though the statements quoted here may refer to the same idea this is far from obvious. When the crucial terms have been emphasized ("independent" and "prefer") it becomes possible to understand Dworkin as referring to two distinct conceptions of neutrality. According to the first quote, political decisions ought to be "independent" of ideas of the good. Thus, what is meant must be that the *justifications* of policies ought to be neutral. According to the second quote, political decisions must not "prefer" one conception of the good to another. But to refrain from "preferring" may well be the same as saying that the state should not promote or support one way of life over another and that is, as we now know, the distinct idea of neutrality of *aims*. Thus, it is unclear whether Dworkin is advocating neutrality in justification or if he also purports to defend the idea of neutrality in aims. Dworkin's ideal of the liberal state therefore seems to be highly ambiguous.[14]

Secondly, take Will Kymlicka's defense of liberal neutrality. Neutrality, he asserts, is the demand "that the state does not *justify* its actions to some public ranking of the intrinsic value of different ways of life."[15] Though this statement gives a relatively clear account of the ideal of neutral justification Kymlicka has, a few pages earlier, characterized the liberal idea somewhat differently. Here neutrality is said to imply the denial of the idea that government should "*act* in order to help some ways of life over others."[16] In this case, the focus is on the actions the state may legitimately undertake, and not on the justifications for these acts. Thus, Kymlicka seems unwittingly to have moved from the idea of neutrality of aims to the idea of neutrality of justification. Perhaps Kymlicka believes that these ideals are inseparable. As we know now, they are not.

Others, recognizing the distinction, appear to believe that it has no political or theoretical importance. For instance, Charles Larmore appreciates the distinction between aims and justifications (in a footnote) only to conclude that it matters little since they always tend to go together. A neutral justification "usually involves a 'neutrality of aim'" according to Larmore. There is a connection between political aims and political justifications because "reasons justifying political principles often concern the aims of action."[17] In effect Larmore argues that a state is necessarily neutral in aims if it justifies its actions and institutions neutrally. That is, whenever the state excludes non-neutral reasons that refer to particular ideas of the good, it is also true that the state acts neutrally and that it does not support one or the other life-style, culture or religious group.

Now I believe Larmore is wrong. It is not true that neutrality of aims follows from neutrality of justification. A decision to promote certain values or forms of life may, for instance, be justified by reference to mere prudential ends. An example of such an end would be that of maximizing profit. This end does not, as observed by Joseph Raz, seem to be ruled out as illegitimate by the liberal idea of neutral justification.[18] Neutrality of justification only applies to conceptions of the good life and comprehensive ideas; e.g., metaphysical or theological doctrines, notions of intrinsic value or theories about how to achieve self-realization or nirvana. Arguments that do not refer to such ideas can legitimately be invoked as justifications for policies and laws. Governments that want to increase economic growth may in other words actively promote ways of life (e.g., consumer-friendly ones) and get away with it without violating the ideal of neutral justification. There is a sense in which the government pursuing these policies is neutral. After all, it does not claim that some ways of life are inherently preferable or better than others. But though the *justifications* in that case may be "neutral" we could not plausibly maintain that this government is acting neutrally. Thus, the acceptance of *neutrality of justification* is compatible with the rejection of *neutrality of aims*.[19]

Once the distinction is made it also becomes clear that neutral aims may be justified non-neutrally. An instance of this reasoning is found in the declaration on religious freedom of the Catholic Church. In this declaration the right to religious freedom has its foundation in the Law that has been "revealed [by the] Word of God."[20] In this case we have an argument to the effect that the state ought to be neutral in aims; no religion is to be deliberately advantaged or disadvantaged by public institutions. Yet, apparently, the justification of this principle is not itself neutral. The Catholic doctrine of freedom of religion is justified by reference to a specific metaphysical doctrine that includes reference to some notion of the good life. Hence, in this case, a non-neutral justification supports the idea of a neutral politics of aims. As Habermas has noted, "to talk of something is not necessarily the same as meddling in another's affairs."[21] Only when the dimension of aims is distinguished from that of justification will we, I think, be able to appreciate the truth of that statement.

We may note that this distinction allows for other logical possibilities. For instance, a government may provide a non-neutral justification of a policy that supports a conception of the good that is *different* from that by which the policy is justified. This is not as awkward as it may sound. As an empirical illustration we may take the case of the established church. It is obvious that where the dominant religious creed is established as official faith, like Anglicanism in Britain, or Lutheranism in Sweden (before the year 2000, that is), the state in fact favors one conception of the good over others. However, the justification of doing this is unlikely to be expressed in terms of these creeds themselves. The Swedish government does not necessarily defend the established Church of Sweden with reference to the truth of Lutheranism. Rather, we may assume, the state claims legitimacy of its non-neutral aims by adhering to the good of maintaining a certain tradition. Thus there is one favored conception of the good (a religious one) that is justified in terms of another (a secular one).

Some of the intricate relations between neutral and non-neutral reasons allowed by the distinction may be further illustrated by a recent constitutional controversy in Germany. A conflict emerged about the constitutionality of enforcing the so-called *Kreuzesbefehl* in Bavarian schools.[22] This law, enacted by the state government of Bavaria, required a cross to be hung in every classroom. Since the cross is closely associated with Christianity, this law provoked a controversy over its consistency with the federal right of religious freedom. In the first instance, the Bavarian Constitutional Court approved of enforcing the Kreuzesbefehl. The justification spelled out by the court in the decision is of relevance to us in that it demonstrates the two dimensions of neutrality.

The Bavarian Court ruled that the cross violates no freedom of religion. It reasoned that, though the cross represents the Christian faith, it might nevertheless be conceived of as a cultural rather than as a religious symbol. Hence, accepting the cross does not necessarily require a religious confession. The only allegiance that is demanded is to that of a "Christian-occidental cultural circle," and since those values are the basis for the entire political system they cannot be ruled out as too controversial. This ruling by the Bavarian Court was later overturned by the Federal Court of Justice, which did not share the view of the cross as a religiously neutral symbol.[23] Yet, what is noteworthy in this case is the explicitness, in the Bavarian Court's ruling, of the idea that the government may have religious aims that are justified by non-religious arguments. The Bavarian Court asserted that the government might favor one religion but it also recognized, implicitly, that such activities require a secular justification. Thereby the Court in fact recognized the distinction between the notion of neutrality in justification (which it did accept) and the notion of neutrality of aims (which it did not accept).

In sum, it seems as if there is a widespread inclination amongst theorists to over-estimate the importance of the notion of neutral justification. It is often believed that a neutral justification is all we need in order to maintain a liberal state that does not promote specific life-styles or conceptions of the good. But that is not true. The fact that we exclude arguments that rest on ideas of the good does not mean that there cannot be other justifications for policies that intend to promote certain life-styles or ideas of the good life. If we want to exclude every measure that promotes some idea of the good there must also be an independent principle of neutrality of aims. This principle will then itself be in need of justification! That is, neutrality of aims does not follow inevitably from the idea of neutral justification.

A Third (and Impossible) Conception of the Neutral State

Political institutions and actions are not merely more or less *justified*, nor do they solely have different *aims*. Typically, institutions and actions have different *consequences* for citizens. A third aspect of neutrality is consequently suggested. Apart from being neutrally justified, or having neutral aims, policies and institutions may be thought to have neutral consequences. Consider the basic institutions of a market economy (laws regulating the making of contracts, the circulation of money, patents, etc.). A legal and political system upholding these institutions may be justified without reference to any specific idea of the good life. Moreover, the legal and political system may claim with some credibility that these institutions are not maintained with the purpose of promoting any particular conception of the good life (unless the purpose is, as of course it may, to create a new, consumerist, type of man). Capitalist institutions may in other words be neutral both in justification and in aims.

In any case, many people would argue that the institutions of the market economy have non-neutral consequences. The market economy will, for instance, make it more difficult for traditional ways of life to survive. Generally, too, people with an idealistic, ecologist, socialist or conservative lifestyle are disadvantaged in a market economy compared to those for whom wealth is the supreme good.[24]

Yet, what could the objection of any member of these groups be? Would they object to the fact that liberal neutrality is not being neutral enough? Or would the accusation concern the pretence, that is the rhetoric, of neutrality? Do those who complain about the non-neutral effects of liberal institutions want more *real* neutrality (making the effects really neutral) or less *talk* of neutrality (making liberal theory correspond to non-neutral reality)?

In either case the important point is—and many writers have affirmed it—that the prospect of ever achieving neutral consequences is chimerical. There cannot be the "same" consequences for everyone, because there is nothing that is "the same" to anyone. The subjective value of a given resource or prohibition is never equal. This is obvious since the tastes, preferences and capacities of individuals differ, so the subjective value of any measure will differ too.[25] Now, the equal distribution of resources is in many cases of extreme significance. But the reason why cannot plausibly be that an equal distribution is having neutral consequences.

Providing all citizens with the right to free education does not mean that all citizens will benefit equally. Thus, the justification of a right to free education cannot be that it makes the consequences of educational programs neutral. Rather, the reason why educational resources should not be distributed unequally is simply that unequal aims or justifications are unacceptable in a liberal democracy. However, unequal consequences are not themselves unacceptable.

Perhaps some would say that limiting the actions of the state would enhance neutrality in consequences. The less that is done, the less there is that can be non-neutral. But the apparent objection to this argument is to point out that a status quo, just like any social state of affairs, is a situation of different value to all.[26] Some will fare better, others will fare worse, but in no sense can doing nothing be described as having neutral consequences.

The apparent futility of an ideal of neutral consequences may explain why liberals, otherwise sympathetic to ideas of neutrality, have rejected it.[27] But it is sensible to be careful about the terminology on this issue. Though the distinction between neutral aims and neutral consequences is analytically clear, it may be difficult to discern which idea is referred to in a text. Consider, for example, Rothstein's claim that neutrality requires that "no particular moral conception should *be favored*" by the state.[28] Let us focus on the meaning of the italicized words in this phrase. Does Rothstein mean that the state must not *intend* to favor any conception of the good? Alternatively, does Rothstein mean to say which a literal reading suggests, namely that no conception of the good must actually *be* favored? Following the first reading, the issue seems to concern neutrality of aims. However, following the second reading, the issue seems to concern the idea of neutral consequences.

A similar ambiguity is found in Joseph Raz's discussion about the idea of neutrality. His analysis ignores the distinction between a political ideal that endorses neutrality of the *intended* consequences (which is equivalent to neutrality of aims) and an ideal that entails neutrality of *actual* consequences. Raz asserts that neutrality of political concern means, "that governments must so conduct themselves that their actions will neither improve nor hinder various conceptions of the good."[29] What matters is in other words what *happens* as the result of official action. Later Raz restates the principle of neutral concern as the idea that the "implementation and promotion of ideas of the good life are not a legitimate matter for governmental action."[30] In this case the intentions, or aims, of the government are in focus.

Now it is apparent that what happens is not necessarily identical to what is intended. Raz, in defining neutrality, consequently seems to refer to two separate ideas. To advocate neutrality in intentions is to advocate a feasible ideal: the government may deliberately choose not to promote virtues. However, to advocate neutrality in consequences is to advocate the unattainable. The government cannot help creating circumstances that benefit some virtues more than others.

One requirement for a fruitful discussion about the merits of an idea is that the discussants concur in their understanding of it— though, of course, they will disagree on how to evaluate it. A further requirement is that the idea discussed represents some state of affairs that belongs to some possible world. The first condition fails when someone is accused of supporting something that he or she does not believe in. The second condition fails when someone is accused of something that is a practical or logical impossibility. In the debate about liberal neutrality the claim is sometimes made that none of these conditions are fulfilled. Yet, as I have tried to demonstrate, such failures are most likely to be restricted to instances when the idea of neutral consequences is at stake. Few liberals endorse this idea, and it does refer to a practical (though not a logical) impossibility.[31]

Reconsidering Neutrality

The distinction between neutrality of aims and of justification is instructive when reassessing the alleged ambiguity of the communitarian position. In my view, the claim that Walzer and Taylor contradict themselves, or that they "really" endorse the ideal of neutrality, is incorrect and presupposes that these distinctions are not made or seen.

At one point Simon Caney refers to a case where Walzer apparently expresses approval of the idea of state-neutrality. At least in some circumstances, Walzer writes, "neutralist liberalism is appropriate."[32] This statement evidently seems to support Caney's conclusion that Walzer accepts neutrality as an ideal. Yet, when we examine the text referred to by Caney, we will actually discern a perplexing statement. "Neutrality," Walzer asserts, "is our idea of the good." That is, Walzer asserts that even if we opt for liberal neutrality this choice has to be done "from within" a conception of the good and justified with respect to it.[33] Though a neutral state is indeed a possibility on Walzer's account, this possibility does *not* comprise a *justification* that is neutral. Only neutrality of aims is an available option for governments according to Walzer. We must therefore conclude that Caney is distorting the facts when he—in apparent contradiction to what Walzer means—asserts that he "defends liberal neutrality."

Taylor's position vis-à-vis liberal neutrality is, at this point, almost identical to that of Walzer's. On many occasions Taylor denounces the possibility of a neutral justification of the liberal state. Liberalism is, Taylor asserts, "the political expression of one range of cultures," and as such it cannot offer any "neutral ground."[34] However, this assertion is, for Taylor, fully compatible with the claim that liberalism necessarily demands a separation of the state from the church. Thus, the argument set forth by Taylor seems to be that the idea of a secular state cannot itself be neutrally justified. To value the separation of politics from religion is to accept a highly culture-specific idea and a particular (liberal) conception of the good. In stating this Taylor does not, in any case, deny that some political *aims* may be described as neutral. It is, in my view, to this latter sense of neutrality, *as restrictions on the aims of government*, that Taylor refers when he claims that he is "not against neutrality in principle."[35]

Now, though both Walzer and Taylor accept the liberal idea of neutrality of aims "in principle," they do not think it holds all the way through. They object to the tendency of extending this idea to all conceptions of the good. In fact, I believe this observation deserves some attention. The disagreement concerning neutrality can to some extent be understood as concerning the *scope* of the restrictions on neutrality. Apparently the communitarian writers believe that a state may legitimately pursue at least some aims inspired by conceptions of the good life. It does seem, for instance, that while they do not think it is appropriate for the state to take a stand on religious issues, they are less concerned about the state taking a stand on cultural aims. Arguably, this distinction accounts for Walzer's remark that neutrality must be "a matter of degree."[36]

Neutrality: Here, There, and Everywhere?

That neutrality (of aims) can be a matter of degree indicates that it may apply to some, but not to all, branches or levels of political institutions. In effect, this idea appears to be similar to that of Rawls; that the subject matter for liberal restrictions is the *basic structure* of society. In Rawls's view, the idea that the scope of liberal theory is restricted in this sense is itself of great importance. The basic structure entails some, not all, political institutions. As a consequence, the requirement that the basic structure of society is neutral in aims is not to say that ordinary political decisions must be neutral in that way too.[37] While the basic set of legal and economic institutions must not be constructed for the purpose of promoting some specific conceptions of the good, such aims *are* permissible for political decisions of less importance.[38] As long as a policy does not infringe on the basic rights of citizens, Rawls could not have any quarrel with appeals to better or worse ideas of the good. For example, as Rawls has recently made clear, he regards the question of whether school prayers can be legally required, as an issue open to democratic decision.[39] It is evident that the idea of neutral aims is not meant to apply on the level of ordinary politics. Critics have not always appreciated the permissiveness of Rawls's theory in these respects. Rawls is frequently understood as defending the view that there should never be non-neutral policies in the liberal state.[40] But that is not what Rawls is saying. The principle he expounds covers the aims of the basic structure and not the aims of ordinary politics.

As has been pointed out, Rawls's account of what belongs to the basic structure and how it should be defined is by no means unambiguous. Which are the so-called "basic" institutions of society that deserve to be justified with particular care? Either we can define as basic those institutions that are of greatest importance, whose effects on the lives of citizens are likely to be most crucial. Alternatively, the basic institutions are defined as those that are the most coercive.[41] Yet, as has been observed by G A Cohen, these definitions are not coextensive. The most coercive institutions are not necessarily the most important (e.g., traffic regulations) and those that are important need not be very coercive (e.g., welfare). The concept of the basic structure is consequently somewhat ambiguous and is probably impossible to identify in a non-controversial way. Which questions are constitutional, and which are not, and whether other institutions such as the family or the economy should be regarded as basic too, is a complex issue.

The point I want to stress is that Rawls, just like Taylor and Walzer, recognizes that a democratic government may legitimately pursue at least some ideas of the good—so long as basic rights and institutions of justice are respected. In other words, the liberal requirement of neutral aims is more narrow in its scope than is sometimes acknowledged. Neutrality of aims applies only to one part of public life, namely the part that is, in some moral sense, of more importance than others.

Yet, liberal writers otherwise sympathetic to the notion of neutrality do not generally endorse the idea that neutrality pertains only to the basic structure of society. As observed by both Rawls and Brian Barry, libertarian (or, neo-liberal) writers generally do not distinguish between the different levels of political life to which liberal neutrality applies.[42] Robert Nozick's theory of rights and neutrality is a case in point. While it is not clear if Nozick accepts neutrality of justification at all,[43] his defense of neutral aims is straightforward.[44] The rationale for neutrality of aims is, according to Nozick, that citizens lead different lives and that they endorse different values. Nozick argues that if the state pursues some specific goal, accepted by only some part of the citizenry, they will "use" the other simply as a means for their purposes. Since this is unacceptable from Nozick's perspective, he contends that the state has to be neutral between its citizens and this applies, he adds, "scrupulously."[45] No value or end may be promoted by the state unless the consent of all citizens is manifest. In our terminology this amounts to a defense of the principle of neutral aims to all issues normally considered to be political. As opposed to Rawls's "narrow" conception of neutral aims, we may characterize Nozick's position as a version of "wide" neutrality of aims.

However, libertarian liberals are not alone in accepting the idea that neutrality of aims applies "widely," or to the political sphere as a whole. This idea is also to be found in the writings of Ronald Dworkin. The aims of any governmental action or law must be neutral between its citizens, since to promote one conception of the good over another would, Dworkin argues, be to "not treat them [citizens] as equals."[46] The aims must be equal in regard to conceptions of the good since people differ naturally in what they believe to be good.

In this respect, Dworkin's positions is obviously reminiscent of that defended by Nozick (which is interesting since they disagree sharply on whether the state should promote distributive justice or not). Just as in the case of Nozick, there are no explicit limits on the applicability of the principle of neutrality. Government decisions, on whatever level, must not deliberately promote any conception of the good according to Dworkin. If taken literally the ideal of neutrality of aims is incompatible not only with support for movements defending metaphysical and ethical ideas. As observed by Rothstein strict neutrality excludes all policies that promotes ideologically defined ends.[47]

The Dimensions of the Neutral State

It is time to sum up the points made here. I have maintained that the communitarian conception of politics *does* pose a challenge to the liberal ideal of political justification. This is so because the communitarian claim that it is impossible to draw a clear line between moral principles and conceptions of the good. Any political and moral justification must, in the end, adhere to ideas of better or worse ways of living and, hence, to ideas involving notions of the good life and virtue. This is not to say that communitarians must challenge every liberal restriction on the aims of governments. To argue that there are no neutral justifications is not to argue that there cannot be *restrictions* on the actions and aims of the government with respect to constitutional, or what Rawls would call "basic," issues. This is why the communitarian position, though dismissive of the prospect of neutral justifications, must be understood as incompatible only with the idea of a wide neutrality of aim. Since Nozick advocates both the idea of a neutral justification and the idea of comprehensive restrictions on the aims of political actions he will, consequently, find himself at a maximum distance from the communitarian standpoint. The libertarian and the communitarian position, in other words, are at odds on both dimensions of neutrality. In contrast, disagreement with a liberal such as John Stuart Mill would be less extensive. Since Mill accepts some specific ideas of the good life as a basis for political principles, we cannot say that he endorses the idea of neutral justification. Yet he would, just like Dworkin, reject the narrow interpretation of the scope of neutrality accepted by communitarians. Rawls and Barry, finally, seem to occupy something like the middle ground. They endorse the doctrine of neutrality of justification but they also believe in a narrow interpretation of that principle.

Figure 6.1
Dimensions of the Liberal Idea of Neutrality

The justification of political decisions is:

		Neutral to ideas of the good	Non-Neutral to ideas of the good
	Not neutral	Neutral principles, no restrictions of aims	Non-neutral principles, no restrictions of aims
The aims of political decisions are :	Narrowly neutral (applies only to basic structure)	Neutral principles, restrictions of aims apply to the basic structure (Rawls, Barry)	Non-neutral priciples, restrictions of aims apply to the basic structure (Taylor, Walzer)
	Widely neutral (applies to politics in general)	Neutral principles, restrictions of aims apply to politics in general (Nozick)	Non-neutral principles, restrictions of aims apply to politics in general (Mill, Dworkin)

Hence, liberal neutrality consists of *two* important ideas as illustrated in the figure above. The first idea is that there are certain fundamental issues into which political decisions, even though legitimized by democratic procedures, must not enter. Such restrictions can vary in scope. In Rawls's theory this idea is represented by the idea of a just basic structure outside the realm of politics. In Walzer's theory this is stated as the need for a separation of "politics itself from the state."[48] Both Rawls and Walzer agree, consequently, that some issues—such as religious ones—should be removed from the discretion of ordinary politics. Other liberals apply the idea of restriction on political action more widely. To them the issue concerns not merely the aims of the constitution and other basic institutions, but the aims of any law, regulation or action that has been enacted by the state or other public authorities. This position is most importantly manifested by Dworkin's theory.

The second idea is that liberal restrictions should, whether wide or narrow, be justified by reasons that are neutral to conceptions of the good life. In other words, liberal neutrality (of aims) claims neutrality (of justification) of itself, which means independence of ideas of the good life. Communitarians reject this way of describing liberal politics. They believe that any restrictions must themselves be justified by reference to some conception of the good life. If some category of reasons is illegitimate, this must be because these reasons are somehow "bad." The wrongness of laws justified by theological or racist ideas does not, that is, consist in the fact that they do refer to some class of reasons (comprehensive reasons) which are politically illegitimate. In the communitarian view, racist justifications are illegitimate because they conflict with our vision of the good life. Thus, if a justification is wrong it is so is because it is substantially wrong and not because it is a justification that belongs to *some* comprehensive doctrine.

In the two chapters to follow I shall examine the rationale for each position taken separately. First, are there any conclusive reasons why the state ought to be neutral *in aims*? Dworkin has, for more than two decades, claimed that such reasons exist. I shall challenge that claim. Second, are there any conclusive reasons why the state ought to be *justified* neutrally? John Rawls has in his highly influential theory tried to qualify that claim. Drawing on the vast literature that has grown up around his work I shall also attempt to challenge the basis of this idea.[49]

Notes

1. Thus Rawls (1993, p 191) writes that "I believe that the term neutrality is unfortunate." Similarly, Bruce Ackerman asserts that it was "perhaps a mistake to popularize the idea of neutrality." (Bruce Ackerman, 1990, p 29.)
2. On neutrality and normative legitimacy, see Peter de Marneffe, 1990, p 255, and Rawls 1993, p 136f.
3. Rawls, 1971, p 332.
4. Michael Walzer, 1990, pp 16ff.
5. Richard Arneson, 1990, p 218; Ludvig Beckman, 1998, pp 52ff; Steven Wall, 1998, pp 32f.
6. Simon Caney, 1993, p 660.
7. Patten, 1996, pp 42f.
8. Charles Taylor, 1995 a, p 250.
9. Walzer, 1997, p 81. See also Michael Walzer, 1983, p 248.
10. Bo Rothstein, 1998, p 31.
11. Rothstein, 1998, p 45.
12. Rawls, 1993, p 9.
13. Dworkin, 1984, p 64 (emphasis added).
14. Raz (1986, p 134 fn 1) has observed the inconsistency of Dworkin's account of neutrality. Raz also observes the contrasts between the positions of Dworkin and

Rawls. See Joseph Raz, 1994, p 109, fn 16. A different view is defended by Jeremy Waldron who charges Dworkin with being unclear about whether he endorses neutrality in aims or in consequences. Jeremy Waldron, 1989, pp 66f.

15. Will Kymlicka, 1992 [1989], p 169 (emphasis added).

16. Kymlicka, 1992, p 166 (emphasis added).

17. Charles Larmore, 1996, p 126, fn 6.

18. Raz, 1986, p 116.

19. Rawls separates *procedural* neutrality from neutrality of aims. However, a procedurally neutral justification would, as Rawls makes clear, rely entirely on formal ideas (such as consistency, non-transitivity etc). Neutrality of justification does not require *that*, but only that no reference is made to comprehensive ideas or to conceptions of the good life. See Rawls, 1993, pp 192ff. Cf Bernard Yack who argues that Rawls *does* aspire to procedural neutrality. Bernard Yack, 1993, p 238. For an attempt (however futile) to provide a procedurally neutral justification (in Rawls's sense) of liberal principles, see Hillel Steiner, 1994.

20. Quoted in Leif Wenar, 1995, pp 42f.

21. Jürgen Habermas, 1994, p 313.

22. An helpful account of the Bavarian case is found in Caygill & Scott, 1996, pp 95–99.

23. The arguments for the repeal of the Bavarian ruling are complex. One reason apparently was the clarification of the right to religious freedom so as to include a right to be free from the "cultural activities of religion." Another, less understandable, idea appealed to by the Federal Court was that describing the cross as a mere cultural symbol—which the Bavarian Court did—conflicts with Christian faith: "[t]o render the cross profane would contradict the self-understanding of Christendom and the Church." [Quoted in Caygill & Scott 1996, p 98.] But why would the fact that a law is justified in terms incompatible with Christianity render that law invalid? Would that not amount to accepting Christianity as relevant to the constitution?

24. See for an example of this critique Beiner (1992, p 69 fn 61). Hardin (1999, pp 50f) argues that neutralist ambitions pertain to political liberalism only, and that economical liberalism is not and cannot be neutral with respect to "what counts as the central value." However, given the fact that economical institutions are always regulated by political institutions it seems odd to say that the non-neutrality of the economy is irrelevant in assessing the neutrality of the political system.

25. See Kymlicka, 1992, p 167.

26. For a good survey of arguments that demonstrate the difficulties with the idea of neutral consequences, see Brian Barry, 1990 [1965], pp 75–79. See also Marneffe, 1990, p 253; Mulhall & Swift, 1992, pp 30f, and George Sher, 1997, pp 22f.

27. Rawls (1993, p 194) makes it clear that he rejects neutrality of consequences (or "effects") for exactly these reasons.

28. Rothstein, 1998, p 45 (emphasis added).

29. Raz, 1986, p 108.

30. Raz, 1986, p 110.

31. See also Michael Sandel's remark (1982, p 13) that the idea of neutral effects "seems ill-equipped to offer an effective critique [of liberal theory]."

32. Michael Walzer, 1992, p 101.

33. Walzer, 1992, pp 102f.

34. Charles Taylor 1995 b [1992], p 249.

35. Taylor, 1995 b, p 250.

36. Walzer, 1997, p 32.

37. By the basic structure Rawls (1993, p 258) has in mind "the political constitution, the legally recognized forms of property, and the organization of the economy, and

the nature of the family." Brian Barry (1995 a, pp 215ff) also defends the idea that liberal restrictions primarily apply to the basic structures of society.

38. "[T]he *basic structure* is not intended to favor any comprehensive doctrine." Rawls, 1993, p 193 (emphasis added).

39. John Rawls, 1997a, p 137.

40. See, for instance, Chantal Mouffe's assertion that Rawls "obliterates all the dimensions of power and antagonism" from "the political." Mouffe, 1994, p 319.

41. Cohen, 1997, pp 11 and 18–21.

42. See Rawls, 1993, pp 262ff, and Barry, 1995 a, p 214.

43. Nozick does not explicitly justify his liberal theory by reference to any ideas of the good nor does he demonstrate that he *wouldn't* need one. This uncertainty is a consequence of what Thomas Nagel has described as Nozick's lack of "moral foundations." See Thomas Nagel, 1975, p 138.

44. See Raz, 1986, pp 110ff.

45. Nozick, 1974, p 33.

46. Dworkin, 1984, p 64.

47. Rothstein, 1998, p 42.

48. Walzer, 1997, p 82.

49. The claim that neutral justifications are never in fact neutral (the communitarian claim) is different from the claim that there are no good reasons for justifying ourselves neutrally. It is the latter claim that I will examine in chapter eight: should we accept the ideal of neutrality of justification?

7

Neutral Aims:
Dworkin and the Liberal State

The principle of neutrality of aims states as a condition for legitimate government that it does not deliberately promote some particular way of life or conception of the good. Thus, in order to be "liberal" the state must not, for instance, act with the intention of making Lutherans better off than Catholics, nor must the constitution or the allocation of rights be designed with any such aim. As argued in the last chapter this principle can be of varying scope. Put crudely, the principle of neutrality of aims may restrict either *all* or just *some* aspects of public authority. In the first case the principle applies widely, in the second it is understood more narrowly.

This difference in scope is of importance to the present task—that of assessing the rationale and the basis for the idea of neutrality of aims. That the state must be restricted in relation to *some* conceptions of the good is perhaps uncontroversial and therefore more easily justified. Few if any believe that a liberal state need not tolerate the free exercise of religion or that a confessional state could be liberal. As we saw, even communitarian critics of liberalism seem to accept that the state should not support particular religious creeds. In that sense, they too accept that neutrality of aims must apply to some issues (i.e., to religious ones). But while there might be something like a consensus about the meaning of liberalism in relation to religion, more controversy surrounds the idea that the state must also be neutral to secular conceptions of the good life. According to that notion the state could not support any life-style, e.g., that of an environmentalist, conservative, socialist or feminist kind. Insofar as these life-styles represent different conceptions of the good life, it follows from the principle of neutrality of aims that they can receive no official support. The government must be neutral, that is, to citizens' choices of life-style.

The purpose of this chapter is to examine whether this idea of neutrality—broadly interpreted as restricting the state in relation to all conceptions of the good—can indeed be given an adequate justification. Are there, that is, good reasons for accepting the idea of neutrality of aims?

The foremost defender of this idea in the contemporary debate is Ronald Dworkin. In his view, the state must not "discriminate against people of any particular ethical party or conviction." Hence, the state must be neutral in its "operation"—the state must not aim at improving, ethically, the lives of the people.[1] Because of the influence of this position and of the pre-eminence of Dworkin's defense of it I shall devote most of this chapter to an examination of his arguments. However, I shall endeavor to demonstrate that he does not provide an adequate theoretical basis for the idea of wide neutrality of aims. In other words, there are no conclusive arguments in his theory for that principle—or so I shall argue. Thus, the idea of neutrality of aims becomes a matter of faith, a tenet without an adequate theoretical foundation.

However, before we reach that conclusion, I shall analyze three different arguments for neutrality of aims that can be reconstructed from Dworkin's theory. The first two arguments represent interpretations of the value of equality. According to them, neutrality of aims is required by a government which—as liberalism demands—wants to treat its citizens as equals. The first form of this argument proposes that neutrality follows from the requirement of *equality before the law*. In the second version neutrality is regarded as required by *respect for citizens as equals*. Both claims, consequently, rely on various interpretations of what it means to treat a person as an equal. The first defends the idea of neutrality by reference to a conception of legal equality. The second understands the meaning of "equal treatment" as more exacting. To treat a person as an equal not only requires equality before the law but also that the state does not generally injure people's sense of being equals.

There is a further argument, however, that is not associated with any interpretation of the value of equality. This argument for the neutral state is based on Dworkin's idea of *life as a challenge*—a notion explored in chapter three. The intriguing question we face is whether accepting that view provides a justification of the idea of neutrality of aims. Dworkin argues that the idea of life as a challenge is fundamental to our understanding of what the good life is and that we, to the extent that we accept this idea, must also accept neutrality of aims. Like the other two arguments this has some force. But, as I will demonstrate, none is forceful enough: the principle of wide neutrality of aims cannot be justified.

Finally it is worth repeating the limitations imposed on the subsequent discussion by my scheme of analysis. As should be clear, the idea of neutrality of aims is distinguished from two other important ideas: that of neutrality of justification and that of individual rights. These two ideas are closely related to the idea of neutrality in aims but are, as I have argued, both conceptually distinct and dependent on separate justifications. The idea that the state must not promote any conceptions of the good is distinct from the idea that the state must not justify its actions with references to any such conception (see chapter six). Moreover, the claim that there are individual rights is distinct from either of these arguments for neutrality. Therefore, although there may be arguments to the effect that the respect for rights implies neutrality of aims, such arguments will not be considered here. When the argument concerns the implications of rights the evaluation takes place in the context of a more general discussion of rights (i.e., in chapter five).

Legal Neutrality[2]

The idea that citizens are equal before the law, and that the law should treat like cases alike, are ideas that may be assumed to be widely accepted. The idea that a law or a judicial body should not treat individuals in the same way appears preposterous to most people. Likewise, the idea that some citizen is entitled to privileges in law, merely by virtue of some personal characteristic, will seem objectionable to most of us. Any political system that aspires to be just is likely to require the law to apply in the same way to all citizens and to recognize citizens as equals before the law.

Now, it is sometimes argued that this common principle of legal justice supports, or even implies, some specific liberal ideas. The idea of equality before the law provides a reason, it is believed, for accepting the idea of neutrality of aims. Only when the government is not pursuing any conceptions of the good, and only when it does not provide support for any such notions, can all citizens be considered equal before the law.

According to this view the idea of equality before the law *entails* the idea of neutrality of aims. An important liberal principle is, in other words, implicit in the idea of legal justice. If this is indeed true, if neutrality cannot be separated from equality before the law, we will have to conclude that any objection to the idea of neutrality is also an objection to the idea of a just legal system. The idea of neutrality is then granted a very strong foundation.

As we shall see, Dworkin does appeal to some notions such as legal equality or equality before the law. He does so, moreover, in an attempt to demonstrate that some political principles are more justified than others. Therefore his legal theory touches on the political and moral question of which aims that are legitimate. Whether Dworkin's legal theory does, in the end, provide an adequate justification of the idea of a neutral state remains to be investigated, however. The legal principles that he takes as integral to equality before the law must be identified and assessed. To do this will be my task in the following section. As I endeavor to argue, Dworkin's legal theory does not support the idea of neutrality of aims.

However, before embarking on the investigation, I shall compare Dworkin's ideas to an argument advanced by Stephen Holmes. I believe this might be instructive, since Holmes tends to ignore some basic distinctions in his defense of liberal neutrality.

The Basis of Legal Equality

According to Stephen Holmes the idea of liberal neutrality is implicit in common ideas such as "law equally applied to all" or "judicial neutrality."[3] If we accept that each citizen ought to be equal before the law, that the judicial system must not be partial or biased in any respect, we must also accept the idea of the neutral state, if we are to remain consistent. Political neutrality to conceptions of the good life is, in effect, implicit in our understanding of what rule according to law means.[4]

However, this may seem like jumping to conclusions. Holmes asserts that judicial neutrality and the idea of the neutral state are closely related notions. By judicial neutrality we commonly refer to the idea that courts should not be biased or partial. Now we may ask what this idea of neutral *adjudication* has to do with the idea that the state should not promote any conceptions of the good life. Though certainly important, the idea of judicial neutrality is not conceptually related to the idea of the neutral state. A law may well be non-neutral in its aims (e.g., supporting only patriotic organizations) and yet be applied in a perfectly neutral way by the courts. Likewise, non-neutral courts may subvert a perfectly neutral law (e.g., supporting all organizations). The adjudication and legislation of law constitute two different contexts of neutrality, and the one is not necessarily related to the other. Holmes' argument is, we must conclude, based on confused assumptions about the meaning of liberal neutrality.[5]

By contrast, Ronald Dworkin seems to provide a more elaborate account of how legal doctrines may provide a basis for political neutrality.[6] According to Dworkin, the idea of equality before the law restricts *legislators* in the pursuit of moral and political aims. The basic assumption is that the government and the agencies of the state must treat "like cases alike." This idea is considered fundamental to a just political system, since it implies that the state acts "in a principled and coherent manner." Thus equality before the law requires that political action is coherent and this, in turn, is "a prerequisite for civilization."[7] Dworkin calls this the idea of *integrity*. By requiring that the law-making agent, the state, acts upon a coherent set of principles it confers a sense of integrity to its actions. The state must speak "with one voice," not "capriciously" or "whimsically."[8] The demand that political principles be coherent is, Dworkin claims, an essential aspect of what "equality before the law" means.[9] To be an equal before the law is, it now becomes clear, to live in a legal and political system based on coherent and general principles.[10]

Now, what normative force does the idea of integrity have? Can the mere principle of equality before the law exclude non-neutral aims? In order to understand the force of this idea we must further examine the notion of integrity in Dworkin's theory. I shall analyze this notion by distinguishing between the elements of generality, universality and coherence. Considered separately or together they represent different normative claims that will not, in my view, justify neutrality of aim.

Integrity, Generality and Universality

That law must be general in form is an important quality in the understanding of what treating like cases alike means. Instead of treating cases one by one, integrity demands that principles recognized as valid in one case are applied in others too. If racist speech is considered to be an infringement of the rights of one particular minority, then that right must be considered in relation to other minorities too. To treat like cases alike is, in other words, to act from principles that are general.

An indication to the effect that Dworkin takes integrity to imply a requirement of generality is found in one of his examples. Imagine, Dworkin writes, a political compromise between those who want to prohibit abortion by law and those who defend the legal right to it.[11] Since neither of the parties is able, in this hypothetical case, to enforce their will, they agree to compromise and to have abortion *both* prohibited and permitted. This is achieved by permitting abortion for women born on even days, while at the same time prohibiting it for women born on odd days. In that way both defenders and the critics of abortion influence the existing law on that issue.

Now, an apparent problem with the imagined compromise is that it makes different laws valid at the same time: abortion is both lawful and unlawful. Thus, we may be faced with a conflict in law, where one prohibits what another permits. But, in fact, that is not the case. Since the law has been made relative to different populations, women born on even days and on odd days respectively, no one need be uncertain of which law applies in her case. That is, the law in question is *not* incoherent.

Yet such laws would be condemned from the perspective of integrity in law. Integrity is a criterion, not of laws but of the principles on which they are based, and it requires that the principles do not conflict. In Dworkin's view any collective decision must "aim to settle on some coherent principle *whose influence then extends to the natural limits of its authority*."[12] The principles on which a decision is based must, that is, be generalized and apply to *all* cases. When one law applies to one set of the population, and another law to a different set, we are in effect allowing two different principles to rule at the same time. But the validity of principles, and this seems to be Dworkin's point, cannot be restricted haphazardly. A principle must apply "to the natural limits of its authority." This is why abortion cannot be unlawful for women born on even days while at the same time being lawful for those born on odd days.[13] The demand for *generality* means that the scope of any principle justifying law must not be restricted arbitrarily.

If this is what integrity means we are faced with the question whether the requirement of generality can, by itself, rebut laws that aim at supporting some conception of the good. What we need to investigate is, in other words, whether generality implies neutrality of aims.

In order to answer this question we need to make a further distinction. As Richard Hare has shown, generality contrasts with specificity while universality excludes only "individual constants." A universal rule must not name persons or groups by name, but it *can* be more or less general or specific.[14] The rule "all cultural minorities are entitled to public support" is more general than the rule "all *indigenous* cultural minorities are entitled to public support." However, both rules are equally universal, since none of them include the names of particular individuals or groups.

Now, does integrity imply a ban on non-universal references? As we know, integrity requires that law is based on a coherent set of principles and that these principles are general. Although Dworkin does not explicitly discuss the case of non-universal categories, it is, I believe, plausible to assume that the claim of generality implies their exclusion.

This conclusion can be defended by considering what the consequences for Dworkin's theory would be did it *not* exclude non-universal references. In that case, any law could explicitly specify some individuals or groups to which it applied. Doing that would, however, undermine the whole idea of general principles underlying laws. No principle would then need to apply generally, since the names of those to which it applied could always be included in the law. So proper names have to be excluded from Dworkin's conception of law, if his idea of generality of principles is to be maintained.[15]

In fact, the idea that laws must be based on general principles, and that they must avoid non-universals, has often been regarded as a prerequisite for any system of law. In the process of making law it has been argued that we must conceive of the law as valid for everyone and that it must not allow for exceptions. This was a basic idea in Rousseau's theory of law. Rousseau defended the view that a law must always consider the people and their acts in general categories and never in particulars.

L'objet des loix est tousjours général, j'entens que la loi considère les sujets en corps et les actions par leur genres ou par leurs espèces, jamais un homme en particulier ni une action unique et individuelle.[16]

Dworkin's theory of integrity in law echoes ideas that have important precedents.[17] But just like Dworkin, Rousseau does not distinguish between the demand for excluding non-universals and the requirement that laws must be general. Rousseau makes no distinction between the requirement that law be general ("L'objet des loix est tousjours général...") and the demand that men and acts be not considered individually ("en particulier").

This takes us to a more challenging problem with the idea of generality. If not naming particular individuals (i.e., universality) is at the heart of the idea of generality, it remains unclear if this really prevents law from targeting specific individuals or groups. In other words, does strict adherence to universality imply that there can be no law that discriminates against individuals or groups? The problem seems to be that even where all non-universal references are banned, the lawmaker will not be obviously constrained in pursuing aims that applies only to specific minorities or individuals. This is so because non-universals can, to a large extent, be reformulated in universal but highly specific terms.

Say, for instance, that the government wants to support one particular cultural minority and not another. Even if the government cannot legitimately *name* the favored minority in the law, it certainly can describe the characteristics of that group in highly specific, albeit universal, terms. Thus if the Swedish government wants to support the immigrant culture of Finns but not of others, then a law can easily be designed so as to describe some of the defining features of the Finnish minority as a criterion for support. Thus the law might say that support is to be directed towards groups "of which it is true that the majority immigrated in the 1960's." But then the implications will be almost tantamount to enacting a law referring to the Finnish minority by name.[18]

An objection to this conclusion is that not all redescriptions of non-universals can be considered as valid. In order for some criterion to be valid it must point at some *relevant* features. After all, the basic reason why non-universals should not appear in legal documents is that individual characteristics are not relevant; a name simply does not count as a reason. Implicit in the notion of "equality before the law" there is an idea of making law immune to subjective or contingent facts about the world. In fact, the desire to make the law non-arbitrary is epitomized by Dworkin's belief that integrity means that the government must not act "capriciously."[19] The law cannot, therefore, contain references to individual characteristics such as names.

This demonstrates that the distinction between universal and general principles is not that strict. The argument that excludes non-universal references also excludes some principles that are universal but which use categories or characteristics that cannot be considered as "relevant." A stronger conclusion would be that, implicit in the demand for *universal* categories, there is a requirement to the effect that laws are as *general* as possible. In other words, a law is more legitimate the more general its form. Thus, granting support to *one* cultural minority is less general, and therefore less legitimate, than granting support to *all* minorities. The conclusion is pushed in this direction since finding relevant criteria for excluding any group must be difficult. Again, using Dworkin's terminology, we might say that any principle must be "extended to its natural limits." Applied to our example above this means that not any reason for discrimination is as good as another. It simply is not reasonable to exclude all cultural minorities but the Finnish from support, merely because the Finnish group immigrated in the 1960s. Though the facts referred to by the law may be true, they need not constitute a plausible reason for public policy.

Yet it remains unclear to what extent laws of high generality will be more easily recommended than a less general law. To say that there is a need for "relevant" criteria is of doubtful merit since our ideas of what *is* relevant are likely to differ a lot. The idea, referred to by Dworkin, that there are "natural limits" to the validity of a principle certainly excludes some cases (e.g., making the applicability of a law depend on when the subject is born). It is obvious, however, that many less than fully general laws may be regarded as "natural" by some people.

Thus, when Charles Taylor defends the right of cultural minorities to have their culture protected by law—even at some cost to the majority—he certainly believes that there are relevant reasons for this. For him, the issue at stake is "cultural survival." When a minority culture is threatened by virtual extinction it may, consequently, be legitimate to enact laws and policies that favor some cultural features (language, signs, traditional industries, etc.) over others. Taylor argues that we must "weigh the importance of certain forms of uniform treatment against the importance of cultural survival."[20] People with different cultural characteristics should not always, then, be treated equally by law. Whether they should or not depends, ultimately, on the need for protecting particular life forms and cultures.

Some people will disagree with Taylor's suggestion. They might wonder, for instance, whether cultural features do in fact set "natural" restrictions for the scope of laws. However, such a suspicion just demonstrates my point. If it is far from obvious that cultural particularities constitute "relevant" reasons for discrimination, it must also be true that these reasons cannot be dismissed on the ground that they are "obviously" irrelevant. There is, in other words, no clear definition of what a "relevant consideration" might be. No *formal*, or natural, way of distinguishing relevant from irrelevant criteria exists. Hayek noted this problem, despite the importance he actually attributed to the idea.

> [I]t must be admitted that . . . no entirely satisfactory criterion has been found that would always tell us what kind of classification is compatible with equality before the law. To say, as has often been said, that the law must not make irrelevant distinctions or that it must not discriminate . . . is little more than evading the issue.[21]

In Hayek's view the requirement of relevant criteria is meaningless since it leaves open the question of which consideration is "relevant."[22] In our case we may see that a decision similar to case B discussed above, where the law indicates by name who is and who is not entitled to public support, will not be excluded by that provision. Only when there is no intelligible motive behind the discrimination, as there cannot be in the case of women born on even and odd days, will this idea have some force. But in most cases considerations that are "relevant" are certain to be found. In sum, the ban on irrelevant considerations, and the claim that any principle must "extend to the natural limits of its authority," does not restrict the government from supporting some particular moral or cultural activities, nor from promoting some particular idea of virtue.[23] Respect for equality before the law does not, in sum, imply that the state must be neutral in the aims of legislation.

Integrity as Coherence

Dworkin's theory tells us that laws should be general and universal in form. Now, in what sense is that a defense of legal *equality*?

Apparently most laws, even bad ones, can be formulated in general and universal terms. For instance, though laws of racial discrimination are less general than laws that do not discriminate on the basis of color or race, a legislature may of course invoke what it considers to be "relevant" considerations in order to justify a lesser degree of generality. The demand of generality means that relevant considerations must be used when discriminating, but since a racist legislature may regard "race" as relevant, this criterion cannot prevent discriminatory laws. Thus, a legal system with "integrity," in Dworkin's sense of the word, is not necessarily a just one. Though integrity, by demanding generality and universality in legislation, secures *legal* equality, it certainly does not exhaust the meaning of *moral* equality.[24]

In this sense Dworkin's reasoning also contrasts with those who argue that a notion of equal treatment is fundamental to law. On that account, to be treated in the same way, or to have equal benefits, is essential to any just legal system. There is, in other words, a *prima facie* form that laws must take.[25] This idea is reinforced by the belief that the simplest meaning of justice is equal treatment. When laws are just and equal, they distribute burdens and benefits equally between citizens unless there are compelling arguments to the contrary. Any entitlement, right, or benefit recognized by law must be accessible to anyone. This idea is based on the belief that "no one can claim a right for himself which another cannot claim."[26]

But to be treated equally—in equal or identical ways—is not the same as being an equal before the law. While equal treatment refers to the outcomes of a law, the idea of equality before the law refers, not to the consequences, but to the structure of law. In the first instance, the test of an equal law is how people are treated or how benefits and burdens are distributed among them. In the second instance the test of an equal law is whether the principles behind that law are endowed with an adequate degree of coherence. While not denying that distributing some good or set of rights equally is often desirable or even an "obvious solution," [27] it is not the same as coherence.

So, integrity requires less than the idea of equal treatment. After all, if equal treatment were the norm, it would require benefits granted to elderly people to be distributed equally between them (but is the idea of equal treatment even compatible with support that discriminates between citizens on the basis of age?). However, the idea of integrity does not seem to require this.

On the other hand, the idea of integrity in law demands something that might be more important. Integrity demands that the principle on which a rule is based is not inconsistent with the principles supporting some other rule. Integrity requires that such principles *cohere*, i.e., that they fit together in an intelligible and systematic manner.[28] So, if elderly people are granted a benefit because they constitute a vulnerable group with poor resources, then that consideration must be valid for decisions concerning other groups too. The idea of integrity, in other words, does expand the principle in question: it requires any particular principle referred to in legislation to cohere with the principles referred to in other places. This is a requirement that the idea of equal treatment does not include. In fact, because integrity applies to principles, and not to the rules or laws justified by these principles, it is a more stringent demand.[29] That is, coherence is a more radical criterion applied to principles than to rules.

This can easily be demonstrated. Two different rules may be coherent in the sense that they do not prescribe behavior that is inconsistent, and yet they may be based on principles that are not easily reconciled. The rule "racist speech on television is prohibited" is not inconsistent with the rule "racist speech on the radio is permitted." However, the principle on which the former rule may be based— i.e., that people have a right not to be confronted with racial prejudice in the media—does not cohere with the principle on which the latter rule rests. These rules will, as a consequence of the incoherence of principles, lack integrity.[30] Discriminatory principles would therefore be difficult to reconcile with a legal system not generally featuring principles of racial inequality.

Another example is the practice in the criminal law of many European countries to punish perpetrators of identical crimes differently according to their current status as citizens. An individual convicted of rape in Sweden is, for instance, generally sentenced to imprisonment for some considerable time. Yet some individuals are also punished by deportation, being forced to leave the country after having served their time. This different punishment applies to foreigners or immigrants who do not possess full Swedish citizenship. Now, we may legitimately ask whether this discrimination can be coherently maintained. It is held that the punishment for rape should depend on the status of citizenship of the offender. Rape by a Swedish citizen merits imprisonment, whereas rape by non-Swedish citizens merits imprisonment and deportation. Now, obviously, what is true about criminal law in the case of rape should also be true about criminal law in relation to other crimes. This is necessary in order for law to be coherent. So, if non-Swedish citizens deserve to be punished more severely for rape, they must deserve to be punished more severely for other criminal offenses too.

The demand for coherence confronts the legislature with a choice. Either it must recognize a discriminatory principle in all spheres of criminal law (and why not also in commercial law, tax law, and public law?). Or, alternatively, the principle of discriminatory punishments ought to be rejected. The preservation of coherence in the legal system requires a decision in one or the other direction.[31] In this case, I believe that the latter choice is the one most faithful to present conceptions of justice in Sweden. The idea of coherence would, if honored, exclude opportunistic exceptions to principles we otherwise would recognize as valid.

"Integrity condemns special treatment," Dworkin argues.[32] However, we know now that the principle of coherence, fundamental to integrity, does not preclude treating different *people* according to different *principles*. This is so because coherence does not rule out distinctions between "different" people as long as they are coherent. Treating "colored" people differently under the law from "whites," or favoring some ethical or cultural values by law, may therefore be done with integrity preserved. However, coherence condemns any law making unjustified exceptions to principles regarded as valid in other spheres. The requirement of coherence is, in other words, incompatible with treating *the same* people according to different principles. Important as this may be, it is far from the liberal principle of neutrality of aims.

Integrity, Like Cases Alike, and Sexual Discrimination

It is sometimes believed that a typical case of sexual discrimination occurs when the ideal of "treating like cases alike" is ignored and set aside.[33] To be treated equally is what the opponents of discrimination want. According to this view a woman is discriminated against whenever she is treated as a man would not be treated in similar circumstances. Similarly, ethnic or cultural minorities are discriminated against when they are treated differently from the majority. The typical way to deal with discrimination is, consequently, to stress the need for scrupulous adherence to the principle "like cases alike."

Yet, the feminist writer Catherine MacKinnon has questioned the relevance of the notion of treating like cases alike. She argues that when law follows the idea of "treating like cases alike and unlike unlike" discrimination is recognized only where women and men are differently treated in similar circumstances.[34] Hence, prevailing anti-discriminatory laws and policies not only take similarity in relation to men as axiomatic, but also take the male-dominated society as the basic line. The doctrine of like cases alike sees no discrimination in the fact that women have positions subordinated to men, and no discrimination in the fact that women lack the bargaining power to change this situation. From the perspective of like cases alike, discrimination only occurs in transitions, but never in the status quo.

Thus, in MacKinnon's view, the doctrine of "treating like cases alike" cannot see "actual disparity as part of the injury of inequality."[35] Inequality in status or in resources is not seen as discrimination, and the doctrine of equality before the law therefore makes the deeper sources of discrimination invisible. Any radical law, sensitive to the aim of remedying the social subordination of women, would in fact be deemed as inconsistent with the idea of equality before the law.

Now, whether one approves of the concerns raised by MacKinnon or not, we can conclude that her critique—though perhaps powerful against the idea that equality before the law only means equal treatment—is less effective against Dworkin's idea of integrity. Dworkin is immune to the critique because he does not claim that equal treatment is essential to treating like cases alike. He need not deny that laws ought to be sensitive to the fact that women suffer from having less social status. Actual inequalities and not merely transitional ones, may therefore be considered as relevant.

Following Dworkin we should definitely treat like cases alike. But all that means is that laws should be founded upon a coherent set of principles—it does not mean that everyone must always be treated in the same way.

The Weakness of Legal Neutrality

In what sense does Dworkin's theory of integrity, as a whole, represent a conception of *equality*? After all, the whole point of the principles of equal treatment and of equality before the law is that they secure a particular aspect of the ideal of equality. The answer to this question points to a complex and ambiguous facet of Dworkin's theory.

On the one hand, integrity may in itself be said to constitute a conception of equality. By requiring coherence and generality in law, integrity guarantees that law is not structured in an arbitrary way. Integrity confers a degree of rationality on law. In that sense, integrity might provide one of the conditions of equality. Laws with the aim to promote some particular individuals for no reason at all will, for instance, be illegitimate.[36]

On the other hand, it is also evident that integrity may be compatible with gross injustices, which are hardly compatible with any idea of equality. A coherent system of racist law may, as we have seen, respect integrity in law. If integrity is a necessary condition for equality *in* law it is definitely not sufficient.[37]

From Dworkin's writings we learn, however, that mere formal criteria for law are not enough. While a racist legal system might constitute "law," even law with integrity, it certainly does not constitute law as we want it to be.[38] Hence, Dworkin connects the idea of integrity to a conception of equality that he believes ought to guide the contents of legislation.[39] The formal character of equality *before* the law is thereby superseded by a substantive notion of equality *in* law.

Dworkin sometimes alludes to this fact. Integrity *and* equality should, on Dworkin's account, guide the contents of legislation: "[integrity] requires that governments pursue some coherent conception of *what treating people as equals means* . . . "[40] Integrity in law does not, then, merely require that laws be made general and coherent. Integrity now implies the much stronger demand that the laws of a country "treat people as equals." In fact, it may be argued that the connections between equal treatment, on the one hand, and coherence and generality, on the other, are very strong. Only when people are treated as equals can coherence and generality in legislation be realized; only when all citizens have the opportunity to express themselves politically can the body politic speak with "one voice."[41]

Whatever the justification of equal treatment may be, the problem is how to interpret this idea. What does it mean to treat someone "as" an equal? Does it mean that the state has to be neutral with respect to conceptions of the good life? Thus, the question we need to answer is whether equality necessarily imposes neutrality on the state, or, whether a non-discriminatory state may legitimately promote some conceptions of virtue.

Neutrality and Treating Citizens as Equals

Laws and policies in a liberal-democratic state are in an important sense based on preferences. The reason why one law rather than another is enacted, or why some policy rather than another is pursued, can be stated in terms of what citizens and officials prefer. The municipality and the state attempt to provide high-quality education because citizens want good education. Likewise, the state punishes murder severely because people are keen on not being murdered. We may therefore say that people's preference for good education and their preference for not being murdered provide the rationale for current policies and laws. Generally, too, we believe this feature of the liberal-democratic system to be valuable and important. The adherence to preferences guarantees that official institutions are, to some extent, responsive to people's wishes.

Now, obviously, the state should not take into account just *any* preferences. When some citizens want to kill another we do not generally believe that their preferences should justify public action. And, in fact, there are many other preferences that we would not like to see aggregated into official laws or policies. So what preferences may legitimately be referred to in law? How can "good" preferences be distinguished from "bad"?[42]

Dworkin has made the influential suggestion that only preferences compatible with the requirement that the state must treat citizens "as equals" may form a legitimate basis for political decisions. Hence, legislators are not only constrained by the demands of integrity that we were confronted with in the previous section. Now the requirement of treating citizens as equals is what provides a justification for neutrality of aims. The neutral state is, from this standpoint, a state that excludes certain, infamous and undesirable, preferences from political life.[43]

My aim in this section is to demonstrate that the attempt to deduce neutrality of aims from the idea of equality cannot be justified. Though I do not intend to question the validity of Dworkin's premise, that the state must indeed treat its citizens as equals, I will question the deduction. I shall dispute the claim that equality of status requires neutrality of aims and I will defend the claim that equality need not be the enemy of virtue

Equal Respect and External Preferences

Any government must, Dworkin argues, treat all citizens "as equals" or "as entitled to equal concern and respect."[44] Now, of course, we need to know what treating someone as an equal means. More specifically, we need to know whether respecting that idea implies the exclusion of all non-neutral aims from political life.

One important idea in Dworkin's work is that treating citizens as equals implies that the state should not be sensitive to the preferences we have about anybody else. There is a distinction between the personal and the external preferences of a person. A personal preference is concerned with the welfare or the status of the person herself and such preferences must, according to Dworkin, be the proper focus for political decisions. Sometimes however, citizens have preferences concerning what others deserve or are entitled to. These preferences are external in the sense that they do not exclusively concern the well-being of oneself. Political measures that take into account external preferences are, Dworkin argues, inconsistent with equality and therefore illiberal.

> [P]eople have the right not to suffer disadvantage in the distribution of social goods . . . just on the ground that their officials or fellow-citizens think that their opinions about the right way for them to lead their own lives are ignoble or wrong.[45]

The idea that all citizens must be treated as equals excludes moralism, or public action based on the external preferences of some citizens. Dworkin takes the example of preferences that are hostile to homosexual behavior. If the government takes such preferences as a basis for a law that prejudices the position of homosexuals, it would, by acting on the external preferences of some citizens, fail to treat homosexuals as equals.[46] They are not equally treated by the government since their life-style is officially condemned. A part of society is allowed to impose its view of which life is good on the rest of society—a minority lifestyle is disparaged by public institutions.

Dworkin's idea of excluding external preferences is not entirely original. Other liberal writers, like John Rawls and David Gauthier, endorse similar ideas. Rawls claims that we should "not take an interest in one another's interest" when choosing basic political institutions.[47] Similarly, Gauthier presents "non-tuism," or the idea that "my preferences do not involve you," as an important assumption for liberal political principles.[48] It may not be an exaggeration to claim that Dworkin's ban on external preferences articulates a widely shared aspect of the liberal ideal.[49] If only the government refrained from acting on the external or tuistic preferences of citizens, neutrality in aims would be achieved.

To begin with we need to know whether the political measures considered in these cases are based on external preferences or not. One reason why a majority of citizens might want to ban prostitution, for instance, can be that they disapprove of "the commodification of the female body." Citizens might want the state to punish those who sell (or buy) sexual services in order to prevent what they believe is an intrinsic evil. However, the preference to make prostitution illegal is certainly external. It is external because it concerns the good or well-being of others. A preference to prohibit prostitution on the grounds that it is an intrinsic evil will consequently conflict with the ideal of the liberal state defended by Dworkin. Similarly, people's external preferences may move them to demand that the state enact policies of affirmative action, or that the state promote the virtue of solidarity through the educational system. Yet Dworkin denies that external preferences can justify public action. Must we then conclude that Dworkin will oppose policies of, for example, affirmative action? No, I do not believe we must. Dworkin recognizes that there may be reasons consistent with the ban on external preferences that will justify such policies. There may in other words be reasons not derived from people's external preferences that justify similar policies. A law punishing prostitution may, to take another example, be based either on moralistic condemnation *or* on a desire to promote equality. Dworkin's criteria would seem to exclude the first but not the second consideration as a basis for such laws. Consequently, a liberal state may punish prostitution or the buying of sexual services for reasons that are consistent with respect for equality. The fact that this law, at the same time, satisfies some external preferences is not a reason to reject it.

In sum, the *analytical* problem concerns the relation between personal and external preferences, on the one hand, and the neutrality of political aims on the other. Does a ban on external preferences lead to neutrality of aims? The *normative* problem is whether the notion of external preferences (rightly understood) indeed captures the wrongness of some non-neutral policies (like racial discrimination). Do the restrictions set on the aims of governmental policies on questions like race, sex and religion, correspond adequately to the distinction between external and personal preferences? I do not think this is the case, and I now intend to justify this claim.

Equal Concern and Affirmative Action: Getting Dworkin Right

Affirmative action deliberately increases the chances of a member of one group achieving a certain position. Affirmative action can, for instance, consist in quotas reserving a number of positions for applicants from an ethnic minority. Now, affirmative action implies, when regulated by law or statute, that the government aims to support one group of people.[50] Does this fact make affirmative action incompatible with the idea of neutrality in aims?

Answering this question from Dworkin's perspective means asking whether external preferences are involved or not. *If* the state, when enforcing a program of affirmative action, acts on the external preferences of some citizens, *then* we will have to conclude that such policies are illiberal.

First, however, we must note that a preference for affirmative action may be "external" in two different senses. People might want to introduce a policy of affirmative action either because they despise those who are at present successful or because they are concerned with those who at present are unsuccessful. Hence, if people want affirmative action to be directed towards blacks, the reason may be either that they are concerned with their welfare or that they want to punish whites. The same distinction could be of relevance to the issue of affirmative action between the sexes. People who have a preference for affirmative action programs that will enhance the chances of female applicants obtaining a position may have that preference for one of two reasons. Either they hate men. Affirmative action in favor of women will then be a means whereby the male community is punished. Or, they want to support women because they believe that this is a way to assist a disadvantaged group.

Thus, preferences may be external in two different senses. The person who favors affirmative action out of hatred has a "hostile" external preference. By contrast, the person favoring affirmative action out of concern for a disadvantaged group has a "supportive" external preference.[51]

It may seem that the distinction made here is of little importance. In his early work Dworkin explicitly rejects policies that depend on both hostile and supportive external preferences. Neither the preference of the racist or the altruist should, Dworkin argues, be considered in political decisions. This is so, because both the racist and the altruist are concerned with the welfare of others rather than their own, and taking their preferences into consideration would therefore be to violate other people's right to equal concern.[52] Thus, since Dworkin appears to claim that *any* external preference is illegitimate, policies of affirmative action cannot be justified.

Mats Lundström reaches the same conclusion. Following Dworkin, he argues that preferences involving the life of others should not be taken into account by political authorities. According to Lundström the idea of favoring one sex at the expense of another is wrong, because "a preference for a certain distribution of sexes is an example of an external preference that should not be respected in a liberal state."[53] Enacting quotas is wrong and comparable to racism when based on the (external) preference for one sex over another.[54] This conclusion may seem too strong in the light of our distinction between hostile and supportive external preferences. After all, a racist preference is necessarily hostile towards some group, whereas the preference for affirmative action may well be supportive. People favoring quotas for women need not be hostile to men, they may just be concerned with the welfare of women. Yet Lundström apparently does not restrict "racism" to preferences that manifest a hostile attitude towards the other sex. In Lundström's view even "'fair racism' is racism." Thus, even supportive preferences for one sex are equivalent to racism. What makes affirmative action racist is not then, that it is based on hatred or prejudice, but that it is based on sexual categories. A policy that depends on the relevance of sexual categories is "racist," Lundström seems to think, for the same reason, that a policy distributing some good according to racial categories would be racist.

Lundström follows Dworkin in rejecting both hostile and supportive external preferences. But doing this is, in fact, not very plausible, and numerous critics have made this point before.

One critic is H L A Hart. Pointing to the discrimination of homosexuals in England, Hart made apparent some of the less attractive implications of excluding supportive external preferences.[55] The point is that the legal reform that made homosexual relations lawful may have been impossible without the support of heterosexual citizens. Only when it became apparent that a majority, or at least a substantial minority, of ordinary citizens felt concern for the situation of homosexuals did Parliament act. In other words, liberal principles were established as a result of supportive external preferences.[56]

Actually, in Hart's example the exclusion of all external preferences becomes perverse from a liberal standpoint. Excluding the preferences some people have on behalf of others may be perverse because, sometimes, this may make society *less* liberal than otherwise. This is clear in the case where the supportive external preferences of heterosexuals were necessary in order to induce legal change. Their external preferences made the abolishment of legal discrimination possible and consequently produced a more liberal society. To remain faithful to Dworkin's ideal may therefore mean being less liberal than what might have been the case if supportive external preferences had been accepted.

For this very reason, however, Hart's example may be inappropriate. In fact, as Raymond Plant observes, the case described by Hart presupposes a situation where unjust laws are already in place (i.e., laws imposed as a result of external preferences).[57] Hart in fact describes a society where some hostile external preferences are already embedded in law. Now Dworkin certainly would not accept that. What is wrong, from Dworkin's point of view, is the law that discriminates against homosexuals, and that law is unjust exactly because it relies on hostile external preferences. That judgement is unaffected by the existence of opposition from benevolent heterosexuals.

However, the deficiency of Hart's example seems not to matter much for the general point he and others have stressed. Whatever the starting point (whether external preferences are institutionalized or not), the point is simply that supportive external preferences are not necessarily harmful.[58] Why, then, exclude them, as Dworkin's theory appears to do? Returning to the case of affirmative action, we may ask what is wrong with having a preference that one group should be supported politically. *Why* is this desire not legitimate? This may seem especially mysterious to someone who believes that there are oppressed or otherwise disadvantaged groups in society, and that the only way to improve their situation is by making other citizens act politically on their behalf.

At this stage it is helpful to return to Dworkin's text and to examine further the idea of excluding external preferences. In fact, I think a careful reading of Dworkin's position makes it clear, that he is *not* excluding external preferences that are supportive. Although writers both sympathetic and critical to Dworkin have interpreted his theory as imposing a general ban on external preferences, this reading is, I now contend, based on a misunderstanding.

In its first formulations Dworkin's view is clearly that all external preferences pose a threat to equality. Dworkin claims that there is a general argument to the effect that "we should not count external preferences *of any form*."[59] In explaining this idea, Dworkin makes clear that external preferences are wrong because "if external preferences are counted...then those constrained suffer . . . because their conception of a proper or desirable form of life is despised by others."[60] Dworkin assumes, apparently, that a political decision concerning the welfare of B, that takes into account A's external preferences about B, does not entirely respect B's equal status as a citizen. The example commonly used by Dworkin is the case of racism. A racist preference typically includes not only what the person who has that preference desires (e.g., "I want to go to school") but also includes what others should or should not have (e.g., "I do not want blacks in my school"). Dworkin rightly argues that the state does not respect the equal political status of blacks if it takes racist preferences into account. However, the objectionable feature of racist preferences, that which makes them illegitimate, seems to be that they express disrespect or even hatred for other citizens. If racist preferences were allowed to influence legislation or policy many people would see their lives "despised" by official institutions. Indeed, the need to protect citizens from being "despised" by the state is explicitly affirmed by Dworkin in the quote above. Yet this is certainly a more specific characteristic of a preference than that of being "external." What we have, consequently, is a theory not of excluding external preferences but of excluding external preferences that are *hostile*.

This interpretation is reinforced by Dworkin's later writings. Here Dworkin clearly states that the aim is to make political decisions immune to prejudiced and contemptuous preferences;

It is exactly that the minority must suffer because others find the lives they propose to live *disgusting* which seems no more justifiable in a society committed to treating people as equals, than the proposition...that some people must suffer disadvantage under the law because others *do not like* them.[61]

Thus, external preferences are not objectionable in themselves; they are objectionable only when they imply that the way of life or the personal characteristics of some citizens are despised or disparaged.[62] If this is the principle that Dworkin expounds, his theory certainly becomes much less vulnerable to the critique expressed by someone like Hart. When some portion of the community engages in the struggle to improve the conditions of another group they definitely want political institutions to respond to their external preferences. But in so far as their external preferences do not include contempt or hatred of anyone, these preferences are fully legitimate according to my reading of Dworkin. No one's sense of being an equal is violated when heterosexuals are supporting homosexuals in their fight against discriminatory laws.

Another consequence is of course that Dworkin's ideas do not exclude policies of affirmative action. As we have seen (above) a decision to establish quotas for some group may be based either on concern for members of that group or on animosity towards members of other groups. When the motive is not based on resentment but on sympathy, we cannot say that anyone's equal status is undermined. Lundström's claim, that "even 'fair racism' is racism," is not a valid inference from Dworkin's theory. The difference between "fair racism" and racism is that the latter, but not the former, is necessarily based on hatred and contempt.

Equality of Status: What Really Matters

One interpretative problem now remains to be solved. One reason for doubting my conclusion concerning Dworkin's position may be that it is contradicted by so many previous commentators. How come these writers did not notice that Dworkin subsequently qualified his ideas? One reason may of course be that Dworkin actually did express his views carelessly. I have already quoted him as saying that "external preferences of any form" must be excluded. Since we later found that he did not believe that, but only that *hostile* external preferences ought to be excluded, some blame must fall on Dworkin himself.[63] However, more problems remain.

Dworkin, in fact, not only did claim that "any" external preferences should be disregarded, he *explicitly* pointed out that "altruistic" preferences must not affect political decisions. This is problematic to us since my thesis is that Dworkin rejects hostile but not supportive external preferences. But aren't altruistic preferences supportive? If so, how can I be right in arguing that Dworkin accepts them? In order to explain this apparent contradiction it is instructive to examine two further examples of altruistic preferences discussed by Dworkin.

The first example concerns a hypothetical situation where local authorities can choose whether to construct a new theatre or a new swimming-pool.[64] The municipality is prepared to bow to the will of the majority of the citizens but, unfortunately, in this case, there is no clear majority to be found. Now imagine, Dworkin says, that some citizens manage to tip the balance in favor of the swimming pool despite the fact that they do not like swimming themselves. The reason why this group of people supports the swimmers may simply be that they "admire athletes." Their preferences are consequently external since they are not concerned about their own good but the good of the swimmers. Likewise, these preferences are "supportive," since they want the swimmers to have what they want and, yet, preferences must not be allowed to count.

In the second example there is a community where "a surprising number of people love Sarah very much" and therefore want her preferences to count more heavily in all future political decisions.[65] Thus, Sarah's interests will, according to the constitution of this community, always be considered more strongly than those of anyone else. Just as in the first example Dworkin believes this would be unjust. Even though Sarah is benefited only because of the altruistic preferences others have—they *want* her preferences to count for more—the equality of citizens is violated.

These examples portray supportive external preferences as in potential conflict with our right to "equal respect and concern." What constitutes this conflict? I think an answer can be modeled on the assumption that political equality is a form of social *status*.[66] This view is well illustrated by Dworkin's remark that the illiberal character of certain discriminatory policies lies in the fact that they presuppose "that some people are worthier or better than others." It is, as Dworkin makes clear, the "inegalitarian premise of status" that makes male-only or white-only suffrage illiberal.[67] Once the notion of "status" is introduced we can see more clearly why some, but not all, external preferences are objectionable. In the case of "Sarah," to grant an individual more extensive political rights than others, violates the idea of equality of status. Thus, a decision to the effect that Sarah's interests must be given more weight not only violates the idea that law must be couched in universal terms—a feature of integrity and equality before the law. The "inegalitarian premise" is, in the case of Sarah, that she is granted superior legal status. A decision to recognize politically others' love for Sarah would, whether or not she would actually benefit by the decision, amount to saying that all other citizens are less worthy. Altruistic preferences (if not put in universal terms) may, in other words, be inegalitarian in a sense similar to that of racist preferences. They are inegalitarian when they express unequal recognition of worth on matters concerning the relation between the individual and the public authorities.

I believe that the notion of equal status also helps to explain Dworkin's relation in the example of the swimming pool. Here, Dworkin considered it objectionable that local authorities should include the preferences of those citizens who supported the construction of a swimming-pool merely because they found "athletes admirable." If this reason were to influence political decisions, some citizens (athletes) would be recognized as worthier than others (theatre-goers). To benefit a group of citizens because they are thought of as "admirable" amounts to recognizing them as worthier than others. The problem is *not*, then, that non-swimmers *support* swimmers. That is not a problem in itself. Indeed, if these non-swimmers supported the construction of a new swimming pool for some other reason (e.g., because they enjoyed sports themselves) there could be no objection.

Conversely, the reason why racist or prejudiced external preferences should be excluded is not that they mean to disadvantage some group more than another. As has been pointed out, blacks *need* not be disadvantaged by a racist law that excludes them from access to some public institution.[68] Whether they will be disadvantaged is an empirical question. Perhaps, all-black universities are as good, and as many, as those reserved for the white population.

Yet our intuition is likely to be that discrimination is discrimination, whether someone is disadvantaged or not. Dworkin explains this intuition. What matters, from Dworkin's perspective, is the status of citizens manifested by a decision. He does not say, then, that any decision that is hostile to someone, in the sense of deliberately conferring disadvantages, is discriminatory.[69] But a decision to exclude people from public education because of the color of their skin does violate the equal status of these citizens. It constitutes such a violation, since such a decision would tell black citizens that they are not entitled to the same respect as others.

The idea that status, and not burdens or benefits, is crucial to discrimination is fortunate for other reasons too. It enables us to distinguish between laws that treat people differently while respecting equality, and laws that treat people differently while *not* respecting equality. To take another example, there is often public support for families with children. Clearly, the law granting these benefits will disadvantage citizens without children. Yet there is an important contrast between this case and one where the benefit is granted to white families only. The second case definitely illustrates a different sort of discrimination from the first. However, the difference does not, indeed could not, reside in the fact that some families are disadvantaged (blacks) compared to others (whites). The fact of being disadvantaged could not be essential, since that would give anyone not having the benefit equal reason to complain. But, surely, white-only child allowances discriminate more against black families than they discriminate against whites without children. In both cases the law disadvantages some citizens. However, the crucial, and intolerable, feature of a law that discriminates on racial grounds is that it regards some people as superior in status than others. When you make the color of the skin a criterion for public support, you are telling some people that they are not of equal value. Liberalism condemns inequality in status and not, primarily, inequality in benefits.

Again, we may say that Dworkin is not against introducing external preferences to politics per se. But neither is it crucial whether an external preference is supportive or hostile to one group or another. What matters is the degree of status recognized to the members of a group. Whereas Dworkin excludes "altruistic" external preferences, he is not excluding external preferences based on solidarity.[70] Another way of stating this point is to say that there is a difference between expressing reverence for someone and expressing one's sympathy and concern.

Equal People, Equal Values?

It is time to shift our attention away from the interpretative issue and to assess Dworkin's defense of neutrality. Is it reasonable to say that the exclusion of non-egalitarian external preferences justifies the principle of neutrality of aims? In other words, is the theory of external preferences also a theory of neutrality?

In one sense it is obvious that Dworkin approves of some non-neutral aims. As we know now, Dworkin may not find objectionable policies that aim at improving the status of some disadvantaged minority. To support homosexuals by changing a law that discriminates against them is a non-neutral aim that Dworkin may consider legitimate. To support women by granting quotas to some public institutions is a non-neutral aim that may also be legitimate. Decisive for the legitimacy of these aims is the reason that justifies them. As long as the reason for supporting some group is not based on inegalitarian premises, stating that some citizens are more worthy than others, doing so will be fully legitimate. If the idea of equal status of citizens justifies some non neutral aims, the conclusion seems to be that Dworkin is in effect defending equality and not neutrality.

But are these examples of non-neutral aims? After all, the aim of these policies is to assist some group, and establish a situation that is *more* neutral. Using non-neutral policies in order to eliminate discrimination is, in other words, not to violate neutrality but to promote it.

Though this point may seem powerful it obfuscates the more precise meaning of neutrality of aims as it is understood here. In fact, it conceals the difference between policies *required* by neutrality in aims, and policies *consistent with but not required* by that idea. The relevance of this distinction can be seen in the case of homosexuals discussed previously.

A liberal state, faithful to neutrality in aims, would certainly be required to abolish any law that, as in England before 1967, punished homosexuality. In this case the remark about using non-neutral policies in order to enhance neutrality seems relevant. The homosexual community is not favored, relative to other communities, by having their rights protected, even if protecting these rights will require more support than is given to others.

A different case applies, however, when the state enacts quotas for women. It would be unreasonable to assume that the main concern for women today is deliberate discrimination. The legal system may cause women to suffer more than men (e.g., by permitting prejudiced employers to favor men), but these consequences are not intentional. That is, the law is not neutral in its aims, and there are in other words no laws that the liberal state is *required* to modify. The case of women is in that sense different from the case of homosexuals, where the law is designed to impose greater burdens on them. Yet, a liberal state *may*, as is recognized by Dworkin, establish quotas for women or other groups.[71] Hence the non-neutral aim of supporting women or some minority is consistent with general liberal principles, although not required by them.

This conclusion is more damaging to Dworkin's pretence of maintaining a principle of neutrality. Surely there are a great number of laws and policies that are not in conflict with the requirement of preserving equality of status, although these laws and policies might not be neutral. The demands of equality of status and neutrality do not, then, coincide in full. Consider, for example, laws establishing some set of virtues as part of the national curriculum for schools. Or consider policies enacting public support to particular organizations on aesethical or moral grounds or, finally, the case of laws punishing prostitution for ethical reasons.

In all these cases the law might be founded on the external preferences of some citizens (that is, on their ideas about what others deserve, should do, or think). Yet the preferences behind such laws need not be inegalitarian, they may fully respect the equal worth of all citizens.

For instance, the view that schools should encourage some virtues and the view that virtuous people are more worthy can be separated. An idea of *what* is valuable need not amalgamate with an idea of *who* is valuable. That is to say, the value of a virtue may be separated from the value of a person.[72] Thus schools may inspire the virtues of intellectual curiosity but need not condemn as unworthy those who do not, for whatever reason, appreciate that virtue.

Another example is the desire to ban activities related to the prostitution of women. A law that makes the commercialization of sexual services unlawful may identify some acts as immoral, but it need not define those performing such acts as morally corrupt. Disgust with the acts is distinguished from disgust with those performing them. In fact, this is exactly the position taken in a Swedish official investigation of the subject: "we may condemn prostitution...but should not condemn prostitutes."[73]

To the extent, then, that external preferences do not express disrespect for particular individuals they may form the basis for political action. This alludes to the possibility of many non-neutral aims being in fact legitimate. A consequence would seem to be that Dworkin's theory does not justify wide neutrality of aims.

But Dworkin *denies* that his theory opens the door to policies based on ideas of what is good and bad in life. He does so because he believes no one can accept that what one cherishes or holds true is treated as less valuable by public institutions. "No self-respecting person," Dworkin writes, "can accept that [her] way of life is base or degrading."[74] No person can, in other words, accept that what he or she finds important in life (e.g., religion, philately, porn...) is condemned by the state. This idea reminds us of the claim, discussed above, that we should not allow "inegalitarian premises of status" to invade public reasoning. The idea is reminiscent since it implies that the state must not express a hostile attitude towards that which citizens believe is essential in life. But in fact this statement is a different one.

If respect for social status is a basic requirement, the state must not act on preferences that express disgust, hatred or disrespect for other citizens. The state has, on my reading of Dworkin, an obligation to treat citizens as of equal status. However, the suggestion that the state must respect whatever the individual believes in is distinct. Dworkin apparently thinks that the latter claim is somehow implicit in the former—that respect for the equal status of citizens implies that what is important in their lives should not be punished or disadvantaged by the state. But desirable as neutrality in aims may be, this idea is *not* implied by recognizing that the state must respect the equal status of citizens. Respecting an individual is one thing, respecting what an individual does is quite another. It does not seem, for instance, that the equal status of prostitutes is ignored because prostitution is made illegal. It does not seem, moreover, that making schools teach the virtue of solidarity ignores the equal status of egoists just because they may reject any morality of solidarity. It does not seem so for the same reasons which are set out by Dworkin in the previous section: that only policies based on an "inegalitarian premise of worth" specifying some citizens as worthier than others, violate the obligation to respect the equal status of citizens. The demand of equal status will exclude reasons that do not respect the status of the citizen as a person. The demand for equal status will not, however, exclude reasons that do not respect all that the citizen does or believes in.

Of course it may be the case that acting against the convictions of citizens will violate some *other* value than the principle of equal status. There may be other aspects of life that conflict with the idea of a politics of virtue. For this reason we need to go further and we need to examine other claims that can be made on behalf of neutrality of aims.

Life as a Challenge and the Neutral State

In chapter four I described Dworkin's idea that life should be conceived of as a challenge: living a good life means responding well to the features of life that we find important. A successful response is defined in relation to the values and convictions of the individual himself—it is the performance that makes a life good. This is the liberal way of life by Dworkin's account, and he believes that this idea justifies the neutral state. If we accept the liberal conception of the good life we will, Dworkin thinks, also accept the liberal conception of the state.

Of course, we may ask why it is so important that people endorse their values. Is it not, for instance, better for people to live in clean, newly built houses, whether they personally want to or not? But the idea of life as a challenge suggests that the answer to that question may be "no." Life is lived from "within," Dworkin writes; what matters is that we perform our lives successfully according to our *own* visions. Provided that a life in filth is the only way a person can live "at peace with himself," a life in filth must also be the best life for him.

In order to assess the merits of this argument it is helpful to focus on two of its assumptions. One is that the endorsement of values is indeed crucial to leading a good life. This assumption is indeed crucial since it excludes all attempts to impose values from "without." But how important can endorsement be, and what is lost when a person cannot live a life that is endorsed by this? Is it not possible, for instance, that endorsement is just one aspect of a good life and that there may be ways to compensate a person for a loss of that value? But if this is so, we cannot generally say that it is bad to impose values on people—even when these values are not endorsed. This question is the focal point of the first part of this section.

The discussion in the second part calls a second assumption of Dworkin's argument in question: that the typical purpose of imposing values on citizens is to make the lives of citizens *better* in a moral or ethical sense. Arguably, the state is paternalistic when it encourages or promotes certain ideas of the good life. This assumption is crucial to Dworkin's argument, since it allows him to conclude that making the life of someone "better" is futile unless that person herself believes that it has been improved. But is the assumption justified? Is the pursuit of virtue necessarily associated with paternalism?

I will argue that an examination of these assumptions will prove that the idea of life as a challenge does not support the idea of a neutral state. Dworkin is therefore unsuccessful in improving on his former defense of neutrality. The last, and third, part of this section endeavors to explain why Dworkin is committed to neutrality of aims despite the lack of rational arguments for that position.

Support for Culture and the Liberal Way of Life

Let us imagine that the government in a democratic state decides to give financial assistance to literature, film and arts of "quality." Thus, films in the category of drama might be more likely to receive public support than films belonging to the category of comedy. Likewise, authors writing serious fiction might be supported more often than those writing whodunits. A liberal insisting on the idea of neutrality in aims will naturally find such policies objectionable.[75] When the state deliberately encourages certain forms of cultural life, it is acting non-neutrally and, therefore, such a state is inherently illiberal.

Dworkin's theory of external preferences seems not to support the liberal in this case. This is so since a decision to support certain forms of culture does not necessarily express disrespect or contempt for any citizen—which is crucial in order for an external preference to be banned. Rather, the government may justify public support for culture of "quality" by the idea that citizens need a rich and stimulating cultural milieu in order to develop into mature human beings. So, the reason why Hollywood productions would be relatively "disadvantaged" by public policy is that the government regards a more varied cultural life as essential to human perfection. Surely, *that* reason does not represent a violation of the idea that citizens are entitled to be considered as of equal status. Public support for culture need not include "inegalitarian premises," because a decision to that effect need not involve contempt or disrespect for any particular individual.

However, from the idea that liberalism recommends a particular way of life, and not merely the protection of equal status, a liberal may in fact be in a position to construct an argument against public support for culture. When the good life is conceived of as a challenge, any policy that does not respect that idea is to some extent wrong or objectionable. Now, what does respecting life as a challenge mean when it comes to public policy?

One clue is given by Dworkin, when he explicitly affirms the view that the government ought to facilitate the liberal way of life: "If living well means responding well to circumstances as these ought to be, then it must be one function of government to try to bring about that circumstances are as they should."[76] Thus the government has an obligation, according to Dworkin, to enable individuals to face the appropriate challenges. What does this mean?

For instance, Dworkin believes that the government has a duty to make available to citizens basic material and educational resources. This conclusion may be unsurprising and perhaps even an implication of the notion that the government should "try to bring about that circumstances are as they should." If citizens need basic resources in order to fulfil their lives, and if the government is committed to promote the liberal way of life, it follows that the government must provide them with such resources.

Yet, this is *not* how Dworkin justifies the claim that the government has an obligation to provide citizens with basic resources. The reason why may be instructive for our purposes too. In fact, Dworkin rejects the common assumption that the government ought to provide basic resources to citizens because they are means for the satisfaction of personal ends. That is to say, the reason why the government must provide basic resources, hence a degree of social justice, is not that it promotes some end thought to be valuable (i.e., to enable an autonomous life). Justice is not a mere background condition for the good life. Instead, Dworkin's argument is that a just distribution of resources is an important *ingredient* in any response to the challenge of life. Social justice, including redistribution of goods and wealth, is a condition for but a part of the good life.

This claim is explained by Dworkin as follows: "Whether my life is good depends, among other things, on whether the share of resources available to me is a just share."[77] A liberal, in Dworkin's view, does not simply want more resources because that would help him lead a satisfying life. A liberal wants a *just* share of resources. Either having too much or having too little, compared to what is just, would make his or her life less successful than it could be. People who profit from what does not belong to them make their lives depend on unjust relations to others. Such lives cannot be called good. Thus, in order to lead a good, liberal life we will have to ensure that the government cares for social justice.

Returning to the previous discussion we may ask if not culture, just as material resources, could be regarded as essential to the good life. Surely, some would say, there are cultural phenomena that are nearly as basic to human well-being as material resources are. Some people might think that a life that is really good must include the enjoyment of Puccini's operas or Mozart's symphonies! Or, more plausibly, some people might believe that the enjoyment of theatre and literature are essential to the good life. So, if we can argue that some features of culture are also basic to the good life why, then, should not the liberal state have an obligation to support them?

The answer to this question, from the perspective of Dworkin's theory, will depend on making two things clear. It will show, firstly, that the case of culture is *not analogous* to that of material resources and, secondly, that the reason why the government is obliged to maintain social justice actually provides a reason *against* recognizing a similar obligation on cultural issues.

To begin with, we may easily demonstrate that culture and material resources are not analogous from Dworkin's point of view. The reason why the distribution of welfare matters to a liberal is, as we now know, that living justly is essential to the liberal way of life. In order to live well, to be able to say that "my life is great," the resources employed must be legitimate—there is no such thing as a good life based on injustice. The role of justice in the good life is illustrated by an example where a person, very contented and happy with his life, is told that his material standard in fact presupposes the enslavement and exploitation of others. Would that piece of information not be likely to affect his perception of how "good" his life is? But perhaps the same person will attempt to ignore the information about the conditions of his life. Instead he may begin to fill his life more intensively with entertaining and enjoyable activities that will, eventually, make him feel happy. Yet will we consider his life a success? Will we say that, because he *feels* happy, his life is a good one?

What is suggested by this example is that justice is not contingently related to the good life. The issue is not, that is, whether someone *could* really be happy in an unjust society. Rather, justice and the good life are *analytically* connected in Dworkin's theory, and this means that they cannot be successfully realized independently from each other. Only a just society allows people to define what the challenge of their lives consists in. To live in a way that responds to the challenges of one's life means having the power to "self-definition" of "ethical identity." This power is denied in a social system that does not provide individuals with adequate resources but instead "predefines different challenges in the lives of different kinds of people."[78] Social injustices not only make it more difficult for individuals to define for themselves their challenges in life. Social injustices contradict the liberal meaning of the good life, the idea that life is a challenge, by "denying the self-definition that is part of our dignity."[79] Thus, since injustices are an "insult" to dignity they affect those who benefit from injustices too. Whether one is oppressed or an oppressor, an unjust system will restrict and distort the challenges of one's life.

The reason why the analogy between culture and material resources fails is plain. It fails because it is not true that any *particular* cultural achievement is necessary in order to define, as an individual, a challenge for life. The absence of opera houses or orchestras will not encroach on the search for "ethical identity" that Dworkin asserts is at heart of the liberal way of life. Hence, exclusion from high culture is not analogous to suffering from injustice.

However, the analogy to material resources might be appropriate if we talk, not about high culture, but about the entire structure of culture. There is a distinction, Dworkin notes, between particular achievements of culture and culture conceived of as a whole.[80] The idea of eliminating all culture (if imaginable), or the idea of narrowing cultural options down to a minimum, *would* in fact conflict with the ideal of life as a challenge. An unjust society undermines the good life and, analogously, a society without a flourishing culture makes it more difficult for people to define what the good life is. Consequently, to uphold, by means of the state, a cultural basic structure is not something to which the liberal would object.[81]

However, suppose that a defender of public support to "high culture" claims that some cultural achievements are, if not basic to life in the same sense as material resources, then at least essential to a life that is "really" good. The claim now is that the *particular* experiences of, for instance, opera and classical music will always improve and enrich life.

Now from the perspective of life as a challenge, this argument for cultural support is not only unjustified but also wrong. It is wrong, not in that it makes a claim about what cannot be right or wrong (namely, that some experiences are "really" good). It is wrong because the claim that high culture always makes life better ignores the *point* of conceiving life as a challenge. To live a successful life, where the appropriate challenges are met and responded to, *includes* the challenge of defining what these challenges are. Thus, though it may be the case that many of those who have listened to operas find them enjoyable we cannot say that those who do not are living lives that are, for that reason, inferior (a conclusion imperative to anyone convinced that opera is "really" good). That is, cultural achievements that are not defined as a challenge by the person cannot make the life of that person better. The challenge of life is defined individually as Dworkin makes clear: "Part of that challenge, in some ways the most important and exciting part, lies in a person's identifying which of the lives he might lead is in fact good for him."[82] What we find valuable is not valuable to a person, unless it is also part of the challenge of his life as he would define it. In Dworkin's terminology, the relation between what is good *for* people, and what they *believe* to be good for them, is defined by the notion of endorsement. When we consider what is good for people, we need to consider which values and ideals they endorse or embrace. Only in relation to these values can we, following Dworkin, assess the goodness of their lives. Endorsement is in other words a condition for a value being valuable to someone.

To this view T M Wilkinson has objected that Dworkin attaches too much importance to the value of endorsement. That people actually endorse what is good is certainly desirable, but it cannot alone be what matters. Surely, people want to be virtuous and to enjoy the fruits of culture—if only they knew how to proceed. Could it not be the case then, that there are some values that would make people respond better to their challenges despite the fact that they do not endorse them? What is good for people (even in terms of meeting the challenge of life) need not, that is, correspond to what they endorse. The upshot of Wilkinson's argument is that whereas endorsement is a value, there are other values too, and no *one* value reasonably exhausts the realm of what makes life good.[83]

Yet, this objection seems to reveal that Wilkinson has not appreciated the full importance of the notion of endorsement. The claim that anything could be good for people, even when they do not endorse these values, is simply nonsense from Dworkin's perspective: "*Nothing* can improve the . . . value of a life unless it is seen as an improvement by the person whose life it is."[84] There is no "balance" to be struck between what is good and what people endorse. For example, we might think being more sociable would improve the life of a loner. But whether or not we succeed in making the loner more sociable, his or her life will not be improved unless he or she actually thinks that being more sociable is a good thing.

Wilkinson, however, insists that meeting the challenges of one's life need not involve endorsement. A life may be a successful performance and, yet, the values that make up the "success" need not be recognized or endorsed by the person whose life it is. Wilkinson takes the example of people who believe that the good life consists in making the most of one's artistic talents. This view, Wilkinson asserts, concurs with the conception, espoused by Dworkin, of life as a challenge. It does so because it describes the goodness of a life as necessarily a "value-to-a-person" and not as something external to that person.[85] Asserting that talent is the highest good in life corresponds to the challenge view, because it denies that the good life consists in making great art or in anything else that is a mere consequence of artistic activity. The goodness of life is not measured by the amount of art produced, but by the extent to which talent within a person is refined and developed.

Now, the point Wilkinson wants to make is that nowhere in this view is endorsement recognized as a necessary feature of the good life. Consequently, the development of talent is good even when this idea is not endorsed: "to develop artistic talents ... would be good ... whether they want those talents developed or not."[86] People developing their talents meet the challenges of their lives whether they endorse this view or not. Endorsement, however desirable, must therefore be treated as only one value among others.

Unfortunately, Wilkinson's argument still does not capture the point Dworkin intends to make. Wilkinson tries to separate the claim that life as a challenge is an attractive ideal from the claim that a value must be endorsed in order to be valuable for a person. But these ideas are inseparable.

We may use Wilkinson's own example in order to explicate this point. Even if developing "artistic talent" would economically improve the life of a person, we cannot say that it would ethically improve the life of that person unless talent is regarded by him or her as essential to life. Artistic talent does not make life better for someone who defines his or her challenge in life differently. Suppose, for example, that Anna's talents were developed, and that this allowed her to earn more and to provide more support to her family. However, let us also assume that Anna does not believe that developing talent is important to her. In that case, would we really improve her life by persuading her to refine her talents? Dworkin's reply is negative, because "how can the life . . . be better . . . when he goes to his grave thinking it has been worse?"[87] Improving the life of a person, making life more successful in terms of performance, is inevitably linked to the idea that life must be seen as improved by the person himself.[88]

Returning to our initial example of culture, the conclusion is that the liberal way of life may provide an argument against public support for particular cultural achievements. Dworkin's argument depends on the idea that values are always integral to individual lives. Thus, it will matter little whether or not high culture is good in itself. It cannot matter because a life cannot become good, or better, simply by imposing good values on it. What makes lives good is performance. Lives are not made good by pouring goodness on them.

Dworkin and Locke: The Value of Conviction

The conclusion reached in the last section is, unsurprisingly, that paternalism is inconsistent with ethical liberalism. If no values are "valuable" unless endorsed, then it would seem to follow that forcing people to do good is pointless. Forcing the polygamist to have only one wife will not make him a better person or make his life a good one, unless he also becomes convinced that monogamy is a better alternative. The conclusion is, in sum, that the use of force or threats cannot be used in order to create good persons.

Actually this argument is not highly original. A very much similar point was made in a famous statement for toleration by John Locke three centuries ago. Joshua Cohen has recently noticed this similarity. Cohen asserts that, in fact, "Dworkin's defense of moral toleration might be seen as generalizing Locke's argument."[89] If Cohen is right it would seem that the virtues of Locke's argument apply to Dworkin too. The opposite will, naturally, also be true: the limits of Locke's position will also apply to Dworkin's argument. However, I believe we should question the assertion that their positions are in fact similar.

Locke's argument has generally been understood as an argument against the rationality of imposing faith. The simple, but nevertheless controversial, point is that forcing the disbeliever or the heretic to recognize true faith is of no avail, and indeed self-defeating, if the aim is to make the heretic a better person. Any attempt to create faith by force is self-defeating because faith presupposes conviction, and force cannot create *that*.

> For no man can, if he would, conform his faith to the dictates of another. All the life and power of true religion consist in the inward and full persuasion of the mind; and faith is not faith without believing.[90]

Locke in effect asserts that a person who does not *believe* in true faith is not made better off by being forced to *do* what "true faith" requires. At first glance Cohen seems to be correct in saying that this argument is similar to that advanced by Dworkin. The paternalistic government that attempts to make people's lives better by force cannot achieve what it intends to. Paternalistic policies are for that reason self-defeating. Paralleling Locke, Dworkin claims that "nothing can improve the value of a life unless it is seen as an improvement by the person whose life it is."[91] And because Dworkin's reasoning is not confined to strictly religious matters, this point may, as Cohen indicates, be seen as a "generalization" of Locke's argument. So, just as a Catholic is not "saved" by being forced to recognize the *Confessio Augustana*, the life of a hard-rock fan is not necessarily improved by being forced to listen to the operas he or she does not like. Any good must be good for the person whose life it is, or else his life is not made any better by having that good.

But although Locke and Dworkin seem to be talking about similar phenomena, and although both appear to justify a degree of neutrality or tolerance, their arguments actually begin from radically divergent premises. In fact, I believe it can be argued that Dworkin and Locke do not have much in common.

To appreciate this we need, firstly, to acknowledge the theological influences on Locke's purportedly liberal position. The basic premise from which Locke derived his argument for toleration is that sincere faith is a prerequisite of salvation.[92] As a Protestant Christian, Locke believed that having the right conviction, rather than doing the right thing, is a necessary condition for mercy: "[T]rue and saving religion consists in the inward persuasion of the mind, without which nothing can be acceptable to God."[93] Of course, if seriousness is at the heart of the religious message, it is easy to see that force and coercion must be inefficient means of conversion. Generally, people will not change their convictions about fundamental matters when they are threatened or coerced. All that the use of force is likely to produce is lip service. Nevertheless, the words Locke uses in explicating this argument reveal some of its main weaknesses. Locke speaks about "torments" and "imprisonment" not being "efficient" in producing faith.[94] Moreover, Locke asserts that "penalties" are "impertinent" in "convincing the mind."[95] He thereby makes clear, again, that the use of force would be foolish, although not necessarily impossible. Locke's argument is, in sum, based on an assessment of the efficiency of using force in converting men, and it is consequently not an argument of principle—it does not show that force *cannot in principle* create "sincere faith."[96] Rather, the strongest and principal claim of Locke's position is the theological point that sincere faith is required for salvation and grace. Though the connection between faith and salvation may be necessary—there is no salvation without faith—the relation between coercion and conviction is contingent. We simply cannot say with certainty that force can never produce true and sincere faith. Persecution of heretics or disbelievers may, that is, be rational if the aim is to "save" them and make them "good." Locke's argument therefore becomes dependent on assessments of probability and costs (What is the probability that A will be converted by persecution? What are the costs of persecuting A?) As a basis for toleration in a liberal society such considerations are less than satisfactory. What the liberal wants is a reason that shows why persecution is wrong in principle.

Compared to Locke, Dworkin's position appears superior.[97] The idea that endorsement of a value is necessary for that value being good for a person derives not from an assessment of the efficiency of means to ends. Rather than being an empirical claim, Dworkin's point is *ethical*.

That this is so might not at first be evident. That a value must be endorsed in order to be valuable could, on the first reading, be understood as nothing more than the innocuous observation that any person must recognize a good *as good* in order for us to say "that is good for her." For example, the parents of a two-year-old girl believe, not implausibly, that the child will feel better when she is clean and fresh. Parents want their children to bathe because they believe this improves their health and, ultimately, the quality of their lives. As it happens, the child might not want to have a bath. Now, gently forcing the child to have a bath will necessarily disappoint the child but may, if her parents are right, make her happier afterwards. Perhaps the child *will* endorse the good in question, and nothing to be deplored has then occurred. Coercion may in other words improve the child's life.[98]

In this example Dworkin's idea plays a role similar to that which Locke allotted to "sincere faith" in Christianity. Like the parents confronting the stubborn child, the authorities confronting the heretic must ask whether force or coercion will actually produce the intended result. Will the child eventually be better off by being forced to take the bath? Will being forced to attend Church save the heretic? The answer *may* of course be "yes" in either case.

Yet the ethical nature of Dworkin's idea of endorsement means that force is never a legitimate means of moral improvement. In order for a life to be ethically improved it is not really enough that a person endorses the values and ideas that define his life. As might be suspected, this would leave the door open to manipulating people into the conviction that they live good lives—and, surely, that is not compatible with the liberal ideal of how life should be lived. Therefore, Dworkin adds the condition that the endorsement must be a "genuine" one.[99] This brings to the fore the close relationship, discussed in relation to Wilkinson's argument, between the idea of performance and the idea of endorsement. The idea that the good life consists in performance means that people should define what is good for them and that they should act on the basis of that understanding. A good life is a life where people accept responsibility for what they think and do. The idea of endorsement means something that is in fact inseparable from this conception. To say that it is good to endorse the values and convictions we live from is just another way to say that it is good to perform our lives at the level of belief. Performance implies, in other words, that we shape our lives in what we do, as well as in what we think. "Endorsement is genuine only when it is itself the agent's performance," Dworkin writes.[100] But if endorsement is another side of performance, the idea of making a person endorse a value, as when the heretic is forced to endorse the true faith, will truly be pointless. Although accepting a value under duress may produce some form of endorsement, doing so will not be compatible with the ideal that sees life as a performance. The child that is forced to bathe, and subsequently thinks it is nice to be clean, is not performing his or her life. The child is not living the good life, as defined by the liberal ideal, and consequently will be no better off (ethically, though perhaps physically) by being forced.

The contrast between Locke and Dworkin is now evident. Where the former sees conviction as *difficult* to create by force, the latter takes it that forced conviction is no conviction at all. A good life must be lived by genuine convictions. No life can be made better by the use of threat or force.

Moralism or Paternalism? A Conceptual Critique

One conclusion seems to be that the idea of life as a challenge is indeed an effective response to the idea of imposing virtues or ideas of the good life. The liberal way of life, as Dworkin spells out that idea, is inconsistent with the government forcing subjects to live according to a certain belief or value—even when citizens come to believe that the policies did in fact improve their lives. But what if the majority of citizens, and their government, do *not* espouse the liberal way of life? What if they do not accept the value of meeting life's challenges, thereby rejecting the ideal defended by Dworkin? How effective are Dworkin's ideas in that context?

The suspicion is, of course, that the strength of Dworkin's argument hinges on the assumption that people accept his philosophy of life. The argument provided by Dworkin will be pointless if directed to an audience that believes the good life to be something else. Liberalism, that is, becomes a theory for liberals and nothing else. This is a criticism that has been leveled against Dworkin by, among others, William Connolly.

Connolly argues that the pretense of Dworkin's liberalism to neutrality is false in that it gives liberals what they want but gives nothing to those who define their lives differently; "...they [non-liberals] find some of their key convictions consigned to the 'private realm' by secular liberal neutrality ... they [non-liberals] are told to leave their bags of faith at the door when they enter the public realm, while Dworkin and his buddies are allowed to bring several suitcases in with them."[101] If this is true, it gives an air of circularity to Dworkin's project. He gives us good arguments against illiberal policies, but for the argument to be good it must be assumed that we accept the liberal life-style. So, we must already be liberals in order to see why non-liberal policies should be rejected. Commenting on Dworkin's early writings, Brian Barry made a similar point; "my guess is that the doctrine [which Dworkin presents] is usually offered for general consumption by people who have no use of it themselves."[102]

Yet, though it is true that the idea of neutrality is a liberal peculiarity, Dworkin in fact believes that his ethical theory would be acceptable to everyone. In fact, Dworkin believes that "*all* understand their different ethical convictions in the fashion of the challenge conception."[103] Although Dworkin may of course be wrong, and it may be true that his theory is only acceptable to liberals themselves, his intention is to establish arguments that anyone will find convincing. In effect, Dworkin's ambition is to provide an account of ethics that is abstract enough to include all different life-styles and conceptions of the good, and to demonstrate that this account justifies liberal institutions. Anyone can perceive his life as a challenge. And if we can all do that, we will also see why the government has no business imposing virtues on us. Therefore, the justification of neutrality hinges on whether "everyone" accepts the idea that life is a challenge.

Now the extent to which people do is an empirical question. How do people conceive the relation between their convictions and their ideas of the good? Whatever the answer is there is a further, and in my view more serious, question that concerns the relevance of Dworkin's argument against paternalism. In fact, I will argue that the defect is that it is an argument against paternalism only.

As we now know, the idea of endorsement implies that conformity without conviction is pointless, since what makes life good is performing our lives ourselves. It is not what *happens* to life but what we *do* that makes a life successful and good. However, it seems that Dworkin's account of ethics excludes from the scenery the idea that some social (e.g., acts, states of mind) or natural (e.g., ecosystems, species) facts are commonly believed to be good in themselves.[104] The idea that all that is good must be assessed in terms of individual challenges does not, for example, provide room for nonanthropocentric worldviews. Ecologists, for instance, may claim that political decisions must give more consideration to the endangered species. In their view, talking about respect for the idea of "life as a performance" is just irrelevant, or at least biased in favor of the human species. What we need to do, according to the ecologists, is to make people respect any form of life.

Moreover, consider the beliefs of religious persons, conservatives, or Marxists. All of them may assert that there are some intrinsic virtues (love, faith and hope, reverence for tradition, social solidarity). Surely, they may say, it is a genuine good to have citizens accepting these values *even* when they do not accept them in a fully reasoned and self-chosen manner. And surely, some of them might continue, the world is a better place to the extent that these virtues are accepted *whether or not* the life of the virtuous individual is actually improved. Telling the truth, being generous, or having respect for nature are good qualities in themselves. Your life may not be improved by these virtues, but the world or the community may be. In order to make your life ethically better, you may have to make it into a good performance. But in order to improve the world we live in, performance can hardly be essential.

The mistaken assumption Dworkin makes seems to be that the political struggle for virtue, or a conception of the good life, is necessarily individualistic. Dworkin assumes that the aim of politics is always to make the individual better off. But once it is recognized that other entities (collective, ecological, theological) may also count as the locus of ethical value, this assumption will seem to be too narrow. Perhaps Dworkin's fallacy may be described as a failure to distinguish *moralism* from *paternalism*.

Following Joel Feinberg, moralism is the idea that the state can legitimately regulate *harmless* acts on the grounds that such actions "constitute or cause evils of other kinds."[105] Using the terminology of Feinberg, moralism is concerned, not with making people better off, but with what is good or bad in itself. The paternalistic state, in contrast, acts with the aim of preventing the individual from harming himself. Paternalism, but not moralism, is in other words concerned with tackling harm and promoting the alleged interests of individuals. Moralism, but not paternalism, is concerned with what is valuable in itself.

By using these concepts we can see that Dworkin's principles afford good arguments against paternalistic aims. They do so for reasons that are now familiar: no one's life is improved by conformity with values or beliefs that he does not himself endorse.[106] But what about the moralistic state? When the aim of the government is not to make people better, but to encourage a sense of care for others or for nature, Dworkin is bereft of arguments. Surely, he will appeal to the value of life as a performance, and he might claim that any policy that does not respect that notion is, to that extent, wrong and illiberal. But the riposte to Dworkin is a simple one. We may grant that endorsement and performance are valuable, and perhaps even indispensable, when thinking about what makes a life good. But there are cases when the aim is a different one. The constraint of endorsement does not apply when the aim of a policy is to create more intrinsic value rather than making the life of citizens better.

It is self-defeating, as Dworkin observes, to try to make people lead better lives by making them conform to ideals they do not endorse. The more we try to make their lives "good," the worse they will be in terms of performance. It is not self-defeating, however, to try to promote what is believed to be of intrinsic value, even when it means that individuals will not perform their lives in full. If there are intrinsic values—and many people think there are—their value is not affected by whether people endorse them or not. Designing institutions so that social solidarity is effectuated might be worthwhile even if people do not endorse the virtue of solidarity. Making men virtuous may be desirable even were it better that people become virtuous by their own fiat and choice.

The Limits of Neutrality of Aims

In this chapter we have examined the arguments in favor of the idea that the state ought to be neutral in aims. The quest for a possible justification of this idea has been undertaken on three different levels. First, on the level of legal principle, we asked whether the idea of equality before the law did provide a justification of the idea of neutrality of aims. Secondly, we asked whether the principle that citizens are entitled to equal concern and respect constitutes a claim to neutrality. On the third level, we approached a specific idea of what is important to life (the idea of life as a challenge). Here we asked whether a liberal idea of the good could justify the principle of neutrality. Arguments on all these levels were reconstructed from Dworkin's legal and political theory. Now, what are the results? Let me briefly recapitulate my conclusions on these three levels.

The principle of equality before the law, understood as the idea of integrity in Dworkin's theory, does establish some restrictions. Most importantly, any law that is enacted must cohere with the principles on which other laws are based. Yet, as I have argued, this formal restriction does not exclude the promotion by law of particular conceptions of the good. A notion of legal equality cannot establish the idea of the neutral state.

Moreover, if we accept the idea of political equality, we are compelled to accept the view that the government should not adopt policies or laws that do not respect the equal status of citizens. Hence, no official action may be based on the assumption that some citizens are more valuable than others. Though this certainly is an important principle, perhaps even the most central idea in liberal theory, it is not the same as neutrality. A state may respect the equal status of citizens and yet prefer some conceptions of the good to others.

A different argument is provided by the idea that the state must respect the liberal way of life. In Dworkin's view the good life is constituted by good performance. Since the liberal way of life accords much value to the *way* in which individuals come to accept their beliefs and values, it seems to provide a good argument against the imposition of any conception of the good. However, despite the merits of this point, I conclude that this idea does not justify the idea of the neutral state. To the extent to which there are values different from that of living a good life such values may plausibly be imposed. Thus, the liberal way of life does not justify the idea of the neutral state—and no argument seems capable of achieving that.

In fact, when we consider the limitations of Dworkin's arguments a further objection becomes apparent. Though the principle he embraces clearly excludes several different ideas from the political sphere, there seems to be no knockdown argument against religious or metaphysical ideas. The liberal state, according to Dworkin, must respect integrity and the equal political status of citizens. Furthermore, a liberal government must respect the liberal way of life in the sense of not acting with paternalistic or moralistic aims. Yet, despite all these reservations, undoubtedly of great importance, there is nowhere an argument that proves that the liberal state must not be a confessional state. Curiously, there is no obvious reason why a religious state could not satisfy all the principles introduced by Dworkin. A peaceful and modest state, that enacts laws and policies that are clearly liberal, might respect the restrictions set out by Dworkin and still be religious in important respects.

And yet, many liberals will feel uneasy about this conclusion. From a liberal point of view a confessional state, proclaiming the truth of a particular theology or doctrine, simply cannot be tolerated. Liberalism is incompatible with a state that heralds metaphysical ideas and justifies its actions, however liberal, by referring to Holy Writ. Such a state might be liberal in its aims, but it cannot be liberal in its justification. There is in other words more to be said about the liberal state than that it should be neutral in its actions. According to other recent liberal theories the idea of political equality means that the political system has to be justifiable to all citizens. "To respect another person as an end is to insist that coercive or political principles be as justifiable to that person as they are to us."[107] What matters in this view is not only what the state should do, but why it should do whatever it is supposed to do. Thus, we need to leave the sphere of aims and action behind and move into the realm of reason.

Notes

1. Dworkin, 1990, pp 111, 116.
2. In this chapter I shall speak of "neutrality" in the sense of "neutrality of aims" except if otherwise indicated.
3. Stephen Holmes, 1993, pp xii, 4. Other notable exponents of this argument include Friedrich Hayek. "[T]hat all rule applies equally to all . . . makes it improbable that any oppressive rules will be adopted." Hayek, 1960, p 210.
4. Holmes (1993, p 238) also claims that the legal norm of "equal and general law" requires the state to "provide important resources that enable citizens to exercise their rights."
5. Apart from not distinguishing between neutrality in legislation and neutrality in adjudication Holmes never specifies which conception of neutrality he refers to.

Thus we cannot say whether his defense of "neutrality" is a defense of neutrality of justification, of aims or of consequences. See Holmes, 1993, *passim.*
6. Dworkin distinguishes clearly between the context of adjudication and legislation. In Dworkin's view equality before the law is applicable in both contexts albeit with slightly different implications. Here, however, the meaning of equality before the law is discussed in relation to legislation only. Ronald Dworkin, 1986, pp 217–219.
7. Dworkin, 1986, p 165.
8. Dworkin, 1986, p 166.
9. "We insist on integrity because [not doing this] would deny what is often called 'equality before the law' and sometimes 'formal equality'." Dworkin, 1986, p 185. In contrast, Peczenik points out that the formal conception of equality before the law only includes the idea that decisions are according to law (i.e., what is often referred to as "legality"). With Peczenik's terminology we are interested in the "material" sense of equality before the law. Aleksander Peczenik, 1995, pp 52f. Bertil Bengtsson, on the other hand, uses a terminology that concurs with that of Dworkin, though Bengtsson warns against the tendency to include specific policy outcomes in the idea of equality before the law. Bertil Bengtsson, 1984, pp 204–208.
10. The basis for integrity, which is a question of little relevance to my inquiry, is discussed at length in Paul Gaffney, 1996, chapter three and *passim.*
11. See Dworkin, 1986, pp 178f.
12. Dworkin, 1986, p 179 (emphasis added).
13. It might be objected that any principle could be the outcome of political compromise. Thus it could be argued that allowing abortion only to women born on odd days is a possible compromise between advocates and critics of abortion in a parliamentary deadlock. Yet Dworkin would deny the legitimacy of such compromises. Though politics certainly must allow for compromises, Dworkin believes it has to be "a compromise about which scheme of justice to adopt rather than a compromised scheme of justice." That is, compromises need to be external to legal justice and not internal to it. Dworkin, 1986, p 179.
14. Richard Hare, 1973, pp 4f. Also Peczenik, 1995, pp 592–596.
15. By contrast Lon Fuller argues that the requirement of *general* laws is crucial and formally entailed by the notion of "law" but that the idea of *universality* (Fuller does not use this term) is not. Fuller claims that avoiding non-universals is a demand of fairness and not a demand of law itself. Lon Fuller, 1969, pp 47f.
16. Rousseau, *Du Contrat Social*, Book III, quoted in Thérèse Björkholm, 1994, p 241.
17. Dworkin explicitly recognizes the analogy between his ideas and Rousseau's. Dworkin, 1986, p 189. A thorough comparison between Dworkin and Rousseau, especially with reference to the role of judicial review, is found in Richard Nordahl, 1997, pp 322ff.
18. However, the requirement to rewrite universal terms in non-universals will occasionally have radical implications. It would seem, for instance, that the Act of Succession in the Swedish Constitution, article one, would fall prey to a strict adherence to this idea: "The right to succession . . . is vested in the male and female descendants of King Carl XVI Gustaf, Crown Prince Johan Babtist Julii, later King Karl XIV Johan's, issue in direct line of descent." Quoted in (1996), "The Act of Succession," *Constitutional documents of Sweden.* Cf Rousseau's point that a law may legitimately establish a hereditary *monarchy* but not elect or name a royal *family.* Björkholm, 1994, p 242f.
19. Dworkin, 1986, p 166.
20. Charles Taylor, 1995, p 247.

21.   Hayek, 1960, p 209. Similarly, Hans Kelsen asserted that equality before the law "merely states that the law should be applied as it is meant to be applied ... regardless of whether this order is just or unjust." Kelsen thereby seems to state the consequences of Hayek's observation more clearly. Quoted in Alfonso Ruiz Miguel, 1997, p 373. For a different view, assuming the clear and unambiguous consequences of equality before the law, see Buchanan & Congleton, 1998, esp chapter one.

22.   See also Björkholm, 1994, pp 247f.

23.   In fact, Dworkin (1986, p 222) admits that the idea of generality does not require principles to be *very* general. "[T]here might be sound reasons of policy why the legislature should not generalize ... integrity is not violated just by accepting these reasons and refusing to make the policy more general."

24.   Cf Raz's (1994, p 322) conclusion that "integrity [in law] is not a conclusive ground for good legislation."

25.   Bo Rothstein, 1994, pp 40–42.

26.   Holmes, 1993, p 239.

27.   Cf Stefan Björklund, 1977, pp 80f, 104f, Rothstein (1994, p 58) and Thomas Gür, 1998, p 10.

28.   Coherence should be distinguished from consistency. The proposition (a) "blacks do *not* have the right to vote" is consistent with the proposition (b) "blacks *do* have the right to public services." Consistency requires that accepting one proposition is not incompatible with accepting another. Yet coherence demands more and requires that all propositions that are accepted can be combined into one systematic set of principles. Thus while (a) and (b) above may be consistent, they are less likely to be coherent. See also Peczenik, 1995, p 628.

29.   For the distinction between principles and rules, see Dworkin, 1977, pp 20ff. In this work the ideal of integrity is termed the idea of "articulate consistency" (p 88).

30.   "The state lacks integrity [when] it must endorse principles to justify part of what it has done that it must reject to justify the rest." Integrity condemns "inconsistency in principle among the acts of the state." Dworkin, 1986, p 184. Cf Raz's contention (1994, pp 319–325) that Dworkin is *not* committed to the value of coherence in law.

31.   Cf Dworkin's (1986, p 404) point that "law as integrity not only permits but fosters different forms of substantive conflicts and tensions within the best overall interpretation of law."

32.   Dworkin, 1986, p 401.

33.   E.g., Gür, 1998, p 10.

34.   Catherine MacKinnon, 1989, pp 216f.

35.   MacKinnon, 1989, p 230.

36.   The most important effect of equality before the law may be, then, that it makes necessary rational justifications. Since only "relevant considerations" are accepted, legislators (and courts) must prove by argument that their decision rests on what is relevant only. In the terminology of Cass Sunstein this amounts to an exclusion of "naked preferences" from politics, i.e., preferences that are justified solely by reference to the will of the subject. See Cass Sunstein, 1993, p 25.

37.   Cf Cass Sunstein's view that "integrity . . . is neither necessary nor sufficient for legitimacy." Cass Sunstein, 1996, p 53. Although seemingly inconsistent with my conclusion it should be observed that Sunstein is concerned with integrity in adjudication, not legislation.

38.   Dworkin (1986, pp 101–104) asks if Nazi Germany had a system of law. Dworkin finds that the question is trivial in one sense, since Nazi Germany certainly did have something similar to what we call "law." But, Dworkin argues, if by law we mean

something like "a flourishing legal system that justifies coercion" then Nazi Germany did not have law, because we would not describe Nazi-law as part of a "flourishing legal system," neither as morally adequate in order to justify coercion. There is in other words a sense in which illegitimate or unjust law is not really "law" and this points at Dworkin's substantive conception of equality as basis for law.

39. Cf Lars Utz McKnight, 1996, p 138, fn 415.
40. Dworkin, 1986, p 223 (emphasis added).
41. This Rousseauan justification of equal concern and respect is suggested by Nordahl, 1997, p 327.
42. Of course the insistence upon individual rights, such as the right to life and to physical integrity, will give us a good indication of where to draw the line. In this section I take the existence of rights for granted and shall instead focus on preferences that, although not violating any rights, are likely to violate the idea of neutrality of aims. Apparently, the distinction between rights and neutrality depends on arguments made in previous chapters (i.e., chapters five and six).
43. This idea also represents Dworkin's attempt to remedy some defects of the utilitarian idea of preference-satisfaction. See, on this point, Leif Lewin, 1988, pp 25f (and references cited therein).
44. Dworkin, 1977, pp 180ff, 272f; Dworkin, 1984, p 62; Dworkin, 1985, pp 84 ff; Dworkin, 1986, p 227.
45. Dworkin, 1985, p 353.
46. Ronald Dworkin, 1983 b, p 32.
47. Rawls, 1971, p 13.
48. David Gauthier, 1986, p 87. Just as Dworkin, Gauthier defends the idea of a state that is "neutral with respect to the aims of its members" (p 350).
49. Cf Michael Freeden's claim that Dworkin's distinction "is not a broadly representative liberal position." Michael Freeden, 1996, p 263. Freeden arrives at this conclusion by comparing Dworkin to a particular brand of English liberalism in the nineteenth century and by ignoring contemporary liberal ideas. I therefore concur with Raz (1994, p 97) in believing that Dworkin here catches a widespread liberal idea.
50. The concept of affirmative action sometimes has a more specific meaning including only the case where separate criteria are used when assessing members of different sexual, racial or cultural groups. A quota, by contrast, refers to the case where a number of seats or positions is exclusively reserved for members of a particular group.
51. The terms hostile and supportive were introduced in this context by Albert Weale, 1983, p 39.
52. "There is a similar corruption when the external preferences that are counted are altruistic." Dworkin, 1977, p 235.
53. Mats Lundström, 1996, pp 61–63 (my translation).
54. Lundström, 1996, p 62. It should be noted that Lundström also claims that affirmative action may sometimes be legitimate and necessary. As a "temporary act" we may be justified, he argues, in discriminating against some individuals (e.g., men) in order for other individuals (e.g., women) to be less discriminated in the future. Cf Gür's (1998) claim that quotas and affirmative action are never justified.
55. In England sexual relations between consenting adults of the same sex was a criminal offense until 1967.
56. Hart, 1992 [1979], p 245.
57. Raymond Plant, 1991, p 121.
58. Actually, a number of writers have previously made this point. John Ely, 1983, pp 285–287; Plant, 1991, p 122; Maureen Ramsay, 1997, pp 128f; Robert Simon, 1979, p 93; Weale, 1983, p 40.

184   The Liberal State and the Politics of Virtue

59. Dworkin, 1977, p 236 (emphasis added).
60. Dworkin, 1977, p 276.
61. Dworkin, 1985, p 367 (emphasis added).
62. Raz (1994, p 98) too observes that Dworkin qualified his notion of external prefer-
     ences in this respect. See also McKnight, 1996, p 138 and Ely, 1983, pp 185ff.
63. In fact, Dworkin seems to recognize this problem of interpretation: "someone
     might have been led to suppose, by my discussion, that what I condemn is any
     political process that would allow any decision to be taken if people's reasons for
     supporting one decision rather than another are likely to lie beyond their own
     personal preferences." Dworkin, 1985, p 368.
64. Dworkin, 1977, p 235.
65. Dworkin, 1985, p 361.
66. The notion of equal status is described by David Miller as an instance of *social
     equality*. This idea should, Miller argues, be distinguished from notions of *distribu-
     tive* equality that are primarily associated with justice. David Miller, 1998, pp 23f.
67. "Political equality must be defined as a matter not of power but of the kind of status....
     Male-only suffrage . . . were inegalitarian because they presupposed that some
     people were worthier or better fit to participate in collective action than others."
     Ronald Dworkin, 1996 b, p 28. An early note on political equality as a form of social
     status is found in Dworkin, 1983 a, p 47. It is noteworthy that neither Dworkin nor
     any of his commentators connect the idea of "equal status" to the distinction between
     external and personal preferences. The closest we get is Robert van der Veen's
     recent observation that Michael Walzer's ideal of a "society of equals" can be under-
     stood in analogy with Dworkin's notion of "equal respect." Robert van der Veen,
     1999, p 246. See also Walzer, 1983, pp 272–280.
68. Rae Langton, 1990, pp 322f.
69. See Dworkin, 1977, p 237, fn 1.
70. Cf Raz (1994, pp 96–98) who claims that Dworkin excludes *any* solidaric prefer-
     ences from politics.
71. E.g., Dworkin, 1985, pp 293–314.
72. This point is made (in relation to Dworkin) in Robert George, 1993, pp 96 and 102.
     See also Haksar, 1979, p 284. Jean Hampton (1989 a, pp 810f) too distinguishes
     tolerance of a *person* from tolerance of the *beliefs* of a person. She asserts that
     while we certainly are required to tolerate any person, it would be absurd to
     require tolerance of every belief. Thus, while persecution and punishment on
     the basis of conviction is definitely illegitimate, persuasion and argumentation is
     not.
73. *Prostitutionen i Sverige*, SOU 1981:71, p 137 (my translation). The full, non-
     translated, quote runs as follows: "Det föranleder mig att göra den reflektionen att
     prostitutionen som företeelse mycket väl kan fördömas men att de enskilda kvinnorna
     som ägnar sig åt prostitution inte bör bli föremål för förakt."
74. Dworkin, 1983 b, p 32. Dworkin speaks in this context of "a sense of equal worth."
     Stephen Wall discusses the same quote but refers to the idea of "a sense of *self-
     worth*" (1998, p 88, my emphasis).
75. E.g., Carl Rudbeck, 1993, pp 10f.
76. Dworkin, 1990, p 98.
77. Dworkin, 1990, p 99.
78. Dworkin, 1990, pp 102f.
79. Dworkin, 1990, p 103.
80. The distinction between particular and structural features of culture is made in
     Dworkin, 1985, p 229.

81. Dworkin writes that "[I] do not mean that the government has no responsibility for the cultural background against which people decide to live." Dworkin, 1990, p 85, fn 44. That Dworkin is, in this case, *not* inconsistent when accepting a non-neutral principle here is clear, I think, from my analogy between material resources and justice. The state may support the structure of culture not because some particular achievements are good, but because the conception of "life as a challenge" is necessarily bound up with *some* culture as a whole. Cf Macleod who claims that Dworkin's recognition of public support to culture is "at odds with the conception of neutrality." Colin Macleod, 1998, p 193.
82. Dworkin, 1990, p 97.
83. Wilkinson, 1996, pp 436f.
84. Dworkin, 1990, p 85.
85. Wilkinson, 1996, pp 438f.
86. Wilkinson, 1996, p 438.
87. Dworkin, 1990, p 80.
88. However, as observed by Macleod (1998, p 36), this does not mean that endorsement is inseparable from Dworkin's ideal of life as a challenge. Other liberal theorists have embraced the endorsement criterion without ever having heard of Dworkin or his theories.
89. Joshua Cohen, 1998, p 216.
90. John Locke, 1963 [1689], p 17.
91. Dworkin, 1990, p 85.
92. E.g., John Plamenatz, 1992 [1964], pp 133f.
93. Locke, 1963, p 19.
94. Locke, 1963, p 19.
95. Locke, 1963, p 21.
96. This is the main argument in Jeremy Waldron, 1988, *passim*.
97. Yet there are passages that might be taken to support a reading closer to the position of Dworkin, i.e., stressing the value of independence. "Neither profession ... [nor] worship can be available to the salvation of souls, unless the truth of the one, and the acceptableness of the other unto God, be thoroughly believed by those that so profess and practice." Locke here claims that to utter the words of the profession of the Church is not enough. Belief in the *truth* of that doctrine is necessary for salvation. By this point Locke probably wanted to emphasize the difficulties of converting men by force. The use of threats is certainly unlikely to save a man's soul if salvation depends on correct beliefs rather than on correct words. Locke's point is still pragmatic, however, compared to Dworkin's idea that the formation of beliefs in truth is part of what has value. Cf Locke, 1963, p 21.
98. Sher believes this point proves that Dworkin's idea of endorsement does not, in the end, exclude a politics of virtue. Sher (1997, p 103) argues that coercion can *lead to* endorsement and that, consequently, imposing virtue may not conflict with the idea of endorsement being essential to the good life; "the use of force [can] indirectly lead [a person] to see the point of accepting the very conception of the good whose acceptance he was originally committed to resisting."
99. Dworkin, 1990, p 79. The idea of "genuine" endorsements is discussed in further detail in chapter three.
100. Dworkin, 1990, p 79.
101. William Connolly, 199, p 124.
102. Brian Barry, 1991, p 35.
103. Dworkin, 1990, p 90 (my emphasis).

104. Thus, it is unclear to what extent this conclusion is consistent with what Dworkin (1993) has said in other contexts about the importance of intrinsic values to people's lives.
105. Joel Feinberg, 1988, pp xx and 324.
106. It should be noted that Dworkin is not opposed to what he calls "superficial paternalism," or "forcing people to take precautions that are reasonable within their own structure of preferences." Dworkin, 1990, p 85. See also Dworkin, 1993, p 259, fn 20.
107. Larmore, 1996, p 137.

8

Neutral Reasons:
The Liberal State Justified

In the previous chapter I examined the idea that the state must be neutral in what it does. In this chapter I am going to examine the idea that the state must be neutral in the justification of its actions. This idea is important, since it rejects reasons for preferring one policy to another that depend, for their validity, on beliefs about the intrinsic value of virtues. Considerations of what is valuable in itself are unacceptable in justifications of public affairs. This is one of the consequences of the liberal principle of neutrality of justification.

In practice the idea of neutrality of justification means that beliefs in virtue cannot be recognized by the state as relevant to political or legal matters. The state must not refer to conceptions of the good or of virtues. But Rawls extends the application of this idea beyond the state so as to include parts of the public life of society. Not only the state must be neutral, citizens that deliberate or argue about the fundamental principles of the state must be neutral too. The reasons of the state *and* of the democratic citizen are, in this sense, restricted by the requirements of liberalism.

Is the idea of neutrality of justification tenable? Are there good reasons for citizens to accept the liberal idea of neutrality? Though the demands of neutrality are fairly modest (compared, let's say, to a defender of a theocratic state who demands that everyone accept some particular faith), it still demands a lot. Citizens may not, according to the idea of neutrality, let their personal morals and political ideals influence fundamental political issues. But why should citizens prefer a political community that ignores the beliefs and reasons that matter most to them? Why should they not, after all, stick to their convictions about what is good or virtuous and try to convince others of their merits? These are questions that have to be answered by a defender of liberal neutrality. In the following I shall discuss the idea of neutrality of justification in relation to the theory of John Rawls. Though Rawls is not the only defender of this ideal, he certainly has given it its most elaborate defense.

A first difficulty for the idea of neutrality concerns its consistency with liberal aspirations. In a liberal society, anyone can say almost anything, no opinions (except perhaps the most extreme ones) need to be hidden. Yet Rawls argues that liberalism imposes the demands of neutrality which restrict what can be said and done politically. Does this not mean that neutrality is at variance with the liberal spirit? The way neutrality is meant to work and the extent to which neutrality can coherently be defended as a liberal ideal will be examined in the first section of this chapter.

However, the emphasis of this chapter is on the arguments for neutrality. The aim is, in other words, to examine the basis for the claim that citizens and the state should *justify* themselves in the liberal way. Rawls's sophisticated theory suggests several reasons for accepting this idea, drawing on a multitude of moral, philosophical and practical considerations. One idea is especially important to Rawls: the assumption that all citizens are political equals. The demand to justify political principles in a neutral way thus follows from the respect that equal citizens owe to each other. Politically speaking, equals are neutral, in other words.[1] The power of this argument to justify neutrality will be appraised in section two of this chapter. Yet, my conclusion is that equality can only play a minor role in the justification of neutrality.

Instead, I argue that the major thrust for neutrality is located in an account of political justification. In Rawls's view, political arguments are characterized by two features: publicity and disagreement. Now the point is that neutrality is a prerequisite for political justifications to be public and for them to be compatible with the fact of disagreement. Rawls's account of publicity and disagreement is at the focus of the discussion in sections three and four.

Publicity is the idea that political institutions must be justified by generally acceptable forms of reasoning. The idea of publicity is, in fact, fundamental to the legitimacy of the state in Rawls's view. Only by adhering to publicity will the justifications of the state be accessible to citizens. And yet commentators of Rawls's work have not

devoted much attention to this fact. The conclusion of the analysis
of the third section is nevertheless that publicity cannot alone vindicate neutrality.

In the fourth section I continue to explore Rawls's account of
political justification and the idea that political arguments must be
reasonable with respect to existing disagreements. In this view,
Rawls's case for neutrality rests on an account of how reasonable
citizens should cope with disagreements on questions of the good
life. The claim is that reasonable citizens should accept the principle
of neutrality when facing pervading political disagreements. In other
words, it is by identifying the conditions of a reasonable justification, and not by insisting on political values such as equality, that
Rawls hopes to convince the non-liberal about the necessity of neutrality in politics. Still, my conclusion is that this strategy must fail.
As the argument stands, it cannot convince the non-liberal that ideas
about virtue and the good life should be rejected.

The guiding idea of my critique is that Rawls does not adequately
appreciate the force of people's moral and ethical beliefs. People
have a wide range of beliefs about what is good or desirable, and
they generally believe these doctrines are true. Without facing the
truth of these beliefs liberalism cannot vindicate the idea of a neutral
state. But Rawls does not want to challenge the truth of people's
beliefs. Rawls's ambition is, as it must be for anyone defending the
idea of a neutral state, that liberal reasons should be compatible with
most people's truths. It is my hope that the discussion which now
follows will serve to explain why this cannot be achieved.[2]

The Ethos of Neutrality

The principle of neutrality is part of the liberal ideal of legitimate
government. Neutrality is also part of the liberal ideal of citizenship.
Not only the government must remain neutral to conceptions of the
good. The ordinary citizen, as well as the judge and the politician,
must remain neutral whenever they engage in a discussion about
fundamental matters of rights and justice. Thus Rawls's liberalism,
in which the idea of neutrality of justification plays this formidable
part, specifies an ethos of neutrality—a public reason—which applies to certain segments of the political sphere.

The ideal of public reason has been criticized for being too extensive. The spirit of liberalism is openness and freedom of argument,

not restraint and censorship. Prescribing neutrality for public debate will, according to one critic, "vitiate just the kind of open and rational atmosphere that Rawls identifies with a liberal society."[3] A second critic argues that the demand of neutrality seems "extraordinarily strong" when applied to the public sphere.[4] A third concludes that the idea of restrictions on public debate seems odd, since liberals typically "seek agreement on what to do rather than exactly how to think."[5]

It can, in other words, be questioned whether the idea of neutrality is consistent with other liberal ideals. In the following I will examine the basis for Rawls's idea that the demands of neutrality should be extended to the public reasoning of citizens. I will argue that public reason is constitutive of liberal justice. Thus, neutrality is not, in Rawls's view, in conflict with liberal principles but integral to them. Moreover, neutrality is not merely a pragmatic idea justified by the fact that it is conducive to the stability and continuity of liberal institutions.

Two Aspects of Neutral Constitutionalism

Why are some arguments excluded from public debate? Why impose neutrality on citizens in the public sphere? In order to understand the rationale of this idea, we need to explore further the basic logic of Rawls's argument.

A fundamental feature of Rawls's ideal of the liberal state is that it proceeds on two levels. There is the level of *choice*, where we choose principles for a just society, and the level of *application*, where we revise and interpret these principles. Rawls's liberal ideal includes an account of both. The reason why it should is easy to see. If, in a society, there is agreement on the principles of justice, but no agreement on how to interpret or apply them, it is unlikely that these principles will remain in place for long. Constitutions change and the principles they embody need to be reinterpreted when new circumstances arise. The fact that society *is* founded on just principles does not mean that we know what those principles will mean in the future. Even the best or most just constitution has to be interpreted.

Thus, when a people is faced with the rare opportunity of constituting its political institutions anew, when people need to reconsider the moral and political basis of the polity, the task is not really one but two. The most pressing challenge is of course the choice of the basic principles: Which powers should the government have? Which basic rights and freedoms are citizens to be granted? Which economic rights and institutions should exist? These questions are typically encountered when new constitutions are designed as, to some extent, in Sweden in the early 1970s, or in many Eastern European countries in the early 1990s. However, a constitutional debate never ends here. Important as the content of a constitution is, its interpretation is at least as important. The question of which rights individuals have is not settled once and for all, just because a Bill of Rights has been agreed on. New, unforeseen, cases will appear, necessitating a revival of the constitutional debate. Do the rights of the constitution include children, fetuses, animals? Unforeseen issues emerge that actuate debates about the meaning of fundamental rights and justice. Moreover, the need to reinterpret basic concepts of justice also follows from the way cultural and political values change and develop.

In theory, Rawls has elaborated two concepts that "model" the conditions under which constitutional decisions ought to be made. At the first level, where the principles of justice are identified and chosen, citizens are to accept the so-called "veil of ignorance." This theoretical construction defines the standpoint from which people should deliberate when engaged in a choice of fundamental principles of justice. One important aspect of this position ("original" position as it is called) is of course the demand for neutrality.[6] Citizens are required not to justify their constitutional arguments in terms of conceptions of the good life.

At the second level, where citizens apply and interpret the principles previously identified, they are guided by what Rawls calls public reason. One of the norms that public reason defines is that of neutrality of justification.

Thus, neutrality restricts both the initial agreement about the contents of justice and the subsequent debate about how to revise or interpret these principles. This is a way to secure that future decisions about justice do not depart too much from the original ideas which have been agreed to. Public reason does in a way perpetuate the ideas identified by citizens in the original position. Thus, the task of public reason can be stated as that of maintaining liberal principles and institutions.

[To] maintain a just and stable democratic society ... it is normally desirable that the comprehensive philosophical and moral views we are wont to use in debating fundamental political issues should give way in public life.[7]

Since the constitution is supposed to be neutral to ideas of the good, it seems natural to accept that the public debate about its meaning and implications ought to be neutral too. The rationale for this idea is that Rawls's ambition is higher than that of identifying just (fair) principles. His ambition is to identify the principles for a society that will continue to be just.[8] We might say that the idea of public reason presents an *ethos* for the liberal society. It is a substitute for the "sanctity" or "reverence" that, in more traditional societies, guarantees adherence to basic principles. Public reason has in an important sense the function of a civil religion.[9]

The objection that the norms of public reason contradict the typical openness of liberalism can now be assessed. In fact the claim that the demands of public reason are "extraordinarily strong," and that they "vitiate" the open atmosphere of liberal society, appears less justified. Public reason imposes neutrality only on questions that concern the basic principles of justice. It does not include the public sphere as a whole. The distinction between "wide" and "narrow" conceptions of neutrality that I proposed in chapter six is also applicable to public reason. According to the narrow conception, neutrality applies in relation to issues concerning the basic structure of society only. In fact, Rawls is rather clear on this point; "the *limits* imposed by public reason do not apply to all political questions but only to those involving what we may call 'constitutional essentials.'"[10]

Rawls's idea is, in this sense, distinct from the idea that every aspect of political life must be neutral. For instance Bruce Ackerman argues that neutrality should, ideally, permeate all social relations. The liberal ideal of neutral debate must, Ackerman contends, apply to the justifications of any institution and not only to political institutions: "every *citizen* could justify every aspect of his power position in a way that [is] *perfectly* consistent with the Neutrality principle."[11]

Even so, Rawls's position is not unambiguous. At one point Rawls alludes to the possibility of expanding the role of public reason. In apparent contradiction to what has previously been said, Rawls argues that it would be "highly desirable" if public reason were invoked in ordinary political debate too.[12] All political conflicts should be solved by means of a neutral political debate and deliberation.

But on what grounds would this be "desirable"? Rawls never explains this and so we can only accept as his the view that public reason ought to guide, ideally, the constitutional level of public discourse.

Neutrality for the Sake of Stability Only?

The conclusion of the previous analysis is that the neutrality of the public sphere is a means whereby liberal institutions are maintained. Public reason is a norm of neutrality that secures the liberal character of constitutional debates. Now the consistency of this account is open to doubt. In fact, my belief is that the instrumental interpretation of public reason is at variance with important ideas of Rawls's liberalism. Though public reason may work in ways that stabilize liberal institutions, this cannot be its main justification. Public reason is not merely an ethos of instrumental importance. I believe that Rawls's ideal should be understood as placing citizens under a moral obligation to restrict their arguments when constitutional matters are at stake. Thus, Rawls's justification of neutrality in the public sphere is based on a moral and not a practical idea. In this part I will explain why.

The idea that neutrality in public life is instrumentally justified is supported by Stephen Holmes. In the terminology of Holmes, Rawls uses the restrictions of neutrality as a form of "gag-rule."[13] Such rules are used to silence, that is gagging, certain questions when we believe that the value of peaceful cooperation is greater than the value of speaking out. In general people do not, for instance, comment on the style and physical appearance of those with whom they cooperate. Comments on such matters are frequently believed to be detrimental to the common project. A certain degree of self-censorship is in other words regarded as prudent.

From Holmes's standpoint this is exactly what Rawls is concerned with but on a larger scale. Rawls's basic idea, according to Holmes, is that citizens "must abstain from questions which elicit radical disagreement." This is so, Holmes continues, because a society "must be able to command the loyalty of individuals." The need for society to elicit loyalty from all citizens motivates the exclusion of some questions from the public agenda.[14]

In Rawls's work we find a similar concern with securing a stable political system. Rawls argues, that the principles of justice must "gain the support of citizens who affirm different ... doctrines." The idea of neutrality rests on the assumption that citizens should be loyal. It also rests on the assumption that loyalty is unavailable where political institutions are marked by conflicting conceptions of the good. The conclusion seems to be clear. Citizens ought to "leave aside ... [their] comprehensive doctrines."[15]

Still I do not think the main purpose for neutrality is to mitigate conflict. I believe in other words that Holmes's suggestion is *not* congenial to Rawls's conception of neutrality.

This is seen once the mutuality of liberal institutions and liberal norms of argumentation is acknowledged. Public reason does support and maintain liberal institutions by excluding controversial issues from the public agenda. Yet liberal institutions also support and maintain public reason. Rawls writes that "the political conception of justice and the ideal of honoring public reason *mutually support one another*."[16] This account of public reason appears to be in conflict with the instrumental interpretation. This is so because public reason cannot be of mere instrumental value if it is itself supported by just institutions. There is a mutual relation between just institutions and the norms of public reasons, and this indicates that the one cannot be subordinated to the other. That is, there has to be something good about public reason.

However, there is one objection to this point. It consists in the fact that, while Rawls believes that the existence of liberal institutions is always a good, he does not believe that strict adherence to the norms of public reason is necessarily good. There are cases when the citizen need *not* speak neutrally on political matters.

Rawls takes the example of the abolitionist movement against slavery in nineteenth-century America. The abolitionists often referred to God's law and religious dogmas in order to convince the public of the evil of slavery. Apparently their arguments did in that sense refer to comprehensive ideas that violated the liberal idea of neutrality. Yet, despite the fact that abolitionists violated neutrality it is not clear, Rawls argues, that they violated any liberal obligation. In fact, ignoring neutrality may sometimes be more liberal than adhering to that idea. In order to adjust the basic structure, and to establish (not merely to interpret, as it were) just liberal principles, the citizen might have to use more powerful arguments than those admitted in times when society is "well-ordered" and just. The abolitionists found themselves in a situation where the basic structure of society was radically unjust. They needed forceful arguments that proved the injustice of the present system. For that purpose the use of diverse comprehensive doctrines may well have been necessary. Thus the *conditionality* of public reason is evident.[17]

The role played by public reason appears, again, to be merely instrumental. The reason why citizens ought to justify themselves neutrally is that this preserves liberal institutions. Consequently, when institutions are not liberal there is no need to speak neutrally. Why use gag-rules when the political system is unjust? Why avoid conflict when you are oppressed?

Yet, the conditionality of public reason does not mean that it is merely of instrumental value. Rather, Rawls's idea is that citizens ought sometimes to ignore its recommendations, because public reason is so important in itself. They ought to do so whenever not adhering to neutrality is "the best way to bring about a well-ordered and just society in which the ideal of public reason could eventually be honored."[18] Thus public reason may, when society is unjust, be "honored" more in the breach than the observance. Thus, the ethos of public reason presupposes that social and political institutions are just. Why is that? Why should not people in an unjust society honor the canons of liberal reason in public?

The reason why justice and public reason are inseparable is that they rest on the same basic idea. In effect, the idea of political justice and the idea of neutrality are two aspects of the same basic idea: that justice is for a person to be treated as an equal and that to be an equal is to be given reasons for why things are as they are. The connection between the demands of justice and the demands of public reason is made explicitly by Rawls.

> [J]ustice as fairness . . . presents itself as a conception of justice that may be shared by citizens as a basis of a reasoned, informed and willing political agreement. It expresses their shared and public political reason.[19]

Just institutions in fact express public reason. To live in a just society is to live in a society whose fundamental principles can be accepted by all and which consequently conforms to the norms of public reason. Public reason holds that neutrality is necessary, because no non-neutral values or beliefs could possibly be agreed to by everyone. Justice holds that neutrality is necessary in that it would be unjust to be treated according to principles one could not possibly agree to. Thus, the norms of public reason are implicit in the idea of justice. As Rawls says, "Justice as fairness is not reasonable unless in a suitable way it can win its support by addressing each citizen's reason."[20] Similarly, the norms of public reason are not worthwhile unless institutions are in fact just.

The idea of neutrality is therefore not a form of strategic self-censorship or "gagging" as Holmes suggests.[21] Neutrality is, in Rawls's view, part of what justice means. It is so, because citizens are entitled to a reason for the institutions, laws and policies they live by, and they will not accept as reasonable reasons that depend on others' conceptions of the good life. Hence, it follows that institutions should be justified neutrally.

Neutrality and Justice

The demands of neutrality are extended beyond the state and to the justifications that citizens present to each other in public. Rawls believes this is a necessary feature of liberal justice. Liberalism, according to Rawls, should "address each citizen's reason." Everyone should be able to accept liberal institutions. The demands of neutrality are part of the liberal ideal and not imposed merely in order to confer stability on liberal institutions. There are no pragmatic reasons for ignoring conceptions of the good life and virtue in the public sphere. Neutrality is not a question of "gagging."

Now, the question remains why it is just for citizens to speak neutrally to each other in public. Why is *this* justice? A number of reasons are suggested. One salient feature of Rawlsian liberalism is its emphasis on equality. Another idea is the requirement that political justifications are public and reasonable. These ideas, equality, publicity and reasonableness, provide potential arguments for the thesis that justice requires neutrality. I shall now assess each one of these claims.

Do Equals Need Neutrality?

The liberal state is a neutral state, the liberal citizen reasons in neutral ways. These are facts of the Rawlsian ideal. Here, we want to know why citizens must accept these restrictions. What reasons are there for citizens and for the state to regard the restriction of neutrality as appropriate for arguments about justice and rights? Why should they adjust their views according to the liberal ideal and not propose principles and ideals in accordance with their personal beliefs on the good life?

In this section I shall examine one potential answer to this question. The reason why citizens ought to accept neutrality is that they ought to accept fellow-citizens as political equals. Assuming that we accept the idea of equality, the citizen will have a conclusive argument for adhering to neutrality in political and constitutional debate.

In chapter seven I discussed the connections between the ideas of equality and neutrality in Ronald Dworkin's writings. However, my analysis at that stage concerned the claim that equality justifies the idea that the state should be neutral in what it does or, using my terminology, in its *aims*. Here, the focus is on the relation between equality and the idea of neutrality of *justification*. Will a state and a citizenry that accepts the idea of equality necessarily have to concede to the idea that justifications of principles, policies and institutions ought to be neutral? The idea of equality is again relevant, but in a different context.

My argument in this section is that equality is not an appropriate basis for the idea of neutrality of justification. Given certain assumptions the appeal to equality *can* provide good reasons for accepting neutrality. But these conditions are controversial. Moreover, they are not prevalent in Rawls's theory. That is the most important reason why the reference to equality is not sufficiently strong to vindicate the idea of the neutral state and the obligation to be neutral in public deliberation.

Reasoning with Persons Who Have Different Interests

It is clear that Rawls believes a basic tenet of liberalism to be that citizens are political equals. More specifically, citizens, in Rawls's words, are "free and equal." The fundamental importance of this commitment is illustrated by the fact that citizens' reasoning on constitutional matters should, according to Rawls, be restricted by the so-called original position that, in turn, is justified because it is believed to secure equality. The basic reason for restricting the permissible arguments and justifications of citizens can consequently be derived from the idea of *equality*. This assumption is clearly stated in Rawls's work: "The original position is regarded as fair [because it] appeals to the fundamental idea of equality."[22]

As we now know the original position imposes neutrality on citizens by assuming a "veil of ignorance."[23] The veil is a metaphor for the idea that citizens disregard some of the knowledge they have about themselves when engaged in constitutional argument. Rawls argues that citizens should disregard any knowledge of their social position, their beliefs about virtues and of the good life. The choice of principles of justice is thereby immunized from the specific interests and convictions that citizens have. As citizens we must reason and argue in ways that do not depend on our interests or ethical beliefs.

The rationale for these restrictions is the idea that equality demands that citizens be situated "symmetrically" when discussing basic political issues.[24] A neutral standpoint allows citizens to be situated symmetrically by making values and beliefs equally accessible to all. No one value or principle may be invoked that is not shared by others. The idea of symmetry derives support from Rawls's idea that a political community is a cooperative venture. The function of the constitution and the basic political and economic institutions is to enable social cooperation between citizens. Thus, the citizen's choice of political principles will in effect identify the conditions for when cooperation is fair. A further assumption is that cooperation in society is always cooperation between equals. This is where Rawls finds the idea of symmetry relevant. Cooperation between equal citizens should be regulated by principles that are themselves agreed on in a situation where citizens are symmetrically situated.[25]

Neutrality is achieved by excluding some contingent facts about life (position and conviction) that usually have great influence on political views. We may feel that there are good reasons for doing this. Here, the question is whether these exclusions are warranted by the idea of *equality*.

Granted that we accept that fellow-citizens are political equals, it seems plausible to demand that the political principles they advance do not depend on their social and economic positions. Not making that demand would amount to saying that a principle of justice can be whatever is in the interests of some group or class. But that is not compatible with the idea of citizens as equals. To say that political institutions should satisfy the interests of some particular social group (white middle-class men, property holders, farmers, etc.) is not compatible with the assumed equality of citizens. The perspective of justice cannot be identical with the interests of one or another social group or individual. Liberal neutrality, understood as an exclusion of interests, will consequently guarantee that basic political principles are unaffected by the struggle between interests that dominate ordinary political life. This is certainly an important idea, though Rawls does not emphasize it. By contrast, the conflict between interest and justice looms much larger in the work of Bruce Ackerman. According to Ackerman liberal neutrality is an answer to the challenges to justice posed by "the struggle for power."[26]

The assumption of equality justifies the part of the "veil of ignorance" that debars citizens with different interests from any knowledge about their social status, work and wealth. To accept citizens as political equals is consequently to accept that a just constitution and a just economic structure cannot be justified in terms of self-interest. Now, Rawls argues that the idea of political equality has further consequences. In Rawls's view, conceptions of the good life are just as inimical to true justice as are interests. Thus, to treat others as equals is to argue without taking recourse to the ideas of virtue and the good life we all embrace. The doctrines of virtue or ethics that each citizen believes in cannot, in Rawls's view, be presented to others without violating their right to equal standing and respect.

Yet to argue that equality is incompatible with self-interest is not the same as to argue that equality is incompatible with moral, philosophical or religious truths. To say that equality requires symmetrical standpoints with respect to interests is one thing. To say that equality requires symmetrical standpoints in respect to conceptions of the good life is quite another.

My belief is that neutrality to interests is a legitimate implication of the principle that citizens are political equals.[27] However, I do not believe that neutrality to beliefs about the goodness of virtue is implied by that principle. Rawls goes too far in that respect. The point I want to make is supported by other commentaries on Rawls's work. Gerald Dworkin notes, for example, that though it is clear that political institutions that depend on the interests of some persons are biased, it is not that clear that political institutions, which depend on what some people believe is true are biased.[28] Interest, not conviction, defines bias. Hence, from the idea that equality demands symmetry we cannot infer that beliefs or convictions are to be excluded.

A further objection is provided by Michael Sandel's critical remark on the interpretation of equality. According to Rawls, equals should not propose political principles that are derived from their conceptions of the good life. However, the question is whether ignoring the truth of the good life is more in harmony with the idea of equality than not ignoring these truths. Will citizens not treat each other more respectfully, more as equals, when they "engage" in and "attend" to what they believe is true rather than ignoring it? If that is so, Sandel concludes, the idea of political equality cannot justify neutrality.[29]

Could Rawls's point be saved? Replying to Sandel and Dworkin, we might wish to say that equals should adopt an impartial attitude in relation to each other's beliefs. When you face another citizen as an equal you must not, by the simple fact that you are adopting a moral perspective, take your ethical truths as the basis for the argument. From this standpoint, to be involved in questions of justice, where we are all equals, is necessarily to be detached in the way prescribed by the idea of justificatory neutrality.

However, we should observe how demanding justice is if we accept this view. Liberal citizens would need to be impartial all the time in order to treat each other as equals. This view parallels Bertrand Russell's vision of the good society. Russell believed people should act on "impartial desires" only. When people are motivated by impartial desires such as the quest for knowledge and feelings of love there will be no conflicts between them. This is so because the satisfaction of an impartial desire does not exclude the satisfaction of another, equally impartial, desire. These desires are in other words "compossible."[30]

It might be conceded that there is a close link between the idea of equality and the notion of impartiality. If murder is wrong, it is wrong to me just as much as it is wrong to you. Morality is impartial in this sense exactly because most of us believe that we are equals from the point of view of morality. But even when this view is accepted, its implications with regard to how we should treat each other remain uncertain. In fact, the view that we ought to act impartially simply because morality is itself impartial is not correct. There is, as has been made abundantly clear in recent writings, an important distinction to be made between *impartial principles* and *impartial attitudes*. That moral rules need to be impartial does not imply that there is an obligation for people to act impartially in each and every case. That is, the principle of impartiality does not necessarily prescribe impartiality. People reasoning impartially may for instance come to the conclusion that it is morally desirable for parents to be somewhat partial in relation to their children. This is simply to say that impartiality of the second-order (principle) need not recommend impartiality of the first-order (attitude).[31]

In connection with this argument, it may be worth repeating a point made in chapter seven, namely, that the principle of equality is distinct from that of equal treatment. That people perceive themselves as equals does not mean that they must be treated equally in each and every particular circumstance. Equals may, consequently, agree to accept that families should receive benefits not accessible to others, or that only qualified people should be allowed to enter schools of medicine.

The point I want to make is that the implications of equality are not self-evident. The moral implications of second-order impartiality are, as Barry notes, an open question.[32] Thus, it is wrong to simply assume that equals should be neutral or impartial when debating questions of constitutional justice. The fact that citizens have an obligation to present arguments compatible with the principle of impartiality does not, then, mean that these arguments themselves need be neutral or impartial. This point is a matter of logic. Another point to be made is empirical. This is the observation that most contemporary ideologies in the West embrace the value of equality in the sense that the principles it adheres to are regarded as valid to everyone. Liberals, conservatives and socialists alike usually endorse equality in this basic sense.[33] Yet, just as with any second-order ideal these ideologies interpret the implications of this claim somewhat differently. A conservative may, for instance, argue that citizens are equals in the sense that they are equal before the mysteries and sanctity of tradition. A Marxist in contrast, may argue that being an equal is to have one's objective needs satisfied. In each case the political and moral imperatives that are believed to follow from perceiving citizens as equals are interpreted differently. The Rawlsian conclusion, according to which equality implies neutrality in relation to comprehensive theories of the good life, is therefore highly controversial.

Different ideologies provide different interpretations of equality and the demands of impartiality. What makes one interpretation better or more persuasive than another is not established merely by referring to the value of equality itself. No one first-order conception of equality or impartiality is right by default. It is therefore a mistake to deduce from the principle of equality the idea of justificatory neutrality.

Reasoning with Persons Who Think They're Better

There is, however, one case where equality warrants the exclusion of some doctrines of what is good and bad in life. That case is when a person claims superiority, not of a particular belief but of a particular person. As noted by Ackerman, people can claim superiority either of their *ideas* or of *themselves*.[34] Though equality does not have the power to exclude all ideas of the good life, it is effective against those that include the view that certain individuals are inherently more worthy. If the idea that citizens are equals means anything, it certainly means that no individuals can claim authority merely by referring to their inherent superiority. "I am better than you" simply is not a very liberal argument.

It might be suggested that the relevant distinction is the one made in chapter seven between universal and non-universal principles. A non-universal principle is, remember, one that identifies a person or a people by name: "Anne is better than John" is an example of such a principle. Universal principles do not, by contrast, refer to names or any features that are highly specific to a particular group or person. To exclude references to the superiority of persons can be seen as equal to the demand that arguments are universal.

Yet this is not so. The demand of universality is different in scope in at least two senses. Universality is a demand that applies, firstly, more narrowly. The requirement that principles are universal stems from the idea that citizens ought to be equal before the law. Thus, the demand restricts primarily the aims and justifications referred to *within* the law. Universality does not, then, exclude non-universal arguments from the debate and discussion that precedes legislation. Legal universality is not necessarily harmed by the fact that the political debate is non-neutral: these are different contexts, and whether an argument from moral superiority results in a universal law or not is an open question. A further difference is, secondly, that whereas universality excludes *any* reference to personal characteristics, the demand not to claim superiority of a person excludes only *that*: non-universal claims need not involve reference to beliefs in intrinsic superiority. An argument or a law may refer to certain individuals without making the claim that they are intrinsically superior. In that case the law violates only the precept of universality. To refer to the family name of the monarch in the constitution (e.g., the Swedish Act of Succession) may be a violation of universality but need not be a violation of the demand not to claim intrinsic superiority of persons.

Thus, the idea that citizens cannot claim intrinsic superiority of persons is distinct from the demand that citizens must not enact laws that refer to the names of persons. Let us take an example in order to illustrate the idea discussed here. Imagine, for instance, an insistent environmentalist. He argues that his ideas of the good life should be incorporated into the constitution. It should be a constitutional duty, according to this view, to revere the mysteries of Nature. Now, let us suppose the environmentalist justifies this claim by referring to the belief that only he is qualified enough to decide on constitutional issues. The environmentalist does not say, then, that his ideas should be accepted because they are true. Instead, he says that only he should have the authority to make decisions about what is true, because only he is sufficiently worthy and qualified. Rawls does not discuss this possibility. To the extent that such claims are prevalent they should nevertheless be easily refuted for reasons of equality. The claim that other citizens are less worthy is exactly the kind of argument that should be excluded by the idea of political equality.

This example shows that the force of insisting on political equality should not be underestimated. Thus, not only adherents of racist ideologies will be confronted with the cutting edge of liberal neutrality. A person with any kind of political, moral or religious belief, who makes the claim that fellow-citizens are less worthy, will have to accept that this claim is illegitimate from the perspective of equality. Aristocrats, racists, and Catholic priests will in other words have to rest their cases in public political arguments. That snobs and racists are in this sense found on the same side of the fence is no surprise. Snobbery is after all, as pointed out by Judith Shklar, the "cousin" of racism.[35]

There is no textual support for the contention that equality is allotted this role in Rawls's work. Rawls does not consider the case where people claim superiority for themselves or others. So the idea that equality excludes beliefs in superior *persons* does not explain why Rawls excludes beliefs in superior *ideas* from political reasoning. Moreover, even if Rawls had argued on such lines, this idea could not have contributed to the defense of neutrality. The point of neutrality is not to silence only supremacist beliefs but to silence any belief in virtue or the good life. And it is a fact that most religious, ecological, socialist and conservative conceptions of the good life do not imply the view that some persons are more worthy or better than others. Hence, not only is it the case that equality does not provide a foundation for neutrality: it *could* not be a foundation for neutrality.

Reasoning with Persons Who Have Different Life-styles

The force of the inference from "equality" to "neutrality" depends, as we have seen, on whether we confront political interests or political beliefs. I argued that the inference is only valid in relation to interests. The equal standing of one citizen is not denied by another citizen insisting that he or she is wrong. The point I make consequently hinges on a distinction between interests and beliefs. Is that distinction plausible? What if there is no real difference between what a person wants and what she believes in?

The upshot is that all conceptions of the good may be regarded as *life-styles* rather than as convictions or as beliefs. What you find valuable in life, the virtues and ideals you cherish, is part of your way of life. Arguably, the beliefs and convictions people have cannot be abstracted from the way they live, from the web of tastes and preferences that constitutes their selves. That some people prefer Mozart to Motörhead is not different from the fact that some people prefer solidarity to egoism. In other words, the political beliefs we have are on par with tastes, preferences or styles. They are subjective in the sense that they are inseparable from the overall configuration of a person's life.

Now, if this is true, the requirement of respecting others as equals will more plausibly support the idea of neutrality in relation to ethical beliefs. If equals should be neutral to the interests of others, and if beliefs are reducible to interests, it follows that equals must be neutral with regard to their beliefs too. The inference from equality to neutrality apparently is much more convincing once this is realized.

But what is wrong with tastes? Let us imagine, for instance, that a majority of citizens are fond of popular music while despising jazz and more "sophisticated" modes of musical expression. Let us imagine, moreover, that this majority of pop-fans want the state to recognize the supreme value of popular music. Since we are now speaking of justifications, not of aims, this means giving popular music a place in the public justification of the basic structure of society. Perhaps extracts from the lyrics of the Rolling Stones or Bob Dylan must be referred to in the constitution. Except for being slightly ridiculous, we may wonder why such references are considered illegitimate according to liberal principles. In this case we may perhaps find it easy to agree with Rawls. A constitution that discriminates between styles of music seems incompatible with the idea that citizens are equals, because taste is one of the respects in which people are equals. This is why it is unfair to incorporate the musical tastes of some portion of the citizenry just because a majority happens to like that kind of music.

It is perhaps reasonable to accept the view that tastes are illegitimate as the basis for political institutions. This means that conceptions of the good life are politically illegitimate once it can be demonstrated that they too are tastes in important respects. But the effectiveness of the argument for neutrality then rests on the assumption that our doctrines and ideals are on a par with tastes and preferences. Beliefs about the good life and intrinsic virtue are then considered subjective in the same sense as musical tastes are. Of course, if moral, religious or political doctrines were considered equally subjective as tastes, it would be as preposterous and unfair to legislate on the basis of them. But are they equally subjective?

My belief is that not all conceptions of the good may properly be described as preferences or tastes. The ideals and beliefs that people have are non-personal in a sense that their tastes are not. A person's ideas about the good life generally include beliefs that he assumes are valid not merely for himself. A person that believes in a socialist community of solidarity does not have an idea merely about his or her own good. To believe that solidarity is the highest good is to endorse an ideal that refers to what is good for others as well as for oneself. Ideals are not typically personal in the way preferences are.

This fact is revealed by the language used to characterize ideas of the good life and tastes respectively. Though people may describe their preference for strawberry ice-cream as a "taste," they would probably describe their socialist ideals somewhat differently. A person does not have a "taste" for a particular virtue. This suggests, I believe, that while tastes are properly described as subjective, conceptions of the good life are not. Moral and political ideals typically involve a reference to what is good or desirable for everyone—or at least to what is good for someone else. What a person wants is "person centered" in a way that political ideals are not, as Peter Jones points out.[36] A person who believes that salvation is the supreme good probably believes that this is good for you and me too. Likewise, a person who believes solidarity is a virtue typically believes that everyone should show attention to this virtue. To value something "is always," as pointed out by Williams, "to go beyond merely wanting something."[37] This is so, because to value something is to assume that what is valuable is recognizable and not just an expression of subjective emotion.

Equality is a forceful idea when invoked in relation to people's interests or tastes. However, in order for the idea of equality to exclude beliefs about the good life something more is required. In other words, an argument to the effect that the principle of equality justifies neutrality with respect to conceptions of virtue and the good life must be based on the assumption that moral ideals and virtues are no more than tastes. Only when Christians, Marxists, conservatives, etc., accept that their beliefs are on a par with preferences or tastes will they have a reason to accept the link between equality and liberal neutrality.

But will they accept that, and should they do so? I do not believe so. Firstly, as we have seen, to regard ethical ideals as preferences or tastes is in a way to commit a mistake: We do not conceive our ideals as similar to tastes. Ideals are plausibly perceived as intersubjectively valid in a sense that tastes are not. To amalgamate ideals with tastes or preferences is therefore to underestimate an important phenomenological difference.[38] Secondly, reducing conceptions of the good to preferences is not in itself a neutral way of describing these conceptions. Patrick Neal neatly encapsulates this point by saying that there is something wrong with liberal "conceptualizations" of the good. To translate all conceptions of the good into the language of "preferences" is to take a stand on a controversial philosophical issue.[39]

If these remarks are correct, it is difficult to maintain the claim that the value of equality is sufficiently strong to motivate the demand of neutrality. This is so since it would require for its success an assumption that not everyone would agree to.

Now, is this objection relevant to Rawls's reasoning? Is Rawls invoking the reductionist assumption about ethical ideals, virtues and conceptions of the good? In his early writings there are clear indications to the effect that Rawls does. At that stage Rawls tended to equate conceptions of the good with "plans of life" and to regard principles of justice as designed with the purpose of achieving "the harmonious satisfaction of *interests*."[40] The obvious way of making people pursue their interests harmoniously, Rawls claimed, is by making justice independent of people's conceptions "of *their* good."[41] People's ideals and beliefs are in other words conceptualized in terms of interests and as ultimately subjective; if you believe in God, you are assumed to have an "interest" in salvation; if you believe that the institution of private property is a moral evil, you are said to have an "interest" in not accumulating wealth and property. As we saw earlier, the veil of ignorance and the demands of symmetry are meant to exclude divergent interests on such matters. And if "beliefs" are on a par with "interests" this exclusion of interests will be effective to beliefs too. But describing our beliefs in terms of personal preferences or interests is to do them injustice. It is a false conceptualization of our ideas of the good life.

However, on closer scrutiny, Rawls does not endorse this reductive conceptualization of the good. Despite the fact that Rawls is somewhat unclear on this point in his early work, it is clear from his recent writings that he has abandoned any reductive language. Now Rawls believes that the purpose of liberal justice is not primarily to allow for different interests and personal goals to flourish. The aim is rather to allow the various "religious, philosophical or moral doctrines" that citizens embrace to flourish together in peace and harmony.[42] It is clear that Rawls now accepts that conceptions of the good are not mere "life-styles."[43] They are "ideals" and should therefore be described as beliefs rather than as preferences.

The conclusion to be drawn is that the inference from equality to neutrality is indeed invalid. The liberal idea that citizens are equals does not have the power to vindicate the idea of neutrality of justification. We should note, moreover, that Rawls did not intend the idea of equality to serve these purposes. Rawls does not, in contrast to what some commentators have asserted, accept the reductive conceptualization of ideas of the good. This means that Rawls could not have justified neutrality in that way.[44] The restraints represented by the notion of the veil of ignorance do not, then, rely solely for their validity on the idea of citizens as equals. The neutrality restraint does not presuppose that ideas of the good are just like tastes.

The Power of Equality

In this section I have examined the relation between the idea of equality and the notion of neutrality of justification. I have assessed the power of equality with regard to interest, personal superiority and life-styles. The thrust of my argument has been that equality does provide a presumption against introducing considerations of these kinds in constitutional arguments. From the point of view of equality, no political and economic system can be justified with reference either to the particular interests of some group, the superior value of a restricted number of people or of their tastes and preferences. Yet this is not to say that equality warrants the exclusion of ethical ideals and conceptions of virtue. I have defended the relevance of a distinction between tastes and preferences, on the one hand, and ethical ideals and beliefs on the other. Thus, when we recognize citizens as equals, we are not also recognizing the idea of the neutral state. Now, the focus in our search for a justification of neutrality must be shifted. This means moving beyond the notion of the veil of ignorance and the demands of equality.

The Demands of Publicity

In a liberal society, Rawls asserts, justice is a *public* idea. A just society is characterized by the fact that every citizen is familiar with the principles guiding basic political and economic institutions. As a normative requirement this idea has certain specific consequences for principles and reasons which are permissible. These consequences are clearly stated by Rawls;

> [P]ublicity ensures, as far as practical measures allow, that citizens are in a position to know and to accept the pervasive influences of the basic structure that shapes their conception of themselves, their character and ends . . . . It means that in their public political life nothing need be hidden.[45]

The ideal state envisaged by Rawls is one where no justifications of policies or institutions "need be hidden" for the people. The principle of publicity expresses the classical liberal idea that citizens, in virtue of being rational creatures, deserve to live by principles and reasons that they can understand. Put in other terms, by Jeremy Waldron, the ideal is the *transparency* of society. The mechanisms, beliefs and institutions that influence our choices and our self-conceptions need to be open for scrutiny and possible to understand.[46] Publicity, or transparency, is therefore an essential aspect of any legitimate social order.[47]

Any political justification is, according to Rawls, a public justification. Any argument to the effect that political and economic institutions ought to be designed in certain ways has to be compatible with the idea of publicity. The precepts of publicity apply to both the citizen and the state.

That publicity is a normative idea implicit in Rawls's theory of liberal legitimacy is rarely acknowledged.[48] The hypothesis I work from is that publicity is a fundamental notion in the liberal ideal of legitimate government. I will conclude that many of the demands of liberal legitimacy can be met by publicity alone. But what does publicity mean? In this section my analysis will discern three distinct components. Arguments justifying a political order need to be understandable, practicable and publicizable in order to satisfy the publicity condition.

Although I will argue in favor of the importance of publicity I will also appreciate its limits. As I shall eventually attempt to demonstrate, the norms of publicity lack the power to exclude all comprehensive ideas and to justify the demand of neutrality. Some other norm or idea is needed in order to arrive at full neutrality to conceptions of the good. This interim conclusion will eventually lead us to a final discussion of Rawls's neutralist liberalism and to an assessment of the idea of reasonableness that underpins the theory of neutrality.

Justice: An Understandable Idea

According to the idea of publicity, facts used to support political principles must be *understandable*. The facts we refer to when arguing about the basic principles of society must, Rawls argues, be compatible with "common sense" and uncontroversial conclusions of "science and social thought." The ideas that are presented should conform, Rawls argues, to generally shared methods of reasoning.[49] Thus Rawls seems to say that publicity requires that the beliefs justifying the principles of justice, but not the principles themselves, must be compatible with certain canons of reason. The rationale for this view is easy to see.

Since it is desirable that citizens should be able to "know and to accept" the basis of the ideas embodied in their basic structure, it certainly is desirable that these ideas are understandable. Metaphysics, alchemy or magic would, probably, be instances of forms of "reasoning" that, if they were used to support the principles of justice, would debar most citizens from understanding. Justice would, then, no longer be an accessible and understandable idea. So, even if the *principles* of justice were reasonable and understandable they would be unacceptable if they rested on some set of obscure *beliefs*.

Rawls illustrates this idea with the attempt by Thomas Aquinas to justify capital punishment for heresy. Aquinas's argument for regarding heresy as such a grave offense is based on the belief that heresy eventually corrupts faith. This corruption is serious, because faith is, in Aquinas's view, the "life of the soul." Heresy does in other words distort the life of the most sacred part of the human creation. Yet, as observed by Rawls, Aquinas's justification is not acceptable from a liberal point of view. This is so because the beliefs Aquinas adheres to cannot be demonstrated by "modes of reasoning commonly recognized."[50] We cannot show the heretic that disbelief will destroy the life of his soul. Aquinas's argument is not compatible with the publicity condition and is therefore disqualified.

We should note that the publicity condition does not rule out the death penalty because it is bad. It does not even say that to punish heresy by death is necessarily objectionable. The fault of Aquinas's position does not reside in the idea that heresy should be punishable by death but in the particular belief by which this principle is defended. It is the factual beliefs by which we justify our opinions that must be public and understandable.

Is this condition reasonable? There are at least *two* possible objections to this view. These objections are united by the suspicion that understandability is too exacting a condition for legitimate government. The first form of this objection points at the uncertain status of moral beliefs. Citizens plausibly refer to their values or ideals in justifying a political principle. But can values be understood in the context of contemporary science and canons of reason? Are values "understandable" in the sense required by publicity? The second form of this objection points at the complexity of existing facts of the world. Many scientific theories that may be referred to in political justifications are extremely complex. This implies, as Stephen Wall notes, that many beliefs compatible with science will not be understood by a majority of citizens.[51]

Let us illustrate the first objection. What if, for example, a person defends a principle by referring to the "fact" that some behavior is morally wrong (e.g., murder)? Obviously, this "fact" is not demonstrable. There is no way to *show* or to *prove* that murder is morally wrong. The idea that political reasons must comply with shared methods of reasoning would seem to make political argument very difficult. Publicity appears to exclude moral notions from public debate and political justification.

However, I believe there is an adequate reply to the first objection. The idea advanced by Rawls is that the "general beliefs about human nature and the way social and political institutions work" must be understandable.[52] Now, I believe we should understand this statement very literally. That is, though our "beliefs about society" must conform to science, nothing is said about our moral convictions. When Aquinas's beliefs are disqualified this is a consequence of his controversial ideas about human nature (the idea that "faith is the life of the soul"). The publicity condition in this sense applies only to some issues. Excluded by publicity are beliefs about society that are false, absurd or obscure. The reason for excluding such beliefs is that it must be possible for citizens to understand the reasons justifying the institutions under which they are to live.

The second objection seems harder to refute: Wall's observation certainly seems justified. Citizens do not apprehend all facts and theories found in contemporary science. How, then, can we expect political principles to be both scientific and understandable? Rawls assumption that citizens are "assumed to be familiar with the methods of science" appears to be presumptuous.[53]

Yet Rawls does not say that everyone must understand everything in order for government to be legitimate. Rawls says that political justifications must be "publicly available." It must be possible, if citizens "wish to," to understand the basic beliefs and reasons of the state.[54] Thus, Wall's objection is in fact not a relevant one. Wall confuses the idea that a justification must be *understandable* with the idea that a justification must be *understood*. And this is easily done. What is essential, from the perspective of publicity, is that all facts can be understood, that is, that facts and theories are understandable or possible to understand by conventional methods of science. What matters then is that there are some established procedures by which citizens could make the basis of their institutions understood.

The importance of available procedures, rather than available knowledge, will explain Rawls's emphasis on the "methods of science." What matters is not that citizens understand all the facts used in political justification. What matters is that there are methods by which such facts could be understood and made intelligible.

In what sense is understandability an aspect of publicity? What does understanding an argument have to do with that argument being public? In one sense the answer is obvious. For a belief to be understandable it must first have been made public. The idea of being understandable implies the further idea of publicizability. Arguments must be *made in public* in order to be understandable. This idea is discussed later in this section. But an argument that is compatible with science is public in a different, and deeper, sense too. A reason that is compatible with shared methods of reasoning is public in the sense that it does not presuppose allegiance to any authority except that of reason. A person does not have to accept the authority of certain canonical texts or mystical methods of interpretation in order to understand scientific facts. No authority "external" to reason is, in Kant's words, necessary.[55]

Justice: A Practicable Idea

I now turn to an examination of the second part of the publicity condition. This is the idea that the principles of justice must "be known to be public." In contrast to the former idea this condition refers to the political principles, not to the beliefs justifying them. Still the meaning of the statement that political principles must be "known to be public" is not very clear. Moreover, this idea is not generally considered to be a part of Rawls's theory.[56] Basically this idea is very simple. It is closely related to the understandability criterion and states that political principles, in order to be "known to be public," need to be principles upon which everyone could act. Let us explain this further.

In his early writings Rawls claimed that we should "evaluate conceptions of justice as publicly acknowledged and fully effective moral constitutions of social life."[57] When assessing the merits of political principles we must not think, that is, merely in relation to ourselves. Instead, we must think about the implications of a principle for society as a whole. A more precise statement about how to achieve this is nevertheless absent in Rawls's work. Which principles could *not* be thought of as "effective constitutions of social life"?

The focus is on the norms for action that people could consistently be committed to. Are there any principles that a people could not act on? One example is principles that allow for arbitrary exceptions. Consider the principle: "taxes should be paid by everyone except me." Though *I* might possibly act on this principle it seems pointless for *everyone* to do so. If everyone thought that they should not pay the taxes but that everyone else should, no one would. The principle would consequently be meaningless. The test is, in other words, whether we could all accept a certain principle without contradiction.

However, we must tread carefully here. The primary problem with a principle such as "everyone but me should..." is not that others would not accept it. Perhaps many people believe they are justified in not paying taxes although they do believe that others should. In that case they will certainly find that principle acceptable and perhaps even just. But it is not whether people accept a principle or not that is the test of legitimacy. The test is rather whether everyone could accept and act on it successfully.

The principle that "everyone but me should pay taxes" is a principle upon which not everyone could successfully act. My acting on this principle presupposes, obviously, that others do *not* act on this principle—since that would mean that nobody paid taxes. Thus, making myself an exception could not be part of a principle on which *everyone* acted and the principle is, in that sense, self-defeating. So, the issue is not whether people will in fact reject that principle or not, but whether we could all act upon that principle simultaneously.

As Onora O'Neill has shown, this Kantian idea will also exclude principles of lying, fraud and deceit. None of these principles could be acted upon by all people at the same time since they presuppose that some people are not following them. Principles such as "everyone but me must always speak honestly" or "everyone but me must always keep promises" become meaningless once everyone accepts them. As general principles for society they are, for that reason, unacceptable.[58]

The idea can be rendered more precise by using the categories developed by Derek Parfit. By using his terminology we can classify the idea that "everyone but me must always speak honestly" as directly collectively self-defeating. By "self-defeating" is meant a principle or a theory that fails in its own terms. Hence, a self-defeating theory does not fail because of circumstances or because it is not adequately followed. A self-defeating theory fails even under ideal conditions.[59]

Now, according to Parfit, theories can fail either indirectly or directly. This is to say that a theory can fail either because everyone is disposed to act on it or because everyone is in fact acting on it. When a theory fails because everyone accepts the dispositions it recommends, the theory is indirectly self-defeating. The disposition to maximize happiness, for instance, may not be the best disposition to accept in order to actually maximize this value.[60] For this reason this disposition is indirectly self-defeating. Yet, this is not our case. We are discussing the case where everyone successfully acts on a principle (to lie, deceive, etc). Thus, since we have already established that such principles are self-defeating they must be *directly* self-defeating in Parfit's terms. Principles such as "no-one shall pay taxes but me" or "no-one shall be honest but me" will fail when everyone acts on them exactly because *everyone* acts on them! It is noteworthy that these principles are only collectively self-defeating. In case only one person acts on the principle, the problem does not emerge. Principles like these are collectively, not individually, self-defeating, using Parfit's terminology.[61]

The distinction between the individually and the collectively self-defeating helps to explain why Rawls suggests that principles must be evaluated as "known to be public." To accept that normative principles should be possible for everyone to accept, forces citizens to consider their own proposals as collective and not as individual principles. In other words, citizens need to universalize their political principles: they have to think of them as valid for everyone and not just for themselves. What is a consistent principle for the individual might turn out to be self-defeating when considered as valid for everyone. Rawls's test of publicity guarantees that the principles suggested as the basis for political life are not self-defeating.

Justice: A Publicizable Idea

Though not presented by Rawls as part of the publicity condition itself, his theory conveys an idea that reinforces some of its normative points. This is the duty to explain our political views to each other. This "duty of civility" demands that citizens and the state defend their political actions in public.[62] In giving a vote on an issue of constitutional importance, or when proposing a measure affecting the basic structure of society, we have a political duty to explain ourselves to other citizens and to listen to their objections. In the following I shall examine the implications of this idea.

Rawls makes it clear that the duty of civility is implicit in the idea of public reason; "[w]hat public reason asks is that citizens be able to explain their vote to one another."[63] According to Rawls "civility" is not merely a willingness to discuss or to talk. We must also have a willingness to *listen* to others. To listen is to have a "fair-mindedness" and to be prepared to make "accommodations" to the opinions of others.[64] Public reasoning is not merely an airing of different views, in Rawls's account. To be civil is to listen and discuss, to be prepared to make a change of opinion.

The duty to defend and explain our views in public seems in fact to be a natural consequence of accepting the idea of publicity. The idea of society as a transparent social order, and the idea that its basic principles should be "known to be public," seems almost to require that a duty of civility is generally accepted. It demands that citizens and the state evaluate basic political principles continually and in public. Thus, the duty to explain our position in public is justified by reference to the idea that basic principles of society must be understandable. Again: legitimacy demands openness, which is ultimately secured by the willingness to undertake a public debate with others.[65]

The notion of publicity has so far been analyzed as two ideas; that beliefs are understandable and that principles are not collectively self-defeating. Now, the third idea is that we should defend our convictions in public, as the duty of civility will want us to do. When we consider whether a specific principle is just or not for our society, we must be prepared to expose our reasons in public, that is, to each other. Accepting this demand is in effect to accept that our *private convictions* will take the form of public *arguments*. Transforming privately held opinions to public arguments might in fact change their contents.[66] Most of us would not, after all, set forth all our wants, desires or convictions as public arguments. Private belief is not, in other words, necessarily acceptable as "constitutions of social life." For example, an aristocrat, with very high thoughts of himself, believes he deserves to be treated with special care and reverence by public institutions. Well, if required to defend this idea in public the aristocrat might hesitate. It is, as Elster and others have pointed out, hard to publicly defend the idea that one should have greater political benefits than others.[67]

This point was also made by Alexis de Tocqueville when he noted that where the *"public* govern . . . pride must be dissembled; disdain dares not break out; selfishness fears its own self."[68] To argue in public will work as a filter that transforms, or merely hides away, some of our preferences and beliefs. "Selfishness fears its own self," Tocqueville writes. The selfish person, who cares for his own reputation should be wise enough not to be egoistic in public. Egoism is in other words an argumentative strategy that is likely to fail. A public discussion of fundamental political matters will consequently be immunized from some of the worst preferences and desires that people have.[69]

Thus, publicity may eventually be said to involve three distinct ideas. The first two are explicit in Rawls's theory; the requirement that political justifications are understandable and that they can be "known to be public" or, that is, practicable in the sense of not being collectively self-defeating. The third idea, the duty of civility, is here captured by the notion of publicizability.

A problem with adding this idea to the previous two is that Rawls seldom explicitly recognizes its normative importance. The idea that arguments defended in public will differ from our private opinion is, in other words, not explicitly considered as a criterion. Perhaps Rawls's silence on this point indicates that we should be careful about interpreting it as such.

One further weakness with this interpretation is that a duty to explain our views in public does not provide us with any criteria by which legitimate and illegitimate reasons can be separated. Even if, as Elster suggests, the mere fact of standing in public will make some views harder to present, we may ask how this *empirical fact* can make normative criteria. If aristocrats cannot defend their selfish principles in public we will be lucky. But what if they can? Will there then be a basis for criticism that does not only rest on the subjective belief of other citizens? What objections can be made against people who dare advance their selfish or mean views in public? The duty of civility provides no answer.

However, in one case Rawls does specify the implications of the duty of civility more clearly. In discussing the role of political parties in a liberal democracy Rawls notes that the options available to parties for raising funds will, to some extent, determine their political role. In the case where public financial support is not available, and private sponsorship is dominant, parties run the risk of becoming dependent on particular private interests. This is obviously a danger for any democratic system. Yet, the point here is not what Rawls actually has to say about the institution of political parties. What is of interest to us, in the context of publicity, is Rawls's particular motivation for rejecting private sponsorship:

> What is necessary is that political parties be autonomous with respect to private demands, that is, demands *not expressed in the public forum and argued for openly by reference to a conception of the public good.*[70]

The problem with privately funded parties is not, in Rawls's view, that some group (e.g., the organized interests of business) may get an undue level of influence on the political debate. Rather, the problem is that by indirectly attempting to influence the political debate— by financial means rather than by arguments—these actors shun the possible moderating effects of public argument. Private funders have not defended their views in public, and yet they are permitted a say on important political matters. The duty of civility is thereby ignored. Views that otherwise might not have entered the political process slip in through the "back door."

However, all this does not make clear which ideas are excluded by publicizability. What kinds of ideas do not stand public scrutiny? A hint is given in Rawls's clearest formulation of this idea: "[p]rinciples are to be rejected that might work quite well provided they were not publicly acknowledged."[71] The duty of civility ex-

cludes ideas that presuppose that they are not made public in order
for them to work. Speaking in public is no longer purely a matter of
psychology: it is not just that certain ideas are hard or embarrassing
to defend in public. Now, the idea of publicizability is said to exclude doctrines that presuppose that they are not generally known in
order for them to be successful. More specifically, such doctrines
share the feature of being "self-effacing" in Parfit's terms. These are
theories that presuppose, in order to be effective, that the subject is
not aware of the doctrine itself. A self-effacing theory, T, tells us to
not believe T in order for the ends defined by T to be realized.[72]
Possibly this idea is of relevance for our understanding of the duty
of civility. It is essential that political doctrines are openly declared
if we want to avoid self-effacing political theories. Thus, the idea of
publicity would seem to be incompatible with the conservatism found
in the work of Friedrich Hayek.

In one interpretation, Hayek's normative theory tells us that liberal societies ought to defend traditional values and habits because
they are instrumental to the maximization of "life-chances." The liberal doctrine of a just basic structure should therefore, on Hayek's
account, incorporate many of the traditional virtues and codes of
behavior. People should be virtuous, not because virtues are good,
but because these virtues contribute to a collective end. People should
be superstitious Hayek thought, because superstition supplies "mul-
titudes with a motive, a wrong motive it is true, for right action; and
surely it is better for the world that men should be right from the
wrong motives than that they should do wrong with the best intentions."[73]

But this reasoning is clearly self-effacing. Hayek's theory presupposes that citizens are unaware of the basic political philosophy of
their country. If citizens knew that the supreme end was "maximizing life-chances," and that their beliefs in virtue and tradition were
means to this end, they would probably reject it. In fact, the motivation to act out of a certain belief would presumably be ruined were it
revealed that the belief was valued merely for its usefulness and not
because of its goodness. The virtues and traditions that were originally believed to be valuable will no longer appear as important if
their sole value is derived from their instrumentality to the abstract
and remote value of "maximizing life-chances." The theory is not,
in other words, publicizable.

Thus, Rawls's duty of civility rejects hypocrisy in public debate.[74] The state cannot legitimately refer to one principle as the basis for its actions and then act in accordance with some other principle. Similarly, citizens must, when asked to explain their political opinion, explain *that* view and not some different doctrine. Public deliberation does in that sense have to be sincere.[75]

In sum, the duty to argue in public has two possible implications. The first is related to the psychological or empirical effect of publicly defending your political views. The second is that doctrines that cannot be made public, will be excluded from political life. Doctrines that are self-effacing will not be possible to justify once it is accepted that only principles that are publicizable are legitimate.[76]

The Power of Publicity

Will the demands that principles and beliefs are publicizable, understandable and practicable, vindicate the idea of neutrality of justification? The criteria lumped together in the idea of publicity evidently exclude a number of ideas from a public political agenda. But in order for Rawls to establish complete neutrality of justification he needs more. Neutrality does not merely aspire to exclude unscientific, egoistic and malicious reasons from public debate. Neutrality aspires to exclude *every* reason that refers to a specific idea of the good life. For instance, a defender of ecological values may insist that the basic principles of justice in society accommodate the intrinsic worth of various ecosystems. The reasons adhered to in such a case are moral; some ecosystems or species are regarded as having intrinsic moral value. In relation to Rawls's theory these reasons clearly violate the *neutrality* criterion. To assume in public argument, that there are intrinsic values, is to adhere to comprehensive and controversial ideas (in this case, substituting an ecocentric for an anthropocentric worldview).[77] Yet, no requirement that can be extracted from the idea of *publicity* has been violated. Clearly, environmentalist ideas need not be self-defeating. Moreover, environmentalists may plausibly defend their views in public without feeling the least inclined to self-censorship. Nor do the reasons they use presuppose concealment or non-publicity in order to be implemented. Finally, the claim that ecological values must be given specific consideration in the constitution need not rely on controversial facts incompatible with "shared methods of reasoning." Since the environmentalist presents a moral claim there are not necessarily any "facts" involved.[78]

Though publicity does not entail neutrality, it draws attention to another facet of public argument. In fact, the duty of civility does not merely say that citizens ought to engage in debate with others and to listen to each other's points of view. To argue in public, to be truly "civil," is also to propose principles that others can accept. This is made clear by Rawls: "each of us must have, and be ready to explain, a criterion of which principles and guidelines we think other citizens may *reasonably be expected to endorse* along with us."[79] In one sense, this is all the idea of publicity is about. The demands that beliefs should be understandable, publicizable, and practicable are necessary in order for others to be able to accept them. But surely it is not enough. The demand that we explain ourselves to others (the duty of civility), must be complemented with a fuller account of what we *can reasonably explain* to others.[80]

The thrust of this section has been to demonstrate that Rawls's idea of publicity entails ideas that are fundamental to any liberal political justification. The idea of publicity articulates some basic truths about how to define an acceptable and legitimate argument. Some justifications, and therefore some political ideas, simply cannot be accepted. In sum, the idea of publicity as analyzed here can be described as consisting of three distinct principles.

Figure 8.1
The Idea of Publicity

Principle	*Criteria*
Arguments are understandable: can be understood by all	Political facts referred to must conform to shared standards of reasoning
Arguments are practicable: can be acted on by all	Political principles are not inconsistent with everyone acting on them
Arguments are publicizable: can be seen by all	Political principles are defensible in public and are not self-effacing

The idea of publicity has a certain force. Yet it does not provide a justification of neutrality.[81] As I have tried to demonstrate, many conceptions of the good life or of virtue are compatible with the idea of publicity. There is, therefore, a reason to explore further the basis of neutrality in Rawls's work. One important path to follow is the one opened up by the idea of arguing in the public. It is not enough to say that one's standpoint does not conflict with publicity. There is also a demand to be reasonable in the choice of principles and ideas which are proposed as the basis for economic and political institutions. To the idea of *reasonableness* we therefore now turn.

The Ideal of the Reasonable Citizen

The publicity condition, analyzed in the previous section, could be understood as taking into account a particular fact: that political arguments are typically presented in public and that they are meant to be effective for social relations. Thus, justifications of institutional arrangements have to comply with the demands of publicity in order for them to be political. However, the "fact" of publicity is not the only one that pertains to attempts to justify a political order. A further fact is, undoubtedly, that people tend to disagree about what values and ends should be pursued by the state and the government. Political discussion, even when it concerns constitutional matters, is marked by conflict and a clash of ideas. There does not seem, then, to be any common set of principles or ideas that are available to citizens. But Rawls believes liberal neutrality is the solution to this problem. If citizens leave their comprehensive ideas and arguments aside, if they accept the idea of a neutral state, they will be able to reach a consensus. What makes citizens accept this restraint is, Rawls now argues, their reasonableness. A reasonable citizen takes the fact of disagreement into account.[82]

However, my argument in this section will be that Rawls ignores a third fact about political debate: *truth*. My belief is that the demands of reasonableness cannot vindicate neutrality, because it does not demonstrate that non-liberal truths are unreasonable. People that believe in the truth of doctrines of virtue will in other words have no reason to abandon their beliefs in favor of the idea of a neutral state. To demonstrate this I will attempt to answer three distinct questions: What does the idea of reasonableness refer to? Why should citizens accept being reasonable? Why is neutrality a reasonable idea?

In the first part of this section I explain why Rawls believes that an account of reasonableness is necessary. The second part analyzes the justification of the idea of reasonableness. In the third part I explore the relation between reasonableness and neutrality. The reasonable citizen is, Rawls claims, a person who accepts the idea of neutrality of justification. But why is that? Here, I explore the discrepancy between the idea of reasonableness and the idea of a neutral political justification.

My conclusion is that the demand of reasonableness, although not itself controversial, does not justify the demands of neutrality. A reasonable citizen need not accept the idea of a neutral state.

Reasonable Citizens: Appreciating the Limits of Arguments

How should a liberal reply to people who insist that political institutions should be designed in accordance with their conception of virtue? I have so far investigated reasons springing from equality and publicity and found the answer wanting. It seems that Gerald Dworkin is therefore right in pointing out that Rawls cannot defend liberalism against non-liberals' beliefs in the truth of their doctrines. Rawls has no adequate reply, according to Dworkin, to a person who believes "authorities should suppress false views."[83] The only answer that will do is to say that there are no moral or political truths except liberal ones.[84]

Yet Rawls could not defend liberal principles in that way. In order to maintain liberalism's neutrality Rawls must not assume that liberal ideas are "truer" than other doctrines. The nature of moral and political truth is a disputed and highly controversial subject: assuming that liberalism is true would in other words be itself non-neutral. A liberal state has to build on assumptions that are acceptable to everyone.

Instead of asserting that liberalism is true, Rawls asserts that liberalism is reasonable. Liberal ideas of ethical neutrality will be acceptable to any *reasonable* person. A crucial step in Rawls's case for reasonableness is the notion of "burdens of judgement." The reasonable citizen is characterized, Rawls writes, by the "recognition of and willingness to accept the consequences of the burdens of judgement."[85] The burdens of judgement refer to an idea of what reason can demonstrate in practical arguments: they identify the limits of argumentation. The message is that arguments may fail to convince, even under ideal conditions, and that disagreements are reasonable to expect.[86] The point is that citizens, when appreciating that arguments are not always convincing, will reduce their expectations on the outcome of political debates and deliberation. Citizens will then realize that insisting on the truth of their conception of the good life will be of no avail.

It is important to Rawls that the burdens of judgements are factual—that is, they do not constitute an evaluative judgement but merely a reporting of facts.[87] To state that arguments often fail to convince is not to say something controversial about the truth or falsity of any particular moral, ethical or political doctrine. Since the burdens of judgement are factual they will not be in conflict with the various beliefs people have.[88] The claim that people may reasonably disagree is a claim acceptable to everyone.

Moreover, the burdens of judgement help to explain, Rawls believes, why disagreements may be reasonable. Since the power of reason is limited, political disputes are likely to persist even when citizens have propounded their views to others as well as they can. The citizen will then have to acknowledge that to *argue* for a position is not the same as to *convince* others of its truth. This fact is comforting though. When disagreements are recognized as reasonable, it will be clear that the indeterminacy of public debate, the absence of consensus, does not necessarily indicate that the debate is defective. Political argument is just like that. Expectations can then be reduced and citizens are provided with a reason for continuing the debate despite continuing disagreements. When arguments are ineffective, the reasonable citizen does not conclude that further argumentation is pointless or irrational.

Reducing expectations of political debate is, paradoxically, essential to Rawls's project of making debate and rational deliberation the basis for a liberal society. Emphasizing the unreasoned aspects of such debate is a way of securing allegiance to the idea of a rational political order. The alternative is the idea of a political order not justified by arguments but by force: an irrational political order is one where justifications do not exist. In order to save our faith in the possibility of a political order that is rationally justified, we may have to appreciate that reason has its limits and that the power of rational argument should not be exaggerated.

By contrast, people that do *not* recognize limits to practical reason are likely to regard persistent disagreement as mysterious. When they explain their case to me as well as they can, and I still disagree, they might conclude either that their explanation was not good enough or that I am incapable of understanding proper arguments. Unconvincing arguments must be either bad or badly understood. But this conclusion would be wrong from a Rawlsian perspective.

Consider, for example, the environmentalists' insistence that nature has intrinsic values and therefore needs constitutional protection. Each species, the environmentalist contends, must enjoy, as humans, the same basic right not to be persecuted. Now, let us assume that a majority of the citizenry remains unconvinced by the environmentalist argument and let us also assume that the environmentalists do not acknowledge the burdens of judgement. Since they consequently do not recognize any limits to argumentation, they will not accept the possibility that a true or rational argument could appear unconvincing. So when their arguments fail to convince, the environmentalists can explain this only in terms of some defect in rationality. In this case, the defect must be located either in people's minds, or in the argument presented by the environmentalists. The environmentalists might be inclined to explain their failure in the first way. Disagreement is explained, that is, in terms of stupidity. That people disagree is not itself taken as a reason for trying another argument.

Recognizing the burdens of judgement is consequently of great importance to liberal society. Unless the citizenry accepts them they will not acknowledge that disagreements may be acceptable. But when citizens do accept such limits they will realize that neither party needs to be entirely wrong. Gerald Dworkin's challenge seems to have been met. Though a person may legitimately claim the power to *know*, no person can claim the power to *convince*. Due to the shortcomings of practical reason, demonstrated by the burdens of judgement, others may *reasonably* disagree. Therefore, any pretense to suppress "false views" can be rejected. Diversity of belief is, in Joshua Cohen's words, "the natural outcome of the free exercise of reason."[89] No one person can say that his or her doctrine is more convincing than that of others. This is, or is most likely to be, a consequence of accepting the burdens of judgement. That impression is reinforced by Rawls's claim that the burdens of judgement are "of first significance for a democratic idea of toleration."[90]

While the demands of publicity were not themselves powerful enough to make convincing the idea of neutrality, the burdens of judgement seem to do the job. Liberal neutrality in the public sphere is justified by the fact that our beliefs about the good life fall within the burdens of judgement and are consequently *reasonably not shared* by others. To insist that one's own ideas of the good should form the basis for the political life of *all* the members of society is therefore unreasonable. Insisting on that is to deny the existence of limits to rational arguments. To acknowledge such limits is, Rawls believes, to acknowledge the reasonableness of neutrality in the justification of political and economic institutions.

Yet the "burdens of judgement" is a slippery notion. Though it is clear that a disagreement can be reasonable and that an argument can on good grounds fail to convince, it is less clear what this implies. This idea does, after all, refer to an empirical fact and not to a normative principle; saying that disagreements are reasonable is to propound a descriptive and not a normative claim. So we need to ask what accepting the existence of burdens of judgements could in fact mean. Rawls believes a reasonable citizen will necessarily accept neutrality. But that conclusion is too hasty Why is it unreasonable to insist on the truth in the face of reasonable disagreements?

Reasonableness and Belief

Rawls claims that political disagreements are generally reasonable. Now do citizens have a reason to accept this view? Could they plausibly object to the idea that there are reasonable disagreements?

In this part I shall discuss one potential objection to Rawls's claim. When believing in a doctrine we normally believe not only in the tenets of that doctrine (e.g., "that solidarity is a virtue"). Generally, believing in a doctrine is also to believe that it is true (that it is most important to believe that "solidarity is a virtue"). Consequently, to argue is both reporting to others what you believe, and making a claim about what the truth is. A person who tells us about the importance of solidarity does in other words claim that the facts and values referred to are correct.

The conceptual relation between simply believing and believing in the truth of something suggests that there is an objection to the idea of reasonable disagreements. The objection stems from the fact that disagreements are obviously incompatible with the truth. If you claim "that X is" and I claim "that X is not," each one of us will definitely believe that the other is wrong.[91] But how can a person be wrong and reasonable at the same time?

Will the industrialist, who rejects the idea of the intrinsic value of nature, seem reasonable to the environmentalist? Will the conservative, who rejects the intrinsic equality of humans, seem reasonable to the socialist? A person who rejects what another person believes to be true does, after all, believe in something that is false. The upshot is that disagreements are not merely about beliefs. Since to believe is to believe that something is true, disagreements are necessarily about truths. Hence, to accept disagreements as reasonable is not merely to accept that people are reasonable in having different beliefs. To accept disagreements as reasonable is to accept that people are reasonable in having different truths. But could we accept this?

Why we could, has been well explained by Joshua Cohen. The idea is that a belief appears differently depending on whose belief one is talking about. A belief appears in one way to the person who believes in it, and in another way to a person who does not believe in it. From the point of view of others, my belief in the doctrine and my belief that the doctrine is true cannot be distinguished. The "truth" of the doctrine cannot be observed by others: they only observe my belief.[92]

So, when environmentalists tell us that caring about nature is the true virtue, the notion "true" does not add anything: it does not provide any new information. The only observable fact is that environmentalists believe that caring for nature is important. The fact that they also believe this virtue to be true does not change that. As a consequence, telling someone that your beliefs are true does not improve the status of your claim. Using the word "true" in order to characterize one's beliefs does not change them or improve them. To others they will remain "beliefs." Recognizing this asymmetry makes it clearer why the burdens of judgements are connected to the idea of neutrality. We now understand that it would be unreasonable for others to accept our views as a basis for political institutions *merely because we believe in them.*[93]

This understanding of the burdens of judgement is ingenious in that it avoids the pitfalls of moral skepticism. Nowhere does this argument depend on the assumption that moral ideas cannot be true. It depends only on the assumption that moral ideas can fail to convince—and this fact has been conceded by all. There is, in sum, nothing controversial about the burdens of judgement.[94]

In this part I have examined one possible objection to the burdens of judgement. The idea examined is that having a belief is always to believe something to be true. Belief and truth are in other words inseparable. This observation might constitute an objection to the burdens of judgement in the sense that it denies that disagreements can ever be reasonable. A person who disagrees must, after all, be wrong! Yet this argument does not constitute a convincing objection. Rawls's point hinges on the plausible idea that, from the outside, a mere belief is not distinguishable from a belief in truth. That is, the truth of a belief is not publicly available: your truths are just beliefs in the eyes of others.

Reasonableness and Truth

Two conclusions are clear concerning the burdens of judgement: they are important to liberals and there are good reasons for everyone to accept them. But why should a person that recognizes the burdens of judgement accept the idea of liberal neutrality? Is it because *talking* about the truth of one's doctrine is unreasonable in the face of disagreements? Or is it because *believing* in the truth of one's doctrine is unreasonable in the face of disagreements? In the following I shall question the assumption, essential to Rawls's argument, that controversial truths need to be avoided in any of these senses.

Do the burdens of judgement require citizens to abolish truth altogether? This conclusion seems to be supported by the fact that, since nobody has the power to convince another person, any doctrine can in fact be true. Rawls does claim that the burdens of judgement imply that the views of others "may be true" and that all views (including our own) may be false.[95] Accepting that you may be wrong you will, moreover, realize that your views cannot plausibly be true. A citizen that acknowledges the burdens of judgement will therefore have to reject his or her belief in truth.

This is an interpretation of Rawls that Cohen makes. Cohen's point is the one referred to in the previous part: that others cannot distinguish a "mere belief" from a belief in the truth. Now Cohen adds to this observation by arguing that once the impossibility of demonstrating truth is acknowledged we must realize that truth is irrelevant. Beliefs are all there is, and claims of truth do not, therefore, make sense. Cohen explains this view in the following way: "what lies between our taking our views to be reasonable and our taking them

to be true is not a further reason, but simply our belief in those views."
There is no difference, in other words, between being convinced
about the truth of one's doctrine and just believing them. The non-
liberal may consequently forsake truth without loss.[96]

However, to require that citizens surrender their belief in truth
would be going too far from a Rawlsian standpoint. Cohen's suggestion does not fit in well with Rawls's claim that, "we need *not* say
that their beliefs are *not true*."[97] Expecting everyone to accept that
his or her ideas of the good are false, or not fully true, will tend to
make liberal neutrality highly controversial. The neutrality of liberalism would thereby be jeopardized. The aim of Rawls's theory is,
remember, to find a shared basis for justice.[98] But apart from being
inconsistent with Rawls's aspirations it also appears to me that
Cohen's conclusions cannot be justified in terms of the burdens of
judgement.

The burdens of judgement inform us about the existence of reasonable disagreements. The burdens of judgement point out that
what may be a good reason to me may not be seen as such to you.
Your rejecting my proposal may therefore be quite reasonable. Now,
the question is why recognizing the existence of reasonable disagreement should motivate citizens to surrender the belief in truth. It is
not a common assumption, to begin with, that a belief is less likely
to be true just because it is contested. To accept the burdens of judgement is to concede to the fact that what one person takes to be true
can reasonably be disputed by others. It is to admit, in effect, that
other and conflicting views may "make sense."[99] But that something makes sense, in the sense of being explicable, does not imply
that it is correct. Thus, conceding that others may reasonably disagree does not imply that they are more likely to be right. I may
believe something to be true that others believe to be false and yet
recognize that their false beliefs are explicable and that they make
sense. In sum, people may consistently accept the burdens of judgement and continue to believe they know the truth.[100]

This brings us to the second possible interpretation. From this
standpoint the burdens of judgement require us to refrain from making any claims on truth. Since others may disagree about the truth,
we should not *talk* about our views as true. This is an idea set forth
by Thomas Nagel that, according to commentators, resembles Rawls's
view very closely.[101] The basic point is that there is a difference

between what could reasonably be believed in and what could reasonably be appealed to. Liberalism needs, Nagel argues, an idea of "epistemological restraint" that excludes claims of truth from the public.[102] Thus, it is the appeal to truth of one way of life that is unreasonable, not the belief in its truth.

One objection to the idea of epistemological restraint is that it may require too much of citizens. Questions about truth cannot be ignored in public debate. Arguing about moral and ethical truths is, as has been suggested by several commentators, what political controversy is all about.[103] Whether this or that ideal, virtue or doctrine is true or not is part of what it means to engage in political debate. To require silence on all controversial issues would be to eliminate the essence of the "political."[104] The mere fact that a person claims to know the truth about, for instance, the dangers of nuclear waste or the beneficial consequences of a free market, cannot be antithetical to liberal aspirations. Facts like these are controversial but they do not necessarily depend on comprehensive doctrines. Opinions about the truth of the workings of society are constantly present in political and constitutional arguments.

But this objection is mistaken. Nagel's idea of epistemological restraint does not apply to truths in general, but only to contestable ethical and moral truths. It should be remembered that Rawls's demand, that arguments conform to publicity, implies that they are "understandable." Thus, all that is required from factual assertions is that they could have been established by commonly accepted forms of reasoning. Opinions about the risks involved in the storage of nuclear waste or ideas about the virtues of free competition are certainly understandable in that sense. Not all beliefs that are considered to be true are therefore excluded. The doctrines Rawls speaks about, which cause most problems for liberalism, are those that entail moral or ethical truths. Such beliefs do not fail the publicity test and yet they are reasonably not agreed to by others. It is only in relation to such doctrines that Nagel wants the non-liberal to stop "appealing to the truth."

It is indeed difficult to see anything objectionable in Nagel's demand. But it is equally difficult too see how it can help to vindicate liberal neutrality. For instance, not claiming the truth is distinct from not arguing for the truth. The ban on "appeals to the whole truth" that Nagel and Rawls seem to advocate will not imply that citizens

cannot advance arguments for what they think is the "whole truth."
Restricting the use of truth-claims is one thing, restricting the topics
to discuss and argue about is quite another. The truth need not be
appealed to in order to be *defended*. A conservative can argue for
the truth of his or her vision of the patriarchal family without actually making the claim that it is true. Similarly, a Marxist need not say
that "Marxism is true" in order to defend Marxism. A non-liberal
could in other words accept that appeals to the truth are pointless
without conceding to the idea of neutrality. Saying that "I am right
because I know the truth" is not a very effective way of presenting
your point of view anyway.

What do the burdens of judgement require? In my view they do
not justify ceasing either to believe or to claim the truth of one's
conceptions of the good. The belief in the good life need not be
abandoned because it is not a valid implication of the burdens of
judgement: I am no less certain about the truth of what I believe
simply because others disagree. The claims of the good life need not
be abandoned, because to do so would be pointless: not speaking
about the truth does not change anything. People are not more liberal simply because they avoid the word "truth."

Yet it appears as if Rawls would deny more than the word "truth."
It appears as if Rawls denies that citizens should present any claims
to the effect that what people believe to be true is challenged or
criticized.

When citizens are reasonable, Rawls tells us, they can discuss
fundamental political issues "without criticizing or rejecting their
deepest religious and philosophical commitments."[105] Cohen makes
a similar point. To be "sectarian," Cohen writes (referring to non-
liberals), "does not require that we condemn as unreasonable everyone who believes what we take to be false."[106] A reasonable citizen
does not, then, criticize or question what other citizens believe to be
true.

To Rawls and Cohen this assumption is important. The idea is that
citizens can agree on liberal principles exactly because they are all
reasonable. Neutrality means that citizens keep their doctrines and
truths private, because they realize the fruitlessness of further attempts to convince others of their truth. But when citizens dispute
the convictions of others, this forum of neutrality threatens to break
down. When one person puts forward his or her doctrine as an alter-

native to justice for everyone, this gives everyone a reason to do the same. Why should you be faithful to neutrality, when others try to convince you of the merits of their conception of the good life? However, when everyone promotes his or her views, no one view is likely to appear convincing. In the absence of neutrality no principles will be agreed to. This is why a ban on criticism is necessary to a liberalism that builds on contractualist assumptions about justice.

Does this ideal rest on plausible assumptions? The basic assumption of this argument is that people will not criticize other doctrines, because they know that many doctrines may be reasonable and because they know that criticism may erode the norms of neutrality. Though Rawls and Cohen vigorously defend this view, they seem unable to present compelling reasons for it that do not merely *assume* the need for neutrality. Why would people not criticize what they believe is wrong? Why, that is, should reasonableness exclude criticism?

The burdens of judgement explain why people disagree by pointing at the many sources of disagreement. These are, for instance, the fact that people have different social experiences and the fact that concepts are vague and difficult to agree on.[107] However, as I have tried to indicate, there are no unambiguous conclusions to draw from the existence of such sources of disagreement. Perhaps a person may just think, as Raz has suggested, that the sources of his or her beliefs are superior and more reliable than the sources of other people.[108] Imagine, for instance, a person whose moral ideas are inspired by ancient Nordic mythology. That person embraces a doctrine according to which the ancient virtues of strength and manliness are the finest. Imagine, further, that these beliefs are to some extent caused by that person's peculiar social experience. Plausibly, that "explanation" will make us understand why he or she believes in Nordic mythology. Why, on the other hand, should this explanation affect how we assess the truth of the beliefs themselves? We may simply contend that the "causes" of these beliefs (his or her experience) are less trustworthy than the causes of our beliefs (our experience). The appeal to the burdens of judgement does not curb the desire to condemn or criticize what is believed to be wrong. Reasonable citizens will not, in sum, be reasonable in the sense of not arguing about the content of the good life, and they will not, consequently, acknowledge the need for neutrality of justification.

The Limits of Neutrality of Justification

If my analysis is sound, it follows that the idea of liberal neutrality remains undefended. Throughout this chapter I have examined three different arguments to the effect that the state and citizens need to justify themselves in neutral ways in political contexts. Yet I have found no conclusive support for this contention.

Firstly, it should be noted that though the idea of equality may constitute an effective argument in certain contexts, it does not justify neutrality in all. This is not to say, of course, that equality is unimportant. For example, citizens faithful to the idea of moral equality cannot coherently present claims which presuppose that some citizens are inherently worthier than others. Moreover, equal citizens cannot coherently accept that the interests, tastes or preferences of only some of them should influence the design of political institutions. There should, as a consequence, be no political and economic system that is justified with reference to the interests, preferences, tastes or beliefs that only a portion of the citizens have. Yet this claim does not show that it would be unreasonable for citizens to maintain and to promote their beliefs about the good life or virtue when engaging in constitutional arguments. Thus, the idea of equality will not justify the idea of neutrality.

Secondly, the idea of publicity is an important aspect of liberalism's pretension of defending the state in a rational and consistent manner. Publicity is the idea that whatever arguments are used to justify the basic political and economic institutions they need to be understandable, publicizable and practicable in the sense of not being collectively self-defeating. These ideas are definitely essential in order to establish a political system justified by the use of reason. In any case, these ideas do not amount to a justification of the idea of a neutral state. Arguably, there are a great number of virtues and conceptions of the good that may be invoked in public without violating the idea of publicity.

Thirdly, I have examined the attempt to explain why the existence of reasonable disagreement leads to neutrality of justification. My argument is that this attempt fails. It fails because the central notion invoked by Rawls in order to explain this argument, the burdens of judgement, is not forceful enough. To recognize the burdens of judgement, that practical arguments are frequently inconclusive, is not to accept a convincing reason for remaining neutral. The burdens of judgement do not deny the existence of moral truths. They deny that such truths are always convincing. Moreover, the existence of the burdens of judgement does not imply that what is believed true *cannot* convince others. That my beliefs *may* fail to convince you is not to say that my beliefs *will* fail to convince you.

However, the observation that there are reasonable disagreements is not entirely pointless. The burdens of judgement clarify why it is unreasonable to expect to achieve complete conversion to one's doctrine. Moral and political arguments generally do not admit to demonstrations of which answer is true or best. This point in fact provides a partial answer to the objections made by Gerald Dworkin. He pointed out that Rawls does not advance any argument which demonstrates why the ardent believer in the truth of a certain doctrine cannot legitimately defend the view that falsity should be suppressed. Now that challenge is responded to. Rawls's idea of the burdens of judgement gives us reason to believe that it is unreasonable to suppress falsity. That some people believe in what is false is a natural outcome of the burdens of judgement. Falsity should not be remedied by the use of force, since it is reasonable to believe in what is false. The burdens of judgement do provide a good basis for toleration.

What the burdens of judgement cannot do, is to provide a case for liberal neutrality. Rawls takes good account of the fact that political doctrines are controversial and that people tend to disagree about them. However, Rawls does not adequately consider the fact that political beliefs are beliefs about what is true. The conclusion of this analysis, therefore, is that the idea of reasonable disagreement, though itself certainly justified, does not strengthen the case for liberal neutrality.

Notes

1.   Henceforth in this chapter I use neutrality as synonymous with the idea of neutrality of justification.
2.   In a way my critique is reminiscent of the critique directed at Rawls from the perspective of "deliberative" or "discursive" democrats. According to them, Rawls does not sufficiently appreciate the value of discussion, dialogue and debate. The norms of liberal neutrality will, it is argued, be unduly conservative in that they exclude radical views from public discourse. E.g., Simone Chambers, 1996, p 75, and Seyla Benhabib, 1989, pp 144 and 154. However, my assessment of Rawls's theory focuses on its internal consistency. I examine the extent to which neutrality is

justified from Rawls's own premises; not whether neutrality coheres with the premises that I, or someone else, would have preferred.

3.   Elizabeth Wolgast, 1994, p 1942.
4.   Chambers, 1996, p 74.
5.   Sunstein, 1996, p 48.
6.   See also chapter four.
7.   Rawls, 1993, p 10. Note that Rawls's term "comprehensive" denotes a wide range of doctrines. Conceptions of intrinsic virtue do not exhaust that category.
8.   See also Thomas Nagel, 1991, p 27.
9.   This is a point made in Simone Chambers, 1995, p 244.
10. Rawls, 1993, p 214 (emphasis added). That these "limits" are identical to the notion of justificatory neutrality is later confirmed; "[O]n fundamental political matters, reasons given explicitly in terms of comprehensive doctrines are never to be introduced into public reason" (p 247).
11. Bruce Ackerman, 1980, p 333. The contrasts with respect to Habermas are also striking. According to Habermas, public debate ought to be regulated by the norms of discourse ethics. The ideal debate should be constructed so that all citizens are guaranteed an equal chance to participate. However, there is no place for restrictions on what can be said in such debates. In contrast to both Ackerman and Rawls, Habermas (1994, p 313) believes that "ethically relevant questions of the good life" should be possible to "thematize," that is, to discuss and argue about.
12. Thus Rawls (1993, p 215) argues that "it is usually highly desirable to settle political questions by invoking the values of public reason."
13. Stephen Holmes, 1995, pp 202ff.
14. Like Holmes, Stuart Hampshire argues that the demand for stability is the main justification of excluding (or "gagging") comprehensive doctrines in Rawls's theory. Stuart Hampshire, 1993, p 45. The concern with stability is criticized as excessive and "fundamentalist" in Paul Campos, 1994, p 1285.
15. Rawls, 1993, pp 24–25, fn 27.
16. Rawls, 1993, p 252 (emphasis added).
17. Since Rawls is so clear on this point it is surprising to find that Sandel misunderstands public reason as to "always" demand neutrality—even in the case where slavery is part of the basic structure. See Michael Sandel, 1994, pp 1776ff.
18. Rawls, 1993, p 250.
19. Rawls, 1993, p 9.
20. Rawls, 1993, p 143.
21. See also the following remark by Rawls: "It is sometimes said that the idea of public reason is put forward to allay the fear of instability or fragility of democracy in the practical political sense. That objection is incorrect." Rawls, 1997 a, p 139, fn 12. See also Chambers, 1996, p 72.
22. Rawls, 1993, p 79.
23. See further the discussion in chapter four.
24. On equality as symmetry, see Rawls, 1971, p 12, and Rawls, 1993, pp 24, 304. Cf Buchanan & Congleton, 1998, pp 43ff.
25. See Rawls (1993, pp 304ff) for the connection between the constraints of the original position, viz the veil of ignorance, and the idea of "fair terms of cooperation."
26. See Ackerman, 1990, pp 30 and 33.
27. I consequently believe it is wrong to argue, as does Jan Narveson, that "egalitarianism" is biased in "empowering some people over others: roughly, the unproductive over the productive." Jan Narveson, 1998, pp 87f. Narveson's claim is wrong

because it assumes that egalitarianism must have neutral consequences. It does not. The point of egalitarianism is that it denies that some citizens are intrinsically superior to others. Charging that idea with being biased is in a way ironic, considering the extent to which Narveson's own favored ideal, the unrestrained market economy, tends to work in favor of the interests of "productive" citizens (i.e., owners of capital).

28. Gerald Dworkin, 1992, p 504.
29. Sandel, 1994, p 1794.
30. See Bertrand Russell, 1931, chapter six.
31. The distinction is made clear in Barry, 1995, pp 11f.
32. Barry, 1995, p 10.
33. The thesis of the ubiquity of equality was first presented by Dworkin, 1986, pp 296ff and later continued by Kymlicka, 1990, pp 4f.
34. Ackerman, 1980, pp 11, 38–41.
35. Shklar, 1984, p 111.
36. Peter Jones, 1989, p 53.
37. Williams, 1985, p 59. Thomas Nagel has, with direct reference to Rawls, pointed out that conceptions of the good typically include "principles that advance the good for everyone." Such beliefs should, consequently, be distinguished from personal interests. Thomas Nagel, 1973, p 226. See also Nagel, 1991, p 10. But cf Waldron, 1989, pp 79f.
38. Thus, Williams (1985, p 86) argues that reducing "ideals or ethical conceptions" to preferences "underestimates their significance."
39. Patrick Neal, 1987, *passim.* Cf Richard Arneson's (1990, p 220) claim that reducing all conceptions of the good to the language of preference is not incompatible with neutrality in justification ("procedural neutrality" in Arneson's terminology). This is so, according to Arneson, because taking values to be a matter of preference does "not amount to the kind of partisanship that the neutrality ideal should be designed to expose and prohibit." There is in other words a difference of degree in the extent to which statements such as "one Christian sect is superior to another" and "values are just like preferences" are controversial. Yet, I do not see how it can be assumed that these statements are not equally sensitive and controversial.
40. Rawls, 1971, p 93 (emphasis added).
41. Rawls, 1971, p 18 (emphasis added).
42. Rawls, 1993, p 38.
43. The change in Rawls's writings on this point has been noted by Raz (1986, p 119) and Barry (1991, pp 31-34). Cf Sher, 1997, p 154.
44. The suggestion that the normative force of the original position can be explained in terms of equality is explicitly rejected by Rawls. The power of the original position depends on many different considerations and ideas and not on equality alone. John Rawls, 1992 [1985], pp 200f, fn 19.
45. Rawls, 1993, p 68.
46. "Society should be a transparent order ... its workings and principles should be well-known and available for public apprehension and scrutiny." Jeremy Waldron, 1987, p 146. In fact, Rawls quotes Waldron in order to explain this idea further. John Rawls, 1995, pp 146f, fn 28.
47. Publicity constitutes an essential element of Rawls's idea of political autonomy: "It is in their public recognition and informed application of the principles of justice in their political life that citizens achieve full autonomy." Rawls, 1993, p 77. The notion of political autonomy, where citizens rule themselves as equals, should not be

conflated with the ideal of moral autonomy, where the individual citizen aspires to self-control and reflection. See further the discussion in chapter four.

48.   The idea of publicity is recognized as an important aspect of Rawls's theory by writers like Stephen Wall and Simone Chambers. See Chambers, 1996, chapter five, and Wall, 1998, chapters four and five. However, Chambers does not present an analysis of the idea of publicity but focuses exclusively on the notion of public reason (discussed in the first section of this chapter). Wall presents an analysis of publicity but does not, I will argue, extend this far enough.

49.   Rawls, 1993, pp 66–67.

50.   Rawls, 1971, p 215. A similar example is used by Wall (1998, p 110): "People who work to defend capital punishment and justify their political action by appealing to a unique moral sense would not give others publicly accessible justification."

51.   Wall, 1998, p 10.

52.   Rawls, 1993, p 66.

53.   Rawls, 1993, p 66.

54.   Rawls, 1993, p 66.

55.   O'Neill, 1989, p 34.

56.   Wall does not acknowledge this idea as part of the publicity condition. This is somewhat surprising since his treatment of Rawls's idea of public justification certainly is the most elaborate hitherto provided. Cf Wall, 1998, pp 111–115.

57.   Rawls, 1971, p 133.

58.   O'Neill, 1996, pp 174f.

59.   Parfit, 1984, p 5.

60.   See Parfit (1984, pp 5, 55) for a definition of the directly and the indirectly self-defeating.

61.   In a more Kantian fashion the same idea can be described as the requirement that the principles we want everyone (the state or citizens) to act from are free from contradiction in conception. Since we cannot imagine everyone successfully acting out of the principle "everyone but me should be honest," that principle must be rejected. See for this aspect of Kant's idea of the hypothetical imperative O'Neill, 1989, pp 95–98.

62.   Rawls, 1993, p 217.

63.   Rawls, 1993, p 243.

64.   Rawls, 1993, p 217.

65.   Empirically speaking this idea is of great importance for the workings of parliamentary democracy. The tradition of public questions in the chamber, or the more recent idea of public hearings, is not merely a way of securing accountability but is essential to the normative legitimacy of political institutions. See also Amy Gutman's and Dennis Thompson's defense of publicity in terms of legitimacy, efficiency and accountability. Yet it remains uncertain whether these various justifications for publicity are consistent. For example, Gutman & Thompson defend secrecy on condition that the net benefit is positive (p 102) but they do not consider whether this is compatible with the idea of legitimacy. Cf Gutman & Thompson, 1998, pp 95–127.

66.   Cf William Godwin's claim that "virtue will always be an unusual spectacle among men, till they have learned to be at all times ready to avow their actions, and assign the reason upon which they are founded." Quoted in Robert E Goodin, 1992, p 125.

67.   Jon Elster, 1983, pp 35f. Elster goes so far as to assert that selfish proposals are "pragmatically impossible" to defend in public. That might be going too far; statements about the superiority of this or that race, sex, nation, etc, seem to be common enough. Also, Goodin, 1992, p 136.

68.   Alexis de Tocqueville, 1998 [1862], p 211.

69. Gutman & Thompson provide some good illustrations of these mechanisms at work. Illustrative is the case when members of the Federal Reserve Board had to publicly defend their previous non-public decision to keep transcripts of meetings secret in *perpetuity*. As they were not able to defend this decision in public, the Board had later to limit the terms of secrecy. Gutman & Thompson, 1998, p 104.
70. Rawls, 1971, p 226 (emphasis added). See also Rawls 1997 b, p 772f.
71. Rawls, 1993, p 69.
72. Parfit, 1984, pp 23, 40.
73. Hayek quoted by Lundström (1993, p 198). Also the conservative writer Edmund Burke, whose ideas in many respects inspired Hayek, believed that certain beliefs, like that in a religion, must be accepted for its usefulness rather than for its truth or intrinsic value. However, at some stage Burke must have realized the weakness of this idea since he emphasized that the upper classes must not themselves think of religion in instrumental terms, as something useful. See Herbert Tingsten, 1965 [1939], p 24.
74. As Rawls notes in a footnote the publicity condition will imply a ban on ideological illusions and a rejection of societies based on "false consciousness." Rawls, 1993, p 68 fn 21.
75. It should be noted that publicizability excludes lying, not insincerity. Publicity is satisfied even when a citizen or a politician defends views that she does not believe in as long as she remains committed to the same views in action. Publicizability excludes discrepancy between public justifications and public actions, not discrepancy between public justification and private beliefs.
76. Again, Kant provides a similar idea of publicizability. As O Neill (1989, p 34) argues Kant thought that it is not whether an argument or doctrine *is* communicated that matters as much as if it *could* have been communicated without contradiction. A self-effacing theory could not have been communicated in public and it is therefore illegitimate. A consequence of this interpretation is that the duty of civility is concerned more with norms of thinking than with norms of action. It is not as important that people in fact stand out in public as it is that they think of their views as consistent with that act.
77. However, the anthropocentric assumption of liberalism is playfully put in question by Rawls in a children's story. The Crocodile, who is speaking for Rawls, asks "why should you assume that you are going to be . . . a human being rather than an animal?" and suggests that " . . . a society can be deemed just only so long as it would be chosen by an animal behind a veil of ignorance." John Rawls, n d, pp 29f.
78. The consequence is that so far as ecologists rest their claims on unproven facts or metaphysical ideas about nature this is a sufficient reason for declaring them illegitimate.
79. Rawls, 1993, p 226 (emphasis added).
80. In this section I have analyzed the implications of the publicity condition in Rawls's theory. I have not been concerned with what, if anything, justifies publicity itself. One suggestion is the Kantian idea that publicity, by constituting a condition for critique, is an aspect of reason itself. See O'Neill (1989, p 37). To the extent that citizens wish to be ruled by a rational political system they should, consequently, accept that its institutions are justified in ways that comply with the requirements of publicity. For the theoretical and historical connections between the ideas of publicity and rationality see, John Christer Laursen, 1989.
81. This conclusion is also reached by Wall (1998, pp 114f). However Wall does not include all the relevant features of publicity in his analysis.
82. In Rawls's theory the notion of the reasonable is sometimes used in ways similar to that of the notion of publicity. Thus Rawls (1993, p 53) claims that citizens accept

publicity *because* they are reasonable; "it is by the reasonable that we enter as equals the public world of others and stand ready to propose, or to accept, as the case may be, fair terms of social cooperation."

83.   Dworkin, 1992, p 503.

84.   Dworkin, 1992, p 506. Jones (1989, p 56) makes a similar suggestion.

85.   Rawls, 1993, p 94.

86.   The burdens of judgement are explained by Rawls (1993, pp 56f) as follows. The fact that concepts are vague implies that we must rely on "judgements within some range where reasonable persons may differ." It is also the case, Rawls argues, that the way we "assess evidence" depends on personal experience. Since "experiences are disparate enough for judgements to diverge" we may arrive at different conclusions in assessing the same facts. Thus, conflicts are inevitable as much as they are reasonable.

87.   In an earlier article Rawls used the term "burdens of *reason*." See John Rawls, 1989.

88.   Sher (1997, pp 89f) notes the importance of the factual character of the burdens of judgement. Cf Gauthier (1986, p 5) who claims that the notion of the reasonable is itself a "morally substantive matter," and Simon Clarke who—wrongly I believe—characterizes this idea as concerned with the nature of knowledge ("an epistemological doctrine"). Simon Clarke, 1999, p 639. If the burdens of judgement are empirical facts then they do not depend for their validity on any moral or philosophical claim.

89.   Joshua Cohen, 1993, p 285.

90.   Rawls, 1993, p 58. This passage is important but is susceptible to misunderstanding. In a critique of Rawls, Leif Wenar (1995, p 43) rightly points out that toleration does not *require* recognition of the burdens of judgement. But Wenar wrongly concludes that the burdens of judgement are therefore "at best unnecessary." This conclusion is wrong in the sense that it rests on a failure to appreciate the argument for tolerance that Rawls, by appealing to the burdens of judgement, presents to citizens. This allows tolerance to be more than a mere matter of faith or coincidence. Rawls's thrust is that there should be reasons for accepting toleration even though they are not necessary in the sense required by Wenar.

91.   "To believe a proposition is to believe that it is true and that contradictory propositions are false." Brink, 1989, p 94. See also Jones, 1989, p 66.

92.   Cohen, 1993, pp 283f. That Cohen has influenced Rawls on this point is acknowledged by Rawls (1993, p 36, fn 37 and 127f).

93.   The success of this argument depends, obviously, on the acknowledgement of others as political equals. There can be no reasonable disagreement about the idea that citizens are equals and that the norms of publicity should apply—disagreements on those questions simply cannot be said to be reasonable. Cf Clarke's (1999, p 640) claim that the argument from the burdens of judgement is "self-defeating" because it may be rejected by appeal to the existence of a reasonable disagreement about such matters. However, the ideas of equality and publicity are tacitly assumed to be valid when we say that disagreements may be reasonable. Only equals that give arguments that are understandable could disagree in reasonable ways.

94.   My aim is not to challenge the existence of the burdens of judgement but to find out whether they justify the idea of neutrality in justification. However, Gaus argues that empirical evidence suggests that the burdens of judgement are not generally accepted. A majority of people interviewed in one investigation thought that what they believed to be true was true whatever evidence or arguments other people could come up with. This means, Gaus concludes, that the burdens of judgement are

"rejected." Gerald Gaus, 1996, p 135. I do not think this interpretation of the results is correct. As I argue above, the point of invoking the burdens of judgement is that citizens cannot count on convincing others of the truth of their doctrines. That is, Rawls is not asserting that people should not believe in the truth. On this interpretation Gaus's evidence rather speaks in *favor* of the burdens of judgement: people do not generally believe that they can be proven wrong. This is exactly Rawls's point.

95. Rawls, 1993, p 58.
96. Cohen, 1993, p 284.
97. Rawls, 1993, pp 127, 153 (emphasis added).
98. Rawls, 1993, p 153.
99. Rainer Forst, 1994, p 169.
100. Charles Larmore (1996, p 173) makes a similar observation: "Generally we have good reasons to believe more than what reasonable agreement with others can secure." The reasons we can agree on do not, in other words, exhaust the reasons which it is reasonable to believe in. It is not unreasonable, then, to believe in what others cannot agree to. It is in a way surprising that Cohen should be susceptible to the point made by Larmore and me, because Cohen *is* aware of the possibility that a person may accept the burdens of judgement and yet reject liberal neutrality. A person may, Cohen (1993, p 283) writes, "acknowledge the idea of reasonable pluralism, and at the same time embrace the sectarian view that our moral views are true . . . these are consistent positions."
101. Barry, 1995, p 188.
102. Thomas Nagel, 1994 [1987], pp 70ff.
103. E.g., Hampton, 1989 a, p 811 and Sandel, 1994, pp 1776ff.
104. That Rawls's liberal ideal is so "thick" that it threatens the free nature of liberal politics is indeed a common objection. See Mouffe (1994) and Wolgast (1994).
105. Rawls, 1995, pp 136, 146, 179. The idea of non-criticism finds its corollary in the constructivist method Rawls adheres to. Rawls (1993, p 127) claims that political philosophy should not "criticize religious, philosophical, or metaphysical accounts of the truth of moral judgements and their validity." The method of liberalism is, then, as agnostic about the good life as the principles justified by this method. Cf David Estlund, 1998, pp 253f.
106. Cohen, 1993, p 283.
107. Rawls, 1993, pp 56f.
108. Raz, 1994, pp 89f.

9

Liberalism and Dogmatism

In the previous chapter it was argued that Rawls's attempt to vindicate the idea of a neutral state is unsuccessful. The most important reason for this conclusion being that Rawls is unable to produce convincing reasons why non-liberals, who believe in the truth of some particular conception of virtue, should remain neutral in a constitutional debate.

In response the liberal might want to take the position of the skeptic. The liberal might want to argue that ethical ideals and conceptions of virtue are all false or nonsensical and that, therefore, everyone should accept the neutral state. If there are no truths about how to live, the state should allow each one to live as he or she wishes. Yet a basic point of departure for this work is that the skeptical argument is fruitless and perhaps even incoherent. Liberal institutions cannot be morally justified, if moral skepticism is conceded. Assuming that ethical notions are nonsensical would in fact undermine the moral legitimacy of the liberal system as much as of any other. This is the essence of the liberal paradox explained in brief in chapter one.

Now, efforts have recently been made to present a defense of liberal neutrality that takes into account the failures of both skepticism and Rawlsian neutrality. The idea, developed by Brian Barry, is that we should be skeptical about ethical certainties rather than about ethical truths.

Arguably liberalism is thereby provided with a cure for the defects of Rawls's theory. At the same time, Barry's notion of "moderate" skepticism is deliberately designed so as to avoid the pitfalls of a full-blown skepticism. It does not claim, as does moral skepticism, that people's moral beliefs are necessarily false. However, it does claim that people's moral beliefs are not necessarily true. Thus, Barry does not deny the existence of ethical truths: he denies the existence of ethical certainties.

A premise of Barry's argument is that there is a difference between dogmas and being dogmatic.[1] From a liberal perspective it is not problematic that people accept dogmas. There is a problem, however, when people accept their beliefs dogmatically—that is, when people believe that the truth is certain and definitive. Although liberalism could not challenge the dogmas people have (since that would be making liberalism too controversial), it can challenge the way people *hold* their dogmas. Once citizens no longer think that their visions of the good life and virtue are certain, they will, according to Barry, be more prone to accept liberal neutrality.[2]

Barry's suggestion goes further than Rawls's idea of the reasonable citizen. The point is that citizens must not only accept that truths are *contested* (Rawls's solution). Citizens must also accept that truths are *uncertain*—contested or not. When they acknowledge the uncertainty of ethical truths, citizens will realize that the state should not take into account any one truth about the good life. Thus, liberal neutrality is a natural consequence of the idea that beliefs in the goodness of virtue are inherently uncertain.

In this chapter I will examine Barry's proposal that uncertainty can cure dogmatic non-liberals of their ills. I will assess the merits of the idea that liberalism can be rescued by requiring that people are uncertain about their beliefs in virtue and the good life. My contention will be that Barry's idea is off the mark. It is so because its basic premise is not correct. In fact, the distinction suggested by Barry between hard-core and moderate moral skepticism, the first rejecting moral truths, the latter rejecting moral certainties, is not exhaustive. People are not necessarily either uncertain or dogmatic about the truth. Thus, I am going to present a different account of political conviction with the implication that Barry's theory appears to be less promising.

The outline of this chapter is as follows. I shall begin by analyzing the basics of Barry's idea of uncertainty and compare it with similar ideas. In the second part I shall examine one of the arguments in favor of the idea of uncertainty. In the third part I shall explain my main objections to Barry's proposal. In the fourth and fifth part I shall explore two further arguments in favor of Barry's attempt to save liberal neutrality. I shall finally make clear why these arguments are either invalid or inconsistent with Barry's own beliefs and values.

Liberalism: A Way to Believe

The idea that liberalism includes an idea of *how* people should hold their political and moral beliefs is not new. Barry's claim, that every citizen must admit some doubt about the truth of his or her ethical beliefs, recalls a classical argument for liberalism. In particular, the idea of a close relation between uncertainty on the one hand and liberalism on the other was common among thinkers such as Bertrand Russell and Karl Popper. Even more strongly than Barry, they emphasized the danger of dogmatic belief. According to Russell certainty is not only unwarranted but in fact excites totalitarian ideas and behavior.

> If you know for certain what is the purpose of the universe in relation to human life ... and what is good for people even if they do not think so ... then you will feel that no degree of coercion is too great, provided it leads to the goal.[3]

Liberalism requires that beliefs are held "tentatively" rather than firmly. The citizen should in other words relinquish the idea that there are definitive truths in morality and politics. In a similar vein, Karl Popper argued that the idea of truth as "manifest"—that truth is certain and definitive—will encourage "fanaticism" and violence.[4] Liberalism requires an awareness of the fact that truths are never definitive but always amenable to change.

The ideas expounded by Russell and Popper are reminiscent of the position defended by Barry.[5] In Barry's terminology, uncertainty must replace certainty. In order for people of different creeds to accept liberal principles, people need to believe more tentatively. The attitude of doubt, or tentativeness, is essential to Barry, because he believes that it is possible to convince citizens not to treat their respective conceptions of the good life as superior to others merely because they believe they are true. Barry believes that liberalism can, eventually, provide rational arguments for a consensus on basic political values and principles.[6] A condition for transcending such divisions, Barry contends, is that we accept our ideas of the good life as uncertain and unlikely to contain the whole truth of the matter.[7]

Moreover, Barry wants us to accept that this uncertainty applies to *every* doctrine, not just our own. When we realize that any doctrine of the good life will be uncertain, we will realize that it is unreasonable to accept one view rather than another as the moral basis for society. Facing the uncertainty of their respective doctrines, the Christian, the Marxist, the ecocentric, the conservative, and all other non-liberals, will be able to accept liberal neutrality. All of them realize that everyone has a good reason, because of the uncertainty of every conception of the good, to reject views different than their own. No one, that is, has a reason to accept *another* doctrine as true. To the extent, then, that citizens are *reasonable* they should propose only principles that others could not reasonably reject.[8] Since one person can reasonably reject the conception of the good of another person, all such conceptions ought to be avoided. This is why the state and citizens should be neutral on questions concerning the good life.

Thus, the notion of uncertainty comes to the rescue of Rawls's idea of neutrality in justification, and it does so at a seemingly low price. All that is needed is to substitute the notion of uncertainty for the idea of burdens of judgement.[9] It is not enough to acknowledge that political disagreements may be reasonable. The fact that political doctrines are not certain must also be acknowledged.

In line with Rawls's ambitions, Barry believes liberal neutrality needs to be justified without reference to controversial ideas. The attractive feature of uncertainty is that it is not metaphysical in the way moral skepticism would be. Moral skepticism denies that there are moral truths or, alternatively, that there are moral facts which could be true. But this is not the idea Barry embraces. All we need to accept is, in Barry's words, that "certainty is ill-founded [not that] *beliefs* are ill-founded."[10]

The position Barry takes can be understood as an elaboration of the distinction between beliefs and attitudes about the truth. On the one hand there are rival approaches to *beliefs* about the truth of ideas of the good life. On the other hand there are different approaches to the *attitude* to the truth of ideas of the good life. People may in other words be skeptical or dogmatic either with regard to what they believe or with regard to the attitudes they have. Figure 9.1 explicates these distinctions.

If liberalism is to be faithful to neutrality it cannot challenge dogmatism at the level of belief. To tell dogmatics that what they believe in is simply false, would make liberalism much too controversial. Liberalism must not claim, then, that there are no true beliefs about

Figure 9.1
Modes of Attitudes to and Beliefs about the Truth

	Scepticism	*Dogmatism*
Belief	No true belief	True belief
Attitude	No certain belief (doubt)	Certain belief (no doubt)

the good life. Instead, using Barry's strategy, dogmatics are challenged on the level of attitude. Liberalism denies certain truths about virtue and the good, not truth itself. This move makes it possible for non-liberals to maintain their dogmas while being less dogmatic about them.

However, there is one question as yet unanswered by Barry: what is the *reason* for accepting the idea about the uncertainty of truth? Why *must* citizens accept that the truth of their doctrines is uncertain?

The Normative Force of Uncertainty

Again, Barry employs a strategy similar to that of Rawls in that he refers to empirical facts in order to vindicate the notion of uncertainty. The empirical facts appealed to by Barry are historical facts concerning the success and failure of different conceptions of the good life. The thrust is that the apparent failure of religious movements to convert people to their respective creeds indicates that their dogmas are far less than certain truths. "It is hard not to be impressed," Barry asserts, "by the fact that so many people have devoted so much effort over the centuries...with so little success in the way of securing rational conviction among those not initially predisposed in favor of their conclusion."[11] Given this fact, the citizen cannot plausibly think that it would be unreasonable for others to reject his or her particular conception of the good. Because all conceptions of the good are "inherently uncertain" others may reasonably disagree about the contents of the good life.[12] Here I am not so much concerned with the correctness of the claim that conceptions of the good life have, historically, appeared as unconvincing.[13] What matters to me is the relevance of this observation. We might ask, for example, why non-liberals should care about the fact that their doctrines appear to be unpersuasive to others? Why would they even be bothered by the fact that the case for the doctrine is a bad one?

246   The Liberal State and the Politics of Virtue

Arguably, some religious believers do not appeal to rational arguments at all in their effort to convert people. Some people believe that reason has nothing to do with the truth of their faith. Using Joshua Cohen's terminology such a person can be called "non-rationalist fundamentalist."[14] Non-rationalist fundamentalists are not merely dogmatic about their dogma, they are also convinced that reason or rationality has nothing to do with the truth of that dogma. The observation that the dogma has met with little success will not be a reason for that person to conclude that the dogma is not true. Indeed, the non-rationalist fundamentalists might even think that the extra-rational character of his or her beliefs is constitutive of them. It is not an uncommon idea, after all, that true "knowledge" of the good can only be achieved by faith. Confronted with the non-rationalist fundamentalist, Barry's historic case for uncertainty might appear unconvincing.

Barry could add however that liberalism's failure in convincing the non-rationalist does not make his case any worse. Of course, a reasonable idea need not appear reasonable to everyone. Of course, people who defy reason will reject liberal ideas. Yet these facts do not imply that liberalism is itself irrational and that it should not be accepted. The idea of uncertainty might very well *seem* unacceptable to people, despite the fact that the idea *is*, in fact, reasonable. Barry makes this clear when he writes that "whether or not dogmatists are actually convinced by the case for skepticism, *they ought to be*."[15] That uncertainty is a reasonable idea does not mean that all of us will accept it. However, it does mean that all of us have reason to accept it.

The Descriptive Accuracy of Uncertainty

Let us grant that there are good reasons why we should be uncertain about the truth of our beliefs in the good life. Now we would like to know, more precisely, what it means to be "uncertain." On this particular point Barry is less than crystal clear; Barry in fact gives very few examples of what embracing uncertainty about the good life would be like. At one point uncertainty is characterized as "doubt." On another occasion uncertainty is described as a rejection of "zealous dogmatism" which is "overly confident."[16]

These statements may seem to correspond to each other; the former stating what uncertainty *is*, the latter what uncertainty is *not*. However, this impression is misleading and not difficult to reveal as such. In fact, a person that is not "overly confident" about the truth and who rejects "zealous dogmatism" does not automatically embrace doubt and uncertainty. That is, to have doubt is not the only alternative. This is seen once we admit that doubt presupposes reason to doubt. I doubt the truth of some proposition because I have reason to believe that it might not be true. But when I find no reason to doubt my beliefs, there are in fact two things I can do. I may conclude that the beliefs I have represent certain and irrefutable truths, or I may conclude that they are simply true. Hence, I may reasonably believe in the truth of a proposition without making the claim that it is an irrefutable or certain truth. People are not automatically dogmatic because they believe that their beliefs are true.

Let us illustrate this with an example. I may, for instance, doubt that authenticity is an aspect of the good life. The doubts I have may perhaps follow from the further belief that people who aspire to be authentic frequently seem to me unhappy. This belief is in other words my reason for being uncertain about the value of authenticity. Suppose, however, that one day I find that a certain amount of melancholy and sadness is a natural part of life and that, therefore, authenticity might not be that bad after all. Consequently, I no longer have a *reason* to doubt the value of authenticity.

Now, if we accept that Barry's dichotomy between dogmatism and doubt is exhaustive, it seems to follow that I have now become a "zealous dogmatic." This must be so because there are only two alternatives according to Barry: being uncertain or being certain. Since I am no longer uncertain about the value of authenticity I must consequently be certain and therefore also dogmatic. But could that be right? In fact, I suggest it is not.

One significant question Barry appears to ignore is the *revisability* of truth. Truths are not just more or less certain, they are also more or less revisable. Barry does not recognize this distinction, and this, I believe, is a serious defect of his argument.

In my view, an important feature of dogmatic belief is the rejection of the possibility of revising the truth. A dogmatic believer denies that new evidence or arguments can be produced that would affect or change what is true. But openness and uncertainty about the truth are not necessarily related to each other. People can believe there *are* no reasons for being uncertain about the truth of the good life and believe, at the same time, that such reasons *could* be produced. To accept that possibility is not, however, to admit that what they now believe true *is* uncertain. To accept that there may later be a reason to doubt a proposition is not a reason for doubting it now. Thus, it is not foolish to be "cock-sure" as de Montaigne once wrote.[17] Insisting on the truth is not stupid as long as one is disposed to listen to new arguments.

Another example concerning factual beliefs may better illustrate the distinction between certainty and revisability. Many think that it is true that "water" is a molecule consisting of two atoms of hydrogen and one atom of oxygen. Most of us have no reason to doubt this truth and most of us are in other words *certain* about the truth of this proposition. Yet few would deny the possibility that one day this truth may in fact be proven false. Perhaps one day scientists will discover some previously unknown structure of atoms that challenges the present understanding of molecules. How could this possibility be rejected? The important point is that accepting the possibility of progress in knowledge need not lead us to doubt the truth of our present theories. That is, we are not more uncertain about present truths merely because we recognize that they may, one day, be disproved.

Barry is busy arguing that uncertainty is not identical to full-blown skepticism. He wants to assure his reader that being uncertain about ethical truths does not amount to the view that such truths do not exist. What we have, Barry asserts, "is skepticism [i.e., uncertainty] on one side and a host of conflicting dogmatisms on the other."[18] But by focusing on the distinction between uncertainty and skepticism he neglects the question of revisability. Barry's statement, that dogmatism is the only alternative to uncertainty, is therefore plainly wrong: we need be *neither* uncertain *nor* dogmatic about the truth.

Introducing two dimensions along which attitudes to truth may vary—revisability and certainty—will demonstrate that Barry is making things too easy for liberalism. Since there are two dimensions of attitudes to truth, not just two different attitudes as Barry suggests, it becomes clear that what we call dogmatic belief may be of two kinds. In fact, I believe dogmatics may be either certain *or* uncertain about the truth. Uncertain dogmatics should be called dogmatic-doubters since they refuse to admit the possibility that what they doubt will no longer be worth doubting.[19] A person is a dogmatic-doubter when, for example, he or she persistently claims to be uncertain about whether the ice on the lake is thick enough to walk on—although people have walked on it for days, the temperature is falling, and so on.

Dogmatic doubters should be contrasted with dogmatic believers that represent the kind of dogmatic Barry is concerned with. The important point is that dogmatic believers and dogmatic doubters are both dogmatics: none of them admit of new evidence or new arguments that could show them that their attitude (of either uncertainty or certainty) is unwarranted.

But if the dogmatic may be of two kinds, so may the undogmatic. In fact, I believe this is a crucial observation. People may be undogmatic in the sense that they recognize that the truth may change and, at the same time, doubt what they presently believe to be true. I will call this view *critical doubt* because it accepts that the truth is uncertain and that what is uncertain is always amenable to change. But all undogmatics need not share this preference for doubt. People that are what I call *critical believers* remain certain about what they believe, though they recognize that the truth may change. Because critical believers acknowledge that what is true today may not be true tomorrow there is nothing dogmatic about them: they do not refuse to listen and they do not deny the relevance of new evidence. Still, they need not be the least uncertain about what they believe at present to be true.[20]

The question of revisability reveals the weakness of Barry's theory of uncertainty. In fact, it suggests that insisting on uncertainty might even be a mistake. This is so because questions of revisability are likely to be much more important than questions of certainty. In

Figure 9.2
Attitudes to Truth

		Is truth certain?	
		Truth is certain	Truth is uncertain
Is truth revisable?	Truth is revisable	Critical believer	Critical doubter
	Truth is not revisable	Dogmatic believer	Dogmatic doubter

order to maintain a political culture where arguments count, where there is faith in political discussion and public debate, people need to see the point in improving their political views by the use of arguments. This means that they need to accept the value of revisability and the idea that truths are never final.[21] Thus, the argumentative and democratic spirit need not be connected with the attitude of doubt or uncertainty. You are not necessarily more inclined to accept the force of the better argument just because you believe that all truths should be doubted. So it does not seem to matter much whether citizens accept truths as certain or uncertain. What matters is that people are prepared to listen and to argue.

In sum, I believe we are entitled to conclude that Barry's emphasis on uncertainty is misguided. This conclusion is warranted primarily for descriptive reasons: it simply is not true that uncertainty has the kind of implications attributed to it by Barry. Yet there may be other reasons that justify the association of liberalism with doubt. In the following sections I shall examine two such notions: the logical basis for uncertainty and the moral basis for uncertainty.

Is Uncertainty More Logical?

It might be argued that doubt is the most rational attitude for a quite simple reason that has to do with the logical possibility of error. Since it is *logically possible* that any one belief is mistaken, there is always a reason to be uncertain about its truth. The stuff of morality and science, the values and facts that we refer to, may logically be quite different than we think they are now and, consequently, everyone has a reason to regard his or her beliefs as uncertain.

However, the appeal of this objection relies on a failure to distinguish between questions concerning what is true and questions concerning our beliefs in what is true.[22] It is one thing to say that the truth is uncertain. It is quite another to say that our beliefs about what is true are uncertain. General philosophical points about truth need not appertain to our particular beliefs about what is true. When you are uncertain about whether some belief is true, this is typically because you have reason to suspect that this belief is not true.[23] But this reason must be specific to the particular belief in question. The claim that "many people are liars" need not make me suspicious about what my wife tells me, since this general claim does not give me a reason to believe that *she* lies. For similar reasons I will not be suspicious about the truth of the proposition "the University of Uppsala was founded in 1477" just because someone tells me that truths are fallible. Claims to the effect that *the truth* is of this or that kind will consequently be of little interest in deciding what we *believe to be true*. The claim that the truth could be anything does not, in other words, mean that we have no reason to believe in something.

This point is further supported by Joseph Raz's observation that uncertainty or doubt presupposes an awareness of a flaw.[24] You need a reason in order to be justified in having doubts. What is more, this reason for doubt must be *specific* in the sense that it pertains to the belief in question. The claim that the world may be different than we presently believe is no specific reason in this sense.[25] I believe Barry disregards this fact, when he asserts that all conceptions of the good life are necessarily uncertain. Barry might be correct in saying that no one belief about the good life is known to be a certain truth. Yet this observation does not provide a specific reason for people to conclude that their beliefs about what the good life is are likely to be false. For that reason alone Barry's thesis cannot be correct.[26]

Is Uncertainty More Moral?

Yet, if uncertainty is not a matter of what we *can* believe, it may be a question of what we *ought* to believe. Doubt should not, then, be understood as warranted by the uncertainty of truth (as an epistemological reason) but by the belief that the moral cost of not accepting that idea is too high. Again, the distinction between epistemological and moral reasons for doubt is rarely made or acknowledged. In contrast to the *epistemic uncertainty* discussed above, which is the affirmation of some flaw or deficiency in the reasons we have for believing true a belief, *moral uncertainty* is the idea that claims to certainty will have bad consequences, or that insisting on knowing the truth in order to be certain is objectionable for some other non-epistemic reason. Thus, the case for uncertainty is supported by appealing to a set of moral beliefs and not by a particular philosophy of knowledge.

One example of such reasoning is found in Russell's writings. Impressed by the dreadful consequences of the Second World War and the threat of a nuclear conflict between the superpowers Russell wrote that "only through a revival of Liberal tentativeness ... can our world survive." In order to prevent a full-scale nuclear war people will have to be less certain about the truth of what they believe in. Hence Russell did not regard the question of whether we should have doubt or not as a philosophical issue.[27] Whether we should embrace liberal tentativeness or not was seen as a matter of simple prudence: we should reject dogmatic belief because that might help us to save the world.

Is the moral case for doubt applicable to Barry's theory? Perhaps it is. As we have seen, Barry refers to the failure of religious movements in order to demonstrate the uncertainty of ideas of the good life; "it became evident [to Catholics and Protestants in post-Reformation Europe] that there was no prospect of one side or the other simply converting the members of the other by a process of rational argument."[28] The upshot of this claim seems to be that the lack of convergence of beliefs concerning virtue and the good life warrants the conclusion that all such beliefs are uncertain.

In an earlier part of this chapter I argued that Barry's thesis does not hold scrutiny if understood as an epistemic claim. From the observation that *some* arguments about the good have failed we are not entitled to conclude that *all* beliefs about the good life are uncertain. Now, what if Barry is not attempting to make an epistemic but a moral case for uncertainty? If that is so the suggestion would be that it is hazardous to believe in the certainty of any one particular idea of the good life. The claim would be that the realization of peace and justice presupposes that people become more uncertain and doubtful.

Yet, the reasoning that would require citizens to adopt truth as uncertain for moral reasons is less convincing than it might seem. In Barry's view, it is crucial that citizens regard their ideas of the good as uncertain in order for them to accept liberal neutrality. Liberal neutrality, in turn, is needed in order to secure liberal institutions. In other words, uncertainty should be accepted because this attitude is conducive to the maintenance of a liberal society.

However, considered as an argument for uncertainty this point is of no use. If the only reason why citizens should be uncertain about truth is that this is necessary in order to justify liberal principles, then the only *motive* that would make people accept this argument must be that they *want* to justify liberal principles. But why, if they already want *that*, should they be uncertain? People who are predisposed to accept liberal principles certainly need not be uncertain about truth in order to endorse them. Similarly, those not predisposed to accept liberal values are unlikely to be impressed by this case for uncertainty. If you do not find liberal values attractive, it is unlikely that you will change your attitude only in order to support these values. In fact, the moral case for uncertainty is not a case at all.

It is ironic that Barry's attempt to justify liberal neutrality falls prey to this objection. This is ironic because Barry once made the same point. In that context Barry observed the meaninglessness of arguments that are directed exclusively to those already disposed towards liberal values. Why elaborate an argument for liberalism that will be accepted only by liberals? "My guess is," Barry wrote, "that the doctrine [of neutralist liberalism] is usually offered for consumption by people who have no use for it themselves."[29] My point is that this objection is valid also in relation to Barry's present position. What use do we have for an argument that presupposes that people already embrace what is to be justified? What use does liberalism have for an argument that will convince no one but the liberal himself?

Why Uncertainty Can't Do the Job

Part of the attractiveness of the neutrally justified government is that it does not appeal to metaphysical constructions or obscure ideas about the essence of the good life. The problem we have discussed here is under what circumstances this ideal is in fact convincing to people who want the state to promote and recognize their particular conceptions of virtue and the good life. In chapter eight, we encountered the force of the arguments from equality, publicity and reasonableness. However, none of these ideas were powerful enough to exclude all or even most conceptions of the good life. What seemed to be needed was some further idea that had the power to undermine the legitimacy of the dogmas people might refer to. Barry suggests one way by introducing the notion of uncertainty. However, my conclusion is that the notion of uncertainty demands both too much and too little in order to justify the neutral state.

In its first form, Barry's argument demands too much. It demands too much because it is not unreasonable to be certain about what one believes true. Barry's distinction between the moderately skeptical liberal and the dogmatic is too crude. A person may be certain

254   The Liberal State and the Politics of Virtue

and yet accept that the truth is not definitive. A person may in other words believe that the truth is certain and revisable. Insisting on uncertainty would be to insist on something that is unreasonable.

In its second form, Barry's argument demands too little. It demands too little because it presupposes that we want to live within liberal institutions. But doing that is in fact to presuppose what is to be justified. The moral reason for uncertainty appears to be insufficient, it does not provide a reason to accept liberal principles, and it will consequently fail to convince the non-liberal.

Notes

1. Barry (1991, pp 37f) makes the distinction between dogmas and dogmatism: "A liberal has no objection to anyone holding a *dogma*, so long as it is not held *dogmatically*" (emphasis added).
2. Barry, 1995 a, section 27.
3. Bertrand Russell, 1955 [1947], p 24.
4. Karl Popper, 1965 [1962], pp 8, 356. An illuminating comparison of the relation between skepticism and liberalism in the work of Popper and Russell is found in Benjamin Barber, 1988, pp 47ff.
5. In contrast to Barry, Popper not only argued that liberalism presupposes uncertainty. Popper (1965, p 352) also argued that the successful pursuit of truth presupposes liberalism. A liberal regime, where openness and critique pervade, is a necessary condition for scientific success.
6. True, Barry uses the notion of *impartiality*, not neutrality, to characterize his theory. However, this term refers to basically the same idea as that of neutrality of justification. Barry's (1995, p 123) definition of impartiality runs as follows: "impartiality ... does not rest on any particular conception of the good."
7. Note that the issue of uncertainty refers to moral and ethical notions only. Barry's point is consequently distinct from the common view that democracy implies that we "must never believe that we have found the final solution" (Rothstein, 1995, p 22).
8. Following Thomas Scanlon, Barry (1995, p 70) argues that what citizens "could not reasonably *reject*" is a better criterion for acceptable principles than what citizens "could reasonably *accept*." The rejection formula is preferable since it avoids the possibility that some citizens take advantage of other, more generous, citizens. Generous people may reasonably accept sacrificing all their property for the pleasure of others, though they may not unreasonably reject giving it all away for that purpose. See also Chambers, 1996, p 81.
9. Jones suggests a similar move; Rawls must shift his attention from the doctrines themselves (i.e., by assuming the burdens of judgement) to how these doctrines are held. This idea seems strikingly similar to Barry's idea that we must regard our conceptions of the good as being somewhat uncertain. Peter Jones, 1995, pp 526f.
10. Barry, 1995 a, p 169.
11. Barry, 1995 a, p 171.
12. Barry takes the experience of the Reformation and the wars of religion to be crucial in this respect. However, neither conservative, Marxist or ecologist notions of the good life, are *religious* truths, nor do they originate from the age of reformation.

Liberal arguments, consequently, seem less powerful in rejecting secular conceptions of the good than in rejecting religious conceptions.

13. Cf Clarke's (1999, p 636) claim that conceptions of justice may have been, in the course of history, as much disputed and controversial as conceptions of the good life.

14. Cohen, 1993, pp 286f.

15. Barry, 1995 a, p 171.

16. Barry, 1995 a, p 169.

17. Michel Eyquem de Montaigne quoted in Shklar, 1982, p 228.

18. Barry, 1995 a, p 172. By dogmatism Barry refers to both the dogmatic belief in truth and the dogmatic denial of truth (which may also be described as philosophical skepticism about knowledge).

19. Cf Laursen's (1989, p 443) observation that Kant denounced "dogmatic doubt" as the wrong-type of skepticism. I have explored some further differences between critical-belief and skepticism in Ludvig Beckman, 1997, pp 121ff.

20. See also Popper (1965, p 49) who describes the "critical attitude" as the view that is "ready to modify its tenets [and] admits doubt." Though Popper seems to regard "doubt" as compatible with the critical attitude, the aspect of revisability appears to loom larger. John Locke also seemed to have no difficulty reconciling certainty with a scientific attitude: "With me to know and to be certain is the same thing: what I know, that I am certain of; and what I am certain of that I know. What reaches to knowledge, I think may be called certainty; and what comes short of certainty, I think may not be called knowledge." John Locke, *Second Letter to Stillingfleet,* quoted in Thomas Spragens, 1981, p 44.

21. See, for instance, Rawls's remark that it is essential that citizens believe "that their political opinions may be revised by discussion with other citizens." Rawls 1997 b, p 772.

22. See Leonard Carrier, 1993, pp 366f.

23. This suggests that all that matters to us is which reasons we can produce and not what is "really" true. Science deals with arguments and not with truth itself. This is Popper's solution to the more general problem of the relation between scientific reasoning and truth. See Popper, 1965, and Dudley Shapere, 1984, p 228.

24. Raz, 1994, pp 100f.

25. Shapere, 1984, p 226.

26. A further point is that doubt does not make your beliefs less likely to be in error compared to the attitude of certainty. If error is indeed a logical possibility it certainly applies to all beliefs equally, whether you are certain or not about them. Thus the claim that error is possible does not seem to justify the conclusion that we should be uncertain. See Ruth Weintraub, 1993, pp 260f.

27. Russell, 1955, p 24.

28. Barry, 1995 a, p 170.

29. Barry, 1991, p 35.

10

Conclusions: The Liberal's Predicament

The modern world resounds with cries for a better and more virtuous life. A wide variety of social movements believe that it is possible to create a good society where there is a place for both virtue and justice. These movements echo the claims of indigenous people, children, environmentalists, feminists, socialists, conservatives, Christians, Moslems, and many others. To many of them, liberalism is an impoverished ideology, because it lacks ethical commitment, and some of them reject the idea of a neutral state with regard to virtues and questions of the good life.

The aim of this study has been to examine the extent to which this critique in fact applies to contemporary liberal theory. Is the liberal state necessarily neutral with regard to ideas about virtue and conceptions of the good life? Do liberal values conflict with notions of virtue and are liberals necessarily indifferent to people's longing for the good life? I have attempted to answer these questions in relation to the writings of contemporary liberal thinkers. Now what is the answer?

First, we should note that there are two distinct issues at stake here. On the one hand, we are concerned with the extent to which the liberal ideology embraces an ideal of the good life. Are there liberal virtues? Is there a liberal way of life? On the other hand, we are concerned with the justification of a particular ideal of the state. Should the state be devoted to the protection of individual rights only? Should the state be neutral regarding conceptions of virtue and goodness?

These issues are distinct, although the position taken at one level is likely to influence the position taken at the other. If you believe that any talk of virtue is ridiculous, you will plausibly defend the view that the state should not be concerned with such notions at all.

However, the skeptical view exemplified by this position is generally regarded as less promising today. Contemporary liberal theories are loath to reject calls for a good and virtuous life as inherently wrong or nonsense. Instead, contemporary liberals seek ways to establish the ideal of an uncommitted state with recourse to moral or ethical principles. In that case the relation between the two questions, whether there are virtues and whether the state should promote them, becomes more complex. In the following I shall summarize my findings on these two issues respectively and, finally, elaborate somewhat on the consequences for our understanding of liberalism and the liberal ideal of the state.

Liberals and the Idea of the Virtuous Life

In chapter two I argued, in contrast to many recent critics that the debate about the place of virtue in liberal thought should be concerned with *which* virtues liberals accept, rather than *if* liberals accept some virtues or not. I consequently rejected the view, defended for instance by Alasdair MacIntyre, that liberalism is necessarily indifferent to the extent to which citizens are virtuous. Liberals are not indifferent to virtue, but they are likely to prefer instrumental justifications of them.

The instrumental approach is well illustrated by Rawls's theory. According to Rawls's *political* liberalism, people need to be virtuous for two reasons. One reason is instrumental; in order to secure liberal institutions and values the individual needs to accept the virtues of justice, cooperation, etc. Another reason is political; each citizen needs to accept that all citizens possess the capacity of choice and autonomy. That is, we all have to realize that everyone might want to be virtuous in the liberal sense. But this is not to say that Rawls would want us all to identify with the virtue of autonomy as argued by William Galston and others. In a Rawlsian society the liberal virtues are either exercised for instrumental reasons or not exercised at all. Liberalism in Rawls's hands does not express an idea about ethics and the good life and therefore does not endorse intrinsic virtues in the terminology used here.

A different view is found in the ethical liberalism of Ronald Dworkin. The interpretation I defend in chapter three shows that Dworkin's theory is essentially a doctrine about the virtue of individuality. The good life is an independent life where authentic ends are pursued in an authentic way. Dworkin's doctrine consequently presents a conception of the liberal way of life—but a peculiar one. What matters is not what people do. The life people lead matters less than how they live it. Dworkin's virtues are, if at all, second-order conceptions.

In sum, there are two distinct version of liberalism: one attempting to avoid questions about the good life, another affirming an individualistic conception of the good life. Even liberalism of the former kind recognizes the instrumental value of a number of virtues. The virtues of justice and cooperation are important to the stability of liberal institutions, although not necessarily part of any particular ethical ideal. The claim that liberalism shuns the domain of virtue seems to be unfounded. Liberal philosophy shows a genuine commitment to a great number of virtues.

Yet it is obvious that the liberal idea of virtue is of a peculiar kind. I believe that it is generally true that liberal virtues are always defined in relation to other ends and values. This is obvious in the case of Rawls's political liberalism. In Rawls's view, a liberal society needs the virtues because they are essential to the realization of certain social, political and economic ends. The virtue of autonomy is, in Rawls's work, accepted because it helps justify liberal institutions— not because it is good that people are autonomous.

By contrast, the instrumental approach is not present in Dworkin's writings. Here, we find an articulation of the virtues of individuality. The virtues of reflection and independence are accepted for intrinsic reasons: they are constitutive elements of the liberal ideal. However, the ideal of individuality is a second-order ideal. This is to say that the virtues of reflection and independence are good, because they allow individuals to pursue other ends and values. In other words, the liberal's second-order virtues are *means*, albeit ethically necessary.

Liberals and the Idea of the Politics of Virtue

The second issue concerns the politics of virtue. Should the state have the authority to pursue conceptions of the good life and virtue? It is clear that contemporary liberals think not: the state should be neutral with regard to conceptions of the virtuous life. Liberal writers have used a great number of reasons and ideas in order to substantiate this conclusion. After all, the idea of ethical neutrality is not supposed to be a mere matter of faith. At a more basic level I distinguished between reasons for neutrality that were based on an account of individual rights and reasons for neutrality that were based on other values. My contention has been that state neutrality cannot be defended in any of these ways.

Traditionally, liberals have emphasized the conflict between the protection of individual rights and policies aiming at the promotion of virtue. The claim is of either empirical or conceptual nature. However, as I endeavored to make clear in chapter five, neither claim is successful. The first claim is that individual rights have been violated in the name of virtue and that, therefore, the politics of virtue ought to be renounced in a liberal society. Yet this observation does not constitute an objection to virtues more than to other values which have, in the course of history, justified policies that have had disastrous results. The idea that the state can be justified in violating the rights of individuals is not theoretically—though perhaps empirically—associated with the idea of virtue. Moreover, I explored the grounds for the alleged incompatibility between notions of virtue and notions of individual rights, and I believe that the conclusion is that it does not bear close examination. The idea that ideals of individual rights are necessarily at variance with ideals of virtues is based on a misunderstanding. This result should perhaps come as a surprise, given the long-standing prestige enjoyed by the position defended by Isaiah Berlin, among others.

Recent liberal theorists put less emphasis on the putative conflict between virtue and rights. Instead of arguing that they are logically or empirically incompatible, liberals like Rawls and Dworkin argue that the idea of a politics of virtue is unjustifiable. Thus, the claim is that the non-neutral state violates certain norms. But what do liberals mean by the *neutral* state?

In chapter six I dissected the idea of the neutral state and found it to have at least three distinct meanings. We can speak about a state being neutral with reference either to its consequences, aims or justifications. Now, I believe there are two common mistakes. One mistake is to accuse liberals of not being neutral enough. The claim, defended by Ronald Beiner among others, is that liberal institutions have non-neutral effects and that, therefore, their neutral ambitions are in vain. However, this objection is irrelevant. Political institutions could never be neutral in consequences and, what is more, liberals advocating neutrality do not pretend that they could. Liberalism is typically committed to the idea of neutrality of aims (Dworkin) or neutrality of justifications (Rawls). A further mistake, now committed by liberals themselves, is that of not making clear the difference between not supporting life-styles and not justifying policies without reference to the superior value of certain life-styles. In other words, the distinction between neutrality in aims and in justification is not always made or seen.

In the remaining chapters, that is, chapters seven, eight and nine, I explored recent attempts to defend the idea of a state that is neutral in aims and justifications respectively. I will not recapitulate the argument in detail, although I believe the general conclusion is clear: notions of equality, publicity or reasonableness cannot vindicate the principle of state neutrality. There is no unambiguous connection between these (undoubtedly liberal) values and the precept of neutrality to conceptions of the good life. In other words, there is a "gap" in contemporary liberalism between its philosophical and political commitments.

The basic difficulty is how to explain to people who do not already accept the idea of neutrality why they should do so. Even when we assume that these people accept that other citizens deserve to be treated as equals, there does not seem to be any further argument that compels them to accept the neutralist conclusion. The amazing result is that this is true even when we grant that citizens accept the rest of the liberal baggage. That is, neutrality does not follow either from the idea of equality before the law (Dworkin), or from the idea that political justifications should be couched in terms understandable to all (Rawls). These principles certainly do present non-liberals with a number of constraints. They do, for instance, imply that there can be no religious justification of policies of virtue in a liberal state. They also exclude justifications that refer to beliefs in the inherent superiority of particular groups or persons. These and other constraints notwithstanding, there do not seem to be a convincing basis for the idea of the neutral state.

However, there are two considerations that, to the liberal, seem more helpful than others. Dworkin's notion of individuality and Barry's idea of moderate skepticism seem, initially, to constitute bullet-proof arguments for the virtue-free state.

The appeal of the notion of individuality is perhaps obvious (I discussed this in chapters three and seven). What matters in this view is that each person is allowed to respond to his or her own life, not that life corresponds to some abstract end or pattern. Only when life is lived according to your own ideals will you be able to develop your individuality in full. Thus, the promotion of individuality is the basic reason why the state should abstain from the pursuit of particular life-styles or virtues. Yet I contend that the argument from individuality is inconclusive, and that it can be successfully invoked against paternalistic aims only. When the government pursues moralistic aims—not intending to improve the life of the individual ethically—the fact that individuality is a good no longer seems to constitute a decisive objection. We may grant that promoting people's individuality is desirable and yet accept that there are other virtues or ends that are important. There is in other words a need for striking a balance between the value of individuality and other values, and this means that neutrality (which would favor individuality only) could not be achieved.

Moderate skepticism, as presented by Barry, is perhaps attractive too. In particular, its appeal is likely to reside in its connotation with a rational and scientific perspective on political matters. The claim is that, when we think about it, we cannot be sure that this or that virtue is really good and that, therefore, we should ensure that the state is neutral with regard to all such beliefs. Liberalism defends a neutral state because liberals hold their beliefs "tentatively," to use Russell's expression.

In my response to Barry I pointed to the fact that tentativeness is distinct from doubt. It may be rational to believe that the beliefs one has about the good life could be improved upon. Yet this is not to say that what we now believe to be true should be doubted. Accepting the liberal call for tentativeness does not, in other words, imply that people cannot defend or insist on what they do in fact believe to be true. The appeal to tentativeness does not, therefore, demonstrate why non-liberals should subscribe to the idea of the neutral state.

The Mythological Element in Liberalism

One important conclusion of this study is that the belief in state neutrality, typical to people of liberal persuasion, cannot be theoretically justified. The belief that the state should not promote conceptions of the good life is in other words comparable to a myth that lacks a rational basis.

What are the implications of this conclusion? Have we no choice but to accept that the government may express a preference for some ways of life, e.g., stating that the national curriculum is based on particular traditions of faith? Is there nothing to say about the state supporting particular virtues, as long as this is done within the confines of the values of equality and publicity?

I believe this conclusion is not correct either. There are justified restraints that apply to the policies pursued by the state or to the reasons that serve to justify them. As we have seen, there are for example good reasons why the state should not force individuals to adopt particular ways of life. Liberals that value individuality, the idea that it is desirable for the individual to be in charge of his own life, have good reason to argue that the state must act with restraint when promoting virtue. Also, the values of equality, publicity and tentativeness, explored in previous chapters, are germane to the question of which virtues the state may legitimately promote.

For instance, liberalism excludes or makes illegitimate the idea that the state may justify policies by reference to metaphysical views. The reason why is that political justifications need to be understandable to all citizens, and that the motivations and aims set out in official sources should conform to generally agreed standards of reasoning. This criterion may in fact exclude many religious justifications from the political sphere.

However, liberal principles are not, as we now know, incompatible with all conceptions of virtue or the good life. Some visions of the good life, some ethical goals and ideals, may quite reasonably be supported by and referred to by the state. That this is a quite reasonable position will perhaps be seen once we realize that many virtues or conceptions of the good are entirely uncontroversial. For example, most people would accept as valid the idea that the good life should involve the experience of love and friendship.[1] Yet such notions are, implausibly I believe, ruled out by the liberal ideal of neutrality.

I believe the most coherent but perhaps also the least attractive option for a liberal would be to concede the possibility of a nonneutral state. Facing the limits of his own principles the liberal will then conclude, however hesitantly, that the case for the neutral state was illusory. In this way the liberal is able to maintain the self-image of being free from prejudices. Paradoxically, he can only do this at the price of allowing the state to adopt what he considers to be prejudiced views and ends.

Yet it seems to me absolutely unavoidable that the liberal creed is strongly associated with the idea of state neutrality. We cannot simply ignore the fact that many liberals believe that neutrality would be a desirable feature of state institutions.[2] Another, less coherent but more attractive, option for the liberal is consequently to affirm the belief in political neutrality and to concede that this belief is endorsed as a matter of faith. Rawls attempted to work out the details of such an ideal, a public reason as he called it, that would guide legislation, adjudication and public debate on certain matters. The idea was that people would find reasonable the restraints of neutrality with regard to what citizens could do or say in a political setting. Now in chapter eight I contested Rawls's conclusion that the idea of a public reason will appear as reasonable to all. Thus the alternative to the idea of a non-neutral state is, to put it somewhat blatantly, to accept that public life is regulated by a myth.

Surely, most liberals would be reluctant to admit that our commitment to liberal institutions depends on beliefs that are non-rational (though not necessarily irrational). There is a tendency to believe that our political values need necessarily be explicable in terms of other, more fundamental, principles or beliefs: we want reasons for our political commitments. And yet, a choice has to be made. Should liberal principles depend on the myth of neutrality, or should liberalism accede to the possibility that liberal democracy may legitimately express people's faith in virtue and the good life? This is the liberal's predicament.

Notes

1.   That many elements of the good life are reasonable is a point elaborated on in Simon Caney, 1998, pp 91f.
2.   As observed by Waldron (1989, p 62) and Hardin (1999, p 50) the term "neutrality" is a recent invention in the tradition of liberal thought and should therefore not be seen as an historical feature of liberalism. However, I assume that contemporary liberals are generally unfavorably disposed to the idea of a politics of virtue.

Bibliography

Ackerman, Bruce, 1980, *Social Justice in the Liberal State*. New Haven and London: Yale University Press.

—, 1990, "Neutralities," in Douglass, Mara & Richardson, 1990.

Alexander, Larry (*ed*), 1998, *Constitutionalism: Philosophical Foundations*. Cambridge: Cambridge University Press.

Altham, J & Harrison, Ross (eds), 1995, *World, Mind and Ethics: Essays on the Ethical Philosophy of Bernard Williams*. Cambridge: Cambridge University Press.

Arblaster, Anthony, 1984, *The Rise and Fall of Modern Liberalism*. Oxford: Basil Blackwell.

Archard, David, 1993, *Children: Rights and Childhood*. London: Routledge.

Arneson, Richard, 1990, "Neutrality and Utility," in *Canadian Journal of Philosophy*, vol 20.

— (ed), 1992, *Liberalism*. Aldershot: Edward Elgar Publishers.

Aspers, Patrik & Uddhammar, Emil (eds), 1999, *Framtidens dygder: om etik i praktiken*. Stockholm: City University Press.

Atwell, John, 1986, *Ends and Principles in Kant's Moral Thought*. Dordrecht: Martinus Nijhoff.

Audi, Robert, 1995, "Acting From Virtue," in *Mind*, vol 104.

Avineri, Shlomo & De-Shalit, Avner (eds), 1992, *Communitarianism and Individualism*. Oxford: Oxford University Press.

Barber, Benjamin, 1988, "Solipsistic Politics: Bertrand Russell and Empiricist Liberalism," in *The Conquest of Politics* (by B Barber). Princeton, NJ: Princeton University Press.

Barker, Paul (ed), 1996, *Living as Equals*. Oxford: Oxford University Press.

Barry, Brian, 1989, *Theories of Justice*. London: Harvester-Wheatsheaf.

—, 1990 [1965], *Political Argument*. Berkeley: University of California Press.

—, 1991, "How Not to Defend Liberal Institutions," in *Essays in Political Theory*, vol 2, *Liberty and Justice*. Oxford: Clarendon Press.

—, 1995 a, *Justice as Impartiality*. Oxford: Clarendon Press.

—, 1995 b, "John Rawls and the Search for Stability," in *Ethics*, vol 105.

Bates, Robert, 1988, "Contra Contractarianism: Some Reflections on the New Institutionalism," in *Politics and Society*, vol 16.

Beckman, Ludvig, 1997, "Going Native or Being a Coloniser?: Liberalism and the Possibility of Cultural Criticism," in Hemmungs-Wirtén & Peurell, 1997.

—, 1998, "Review of *Just Institutions Matter*," in *Tidskrift för Politisk Filosofi*, no 3.

—, 1999, "Föräldrars dygder och barns rättigheter," in Aspers & Uddhammar, 1999.

Beiner, Ronald, 1992, *What's the Matter with Liberalism?* Berkeley: University of California Press.

Beiner, Ronald & Booth, William James (eds), 1993, *Kant & Political Philosophy: The Contemporary Legacy.* New Haven: Yale University Press.

Bellamy, Richard (ed), 1989, *Liberalism and Recent Legal and Social Philosophy* (Archiv für Rechts- und Sozialphilosophie no 36). Stuttgart: Franz Steiner Verlag.

Bellamy, Richard, 1992, *Liberalism and Modern Society: An Historical Argument.* London: Polity Press.

—, 1996, "Pluralism, Liberal Constitutionalism and Democracy: A Critique of John Rawls's (meta) Political Liberalism," in Meadowcroft, 1996.

Bengtsson, Bertil, 1984, "Om lagrådsgranskningens gränser," in *Förvaltningsrättslig tidskrift,* vol 47.

Benhabib, Seyla, 1989, "Liberal Dialogue versus a Critical Theory of Discursive Legitimation," in Rosenblum, N, 1989.

Bennich-Björkman, Li, 1991, *Statsstödda samhällskritiker: författarautonomi och statsstyrning i Sverige.* Stockholm: Tiden,

Berger, Fred, 1984, *Happiness, Justice, and Freedom: The Moral and Political Philosophy of John Stuart Mill.* Berkley: University of California Press.

Bergström, Lars, 1990, *Grundbok i värdeteori.* Stockholm: Thales.

Berkowitz, Peter, 1999, *Virtue and the Making of Modern Liberalism.* Princeton, NJ: Princeton University Press.

Berlin, Isaiah, 1984 [1969], "Two Concepts of Liberty," in Sandel, 1984.

—, 1990 [1988], "The Pursuit of the Ideal," in *The Crooked Timber of Humanity: Essays in the History of Ideas.* London: John Murray.

Binswanger, Harry, 1986, *The Ayn Rand Lexicon.* New York: New American Library.

Björkholm, Thérèse, 1994, *Liberté and Loi: A Reading in the Political and Legal Philosophy of Jean-Jacques Rousseau,* (diss). Uppsala.

Björklund, Stefan, 1977, *Den uppenbara lösningen.* Stockholm: Bonniers.

—, 1991, *Forskningsanknytning genom disputation.* Stockholm: Almqvist & Wiksell International.

—, 1993, "Kan statsvetare ta ställning i politik?," in *Statsvetenskaplig Tidskrift,* vol 96.

Blomgren, Roger, 1998, *Staten och filmen.* Hedemora: Gidlunds förlag.

Bock, Gisela, Skinner, Quentin & Viroli, Maurizio (eds), 1990, *Machiavelli and Republicanism.* Cambridge: Cambridge University Press.

Bohman, James & Regh, William (eds), 1997, *Deliberative Democracy: Essays on Reason and Politics.* Cambridge, MA: Cambridge University Press.

Brecht, Arnold, 1959, *Political Theory: The Foundations of Twentieth-Century Political Thought.* Princeton, NJ: Princeton University Press.

Brink, David O, 1989, *Moral Realism and the Foundation of Ethics.* Cambridge: Cambridge University Press.

Buchanan, James, & Congleton, Roger, 1998, *Politics by Principle, not Interest.* Cambridge: Cambridge University Press.

Callan, Eamond, 1997, *Creating Citizens*. Oxford: Oxford University Press.

Campos, Paul, 1994, "Secular Fundamentalism," in *Columbia Law Review*, vol 94.

Caney, Simon, 1993, "Liberalisms and Communitarianisms: A Reply," in *Political Studies*, vol XLI.

—, 1998, "Impartiality and Neutrality," in Kelly, 1998.

Carrier, Leonard, 1993, "How to Define a Non Skeptical Fallibilism," in *Philosophia*, vol 22.

Caygill, Howard & Scott, Alan, 1996, "The Basic Law Versus the Basic Norm?: The Case of the Bavarian Crucifix Order," in Richard Bellamy & Dario Castiglione (eds), *Constitutionalism in Transformation: European and Theoretical Perspectives*. Oxford: Blackwell

Chambers, Simone, 1995, "Discourse and Democratic Practices," in White, 1995.

—, 1996, *Reasonable Democracy*. Ithaca, NY: Cornell University Press.

Chapman, John & Galston, William (eds), 1992, *Virtue*. New York: New York University Press (*Nomos* 34).

Clarke, Simon, 1999, "Contractarianism, Liberal Neutrality, and Epistemology," in *Political Studies*, vol XLVII.

Clor, Harry, 1985, "Mill and Millians on Liberty and Moral Character," in *The Review of Politics*, vol 47.

Cohen, Gerald A, 1997, "Where the Action Is: On the Site of Distributive Justice," in *Philosophy and Public Affairs*, vol 26.

Cohen, Joshua, 1993, "Moral Pluralism and Political Consensus," in Copp, Hampton & Roemer, 1993.

—, 1998, "Democracy and Liberty," in Elster, 1998.

Connolly, William, 1993 [1974], *The Terms of Political Discourse*. Princeton, NJ: Princeton University Press.

—, 1995, *The Ethos of Pluralization*. Minneapolis: Minnesota University Press.

Constitutional Documents of Sweden, 1996. Stockholm: The Swedish Riksdag

Copp, David, Hampton, Jean & Roemer, John (eds), 1993, *The Idea of Democracy*. Cambridge: Cambridge University Press.

Corlett, J Angelo (ed), 1991, *Equality and Liberty: Analyzing Rawls and Nozick*. London: Macmillan.

Crisp, Roger, 1992, "Utilitarianism and the Life of Virtue," in *The Philosophical Quarterly*, vol 42.

Dagger, Richard, 1997, *Civic Virtues: Rights, Citizenship, and Republican Liberalism*. New York: Oxford University Press.

Dascal, Marcelo & Gruengard, Ora (eds), 1989, *Knowledge and Politics: Case Studies in the Relationship Between Epistemology and Political Philosophy*. Boulder: Westview press.

Douglass, R B, Mara, G M & Richardson, H S (eds), 1990, *Liberalism and the Good*. New York: Routledge.

Dunn, John, 1990 [1984], "Liberty as a Substantive Political Value," in *Interpreting Political Responsibility: Essays* (by J Dunn). Cambridge: Polity Press.

Dworkin, Gerald, 1992, "Non-Neutral Principles," in Arneson, 1992.

— (ed), 1994, *Morality, Harm, and the Law*. Boulder: Westview Press.

Dworkin, Ronald, 1977, *Taking Rights Seriously*. London: Duckworth.
—, 1978, "Soulcraft," in *New York Review of Books*, October 12.
—, 1983 a, "What Liberalism Isn't," in *New York Review of Books*, January 20.
—, 1983 b, "Why Liberals Should Believe in Equality," in *New York Review of Books*, February 3.
—, 1985, *A Matter of Principle*. Cambridge, MA: Harvard University Press.
—, 1986, *Law's Empire*. London: Fontana Press.
—, 1990, "Foundations of Liberal Equality," in Petersen, 1990.
—, 1993, *Life's Dominion: An Argument About Abortion and Euthanasia*. London: Harper Collins.
—, 1996 a, "Do Liberty and Equality Conflict?," in Barker, 1996.
—, 1996 b, *Freedom's Law*. Oxford: Oxford University Press,
Elster, Jon, 1983, *Sour Grapes: Studies in the Subversion of Rationality*. Cambridge: Cambridge University Press.
— (ed), 1998, *Deliberative Democracy*. Cambridge: Cambridge University Press.
Ely, John, 1983, "Professor Dworkin's External/Personal Preference Distinction," in *Duke Law Journal*, vol 1983.
Englund, Tomas, 1986, *Curriculum as a Political Problem: Changing Educational Conceptions, with Special Reference to Citizenship Education* (Uppsala studies in education, 25). Lund: Studentlitteratur/Bromley: Chartwell-Bratt.
Erixon, Dick, 1999, *Svaghetens moral*. Stockholm: Timbro.
Estlund, David, 1998, "The Insularity of the Reasonable: Why Political Liberalism Must Admit the Truth," in *Ethics*, vol 108.
Etzioni, Amatai (ed), 1995, *New Communitarian Thinking: Persons, Virtues, Institutions, and Communities*. Charlottesville: University of Virginia Press.
Feinberg, Joel, 1966, "Duties, Rights and Claims," in *American Philosophical Quarterly*, vol 3.
—, 1988, *Harmless Wrongdoing*, vol 4, *The Moral Limits of the Criminal Law*. Oxford: Oxford University Press.
Fishkin, James, 1986, "Liberal Theory and the Problem of Justification," in Pennock & Chapman, 1986.
Flathman, Richard, 1996, "Strains in and Around Liberal Theory: An Overview from a Strong Voluntarist Perspective," in Meadowcroft, 1996.
Fogelin, Robert, 1987, *Understanding Arguments: An Introduction to Informal Logic*. San Diego, CA: Harcourt Brace Jovanovich.
Forst, Rainer, 1992, "How (not) to Speak About Identity: The Concept of the Person in *A Theory of Justice*," in *Philosophy and Social Criticism*, vol 18.
—, 1994, "Political Liberalism," in *Constellations*, vol 1, 169.
Frankfurt, Harry, 1971, "Freedom of the Will and the Concept of a Person," in *Journal of Philosophy*, vol 68.
Freeden, Michael, 1996, *Ideologies and Political Theory*. Oxford: Clarendon Press.
Fuller, Lon, 1969, *The Morality of Law* (rev ed). New Haven: Yale University Press.

Gaffney, Paul, 1996, *Ronald Dworkin and Law as Integrity*. Lewiston, NY: The Edwin Mellen Press.

Galston, William, 1988, "Liberal Virtues," in *American Political Science Review*, vol 82.

—, 1991, *Liberal Purposes: Goods, Virtues, and Diversity in the Liberal State*. Cambridge: Cambridge University Press.

—, 1992, "Introduction," in Chapman & Galston, 1992.

Gaus, Gerald, 1996, *Justificatory Liberalism*. Oxford: Oxford University Press.

Gauthier, David, 1986, *Morals by Agreement*. Oxford: Oxford University Press.

Gellner, Ernest, 1994, *The Conditions of Liberty*. London: Hamish Hamilton.

George, Robert, 1993, *Making Men Moral: Civil Liberties and Public Morality*. Cambridge: Cambridge University Press

Gewirth, Alan, 1960, "Positive 'Ethics' and 'Normative' Science," in *The Philosophical Review*, vol LXIX.

Glendon, Mary Ann, 1991, *Rights Talk: The Impoverishment of Political Discourse*. New York: Basic Books.

Goodin, Robert & Reeve, Andrew (eds), 1989, *Liberal Neutrality*. London: Routledge.

Gorr, Michael, 1991, "Rawls on Natural Equality," in Corlett, 1991.

Graham, Gordon, 1996, "Tolerance, Pluralism, and Relativism," in Heyd, 1996.

Gray, John, 1996 a [1983], *Mill on Liberty: A Defence*. London: Routledge.

—, 1996 b, "Postscript," in Gray, 1996 a.

Griffin, James, 1986, *Well-Being: Its Meaning, Measurement, and Moral Importance*. Oxford: Clarendon Press.

Gutman, Amy & Thompson, Dennis, 1998, *Democracy and Disagreement*. Cambridge, MA: Harvard University Press.

Gür, Thomas, 1998, *Positiv särbehandling är också diskriminering*. Stockholm: Timbro.

Habermas, Jürgen, 1987 [1981], *The Theory of Communicative Action: The Critique of Functionalist Reason* (vol 2). Cambridge: Polity Press.

—, 1994, *Between Facts and Norms*. Cambridge: Polity Press.

Haksar, Vinit, 1979, *Equality: Liberty and Perfectionism*. Oxford: Oxford University Press.

Hampsher-Monk, Ian, 1995, "Rousseau and Totalitarianism: With Hindsight," in Wokler, 1995.

Hampshire, Stuart, 1993, "Liberalism: The New Twist," in *New York Review of Books*, August 12.

Hampton, Jean, 1989 a, "Should Political Philosophy be Done Without Metaphysics?," in *Ethics*, vol 99.

—, 1989 b, "Hobbes's Science of Moral Philosophy," in Dascal & Gruengard, 1989.

Hardin, Russell, 1995, *One for All: The Logic of Group Conflict*. Princeton, NJ: Princeton University Press.

—, 1999, *Liberalism, Constitutionalism, and Democracy*. Oxford: Oxford University Press.

Hare, Richard, 1973, "Principles," in *Proceedings of the Aristotelian Society*, vol 73.

Harman, Gilbert, 1977, *The Nature of Morality*. New York: Oxford University Press.

Harrison, Jonathan (ed), n d, *Time-Travel for Beginners and Other Stories*. Printed by the University of Nottingham, probably 1990.

Harsanyi, John, 1982 [1977], "Morality and the Theory of Rational Behaviour," in Amartaya Sen & Bernard Williams (eds), *Utilitarianism and Beyond*. Cambridge: Cambridge university Press.

Hart, H L A, 1992 [1979], "Between Utility and Rights," in Arneson, 1992.

Hayek, Friedrich, 1960, *The Constitution of Liberty*. London: Routledge.

Hermansson, Jörgen, 1997, "Att nalkas det storslagna," in *Svensk Juristtidning*, vol 81.

Hemmungs-Wirtén, Ewa & Peurell, Erik (eds), 1997, *The Interpretation of Culture and the Culture of Interpretation*. Uppsala: Publications from the section for sociology of literature, no 36.

Heyd, David (ed), 1996, *Toleration: An Elusive Virtue*. Princeton, NJ: Princeton University Press.

Hobbes, Thomas, 1985 [1651], *Leviathan*. London: Penguin Books.

Holmes, Stephen, 1989, "John Stuart Mill: Fallibilism, Expertise, and the Politics-Science Analogy," in Dascal & Gruengard, 1989.

—, 1993, *The Anatomy of Antiliberalism*. Chicago: University of Chicago Press.

—, 1995, *Passions and Constraint*. Chicago: University of Chicago Press.

Horton, John (ed), 1994, *After MacIntyre*. Oxford: Polity Press.

—, 1996, "Toleration as a Virtue," in Heyd, 1996.

Horton, John & Mendus, Susan (eds), 1985, *Aspects of Toleration*. London: Methuen.

Hurka, Thomas, 1993, *Perfectionism*. Oxford: Oxford University Press.

Hägerström, Axel, 1966 [1911], "Om moraliska föreställnigars sanning," *Socialfilosofiska uppsatser*, Stockholm: Bonniers.

Höög, Victoria, 1999, *Upplysning utan förnuft: begär och upplysning hos Thomas Hobbes, John Locke, David Hume och Montesquieu*, (diss). Eslöv: B Östlings bokförlag Symposion.

Jones, H S, 1992, "John Stuart Mill as a Moralist," in *Journal of the History of Ideas*, vol 53.

Jones, Peter, 1989, "Liberalism, Belief, and Doubt," in Bellamy, 1989.

—, 1994, *Rights*. London: Macmillan.

—, 1995, "Two Conceptions of Liberalism, Two Conceptions of Justice," in *British Journal of Political Science*, vol 25.

Kateb, George, 1989, "Democratic Individuality and the Meaning of Rights," in Rosenblum, 1989.

Kelly, Paul, 1994, "MacIntyre's Critique of Utilitarianism," in Horton, 1994.

— (ed), 1998, *Impartiality, Neutrality and Justice: Re-reading Brian Barry's Justice as Impartiality*. Edinburgh: Edinburgh University Press.

Körner, Stephan (ed), 1974, *Practical Reason*. Oxford: Basil Blackwell.

Korsgaard, Christine, 1983, "Two Distinctions in Goodness," in *The Philosophical Review*, vol XCII.

Kuhn, Deanne, 1991, *The Skills of Argument*. Cambridge: Cambridge University Press.

Kymlicka, Will, 1990, *Contemporary Political Philosophy*. Oxford: Basil Blackwell.
—, 1991, *Liberalism, Community and Culture*. Oxford: Clarendon Press.
—, 1992 [1989], "Liberal Individualism and Liberal Neutrality," in Avineri & De-Shalit, 1992.
Langton, Rae, 1990, "Whose Right? Ronald Dworkin, Women and Pornographers," in *Philosophy and Public Affairs*, vol 19.
Larmore, Charles, 1996, *The Morals of Modernity*. Cambridge: Cambridge University Press, 126.
Laslett, Peter & Fishkin, James (eds), 1979, *Philosophy, Politics and Society: A Collection* (5th series). Oxford: Blackwell.
Laursen, John Christer, 1989, "Scepticism and Intellectual Freedom: The Philosophical Foundations of Kant's Politics of Publicity," in *History of Political Thought*, vol 10.
Lewin, Leif, 1988, *Det gemesamma bästa*. Stockholm: Carlssons.
Locke, John, 1963 [1689], *A Letter Concerning Toleration*. The Hague: Martinus Nijhoff.
Louden, Robert, 1997 a, "Kant's Virtue Ethics," in Statman, 1997.
—, 1997 b [1984], "On Some Vices of Virtue Ethics," in Statman, 1997.
Lukes, Steven, 1973, *Individualism*. Oxford: Basil Blackwell.
Lundström, Mats, 1993, *Politikens moraliska rum*, (diss). Stockholm: Almquist & Wiksell International.
—, 1996, *Jämställdhet eller sexistisk rättvisa?* Stockholm: Studieförbundet Näringsliv och samhälle.
McCloskey, H J, 1963, "A Note on Utilitarian Punishment," in *Mind*, vol 72.
—, 1974, "Liberalism," in *Philosophy*, vol 49.
Macedo, Stephen, 1990, *Liberal Virtues: Citizenship, Virtue, and Community in Liberal Constitutionalism*. Oxford: Oxford University Press.
MacIntyre, Alasdair, 1985, *After Virtue*. London: Duckworth.
MacKinnon, Catherine, 1989, *Toward a Feminist Theory of the State*. Cambridge, MA: Harvard University Press
McKnight, Utz Lars, 1996, *Political Liberalism and the Politics of Race*, (diss). Lund: Lund University Press.
McLellan, David (ed), 1977, *Karl Marx: Selected Writings*. Oxford: Oxford University Press.
Macleod, Colin, 1998, *Liberalism, Justice, and Markets: A Critique of Liberal Equality*. Oxford: Oxford University Press.
McNaughton, David, 1988, *Moral Vision*. Oxford: Blackwell.
Manning, D J, 1976, *Liberalism*. London: J M Dent & Sons Ltd.
Mason, Andrew (ed), 1998, *Ideals of Equality*. Oxford: Blackwell.
Marneffe, Peter de, 1990, "Liberalism, Liberty and Neutrality," in *Philosophy and Public Affairs*, vol 19.
Marx, Karl, 1977 [1875], "Critique of the Gotha Programme," in *Karl Marx: Selected Writings* (ed D McLellan). Oxford: Oxford University Press.
Meadowcroft, James (ed), 1996, *The Liberal Political Tradition: Contemporary Reappraisals*. Cheltenham: Edward Elgar.

Mendus, Susan (ed) 1988, *Justifying Toleration*. Cambridge: Cambridge University Press.
—, 1989, *Toleration and the Limits of Liberalism*. London: Macmillan.
Miguel, Alfonso Ruiz, 1997, "Equality Before the Law and Precedent," in *Ratio Juris*, vol 10.
Mill, John Stuart, 1969 [1861], *Utilitarianism*, vol 10 of *Collected Works of John Stuart Mill*. Toronto: Toronto University Press.
—, 1977 [1859], *On Liberty*, vol 18 of *Collected Works of John Stuart Mill*. Toronto: University of Toronto Press.
—, 1985 [1869], *The Subjection of Women*. London: Everyman's Library.
Miller, David, 1976, *Social Justice*. Oxford: Clarendon Press.
—, 1977, "Socialism and the Market," in *Political Theory*, vol 5.
— (ed), 1987, *The Encyclopaedia of Political Thought*. Oxford: Blackwell.
—, 1998, "Equality and Justice," in Manson, 1998.
Mouffe, Chantal (ed), 1992, *Dimensions of Radical Democracy*. London: Verso.
—, 1994, "Political Liberalism, Neutrality and the Political," in *Ratio Juris*, vol 7.
Mulhall, Stephen & Swift, Adam, 1992, *Liberals and Communitarians*. Oxford: Blackwell.
Murray, Charles, 1998, *What It Means to Be a Libertarian: A Personal Interpretation*. New York: Broadway Books.
Nagel, Thomas, 1973, "Rawls on Justice," in *Philosophical Review*, vol 82.
—, 1975, "Libertarianism Without Foundations," in *Yale Law Journal*, vol 85.
Nagel, Thomas, 1979, "The Fragmentation of Value," in *Mortal Questions* (by Th Nagel). Cambridge: Cambridge University Press.
—, 1991, *Equality and Partiality*. Oxford: Oxford University Press.
—, 1994 [1987], "Moral Conflict and Political Legitimacy," in G Dworkin, 1994.
Narveson, Jan, 1998, "Egalitarianism: Partial, Counterproductive and Baseless," in Mason, 1998.
Neal, Patrick, 1987, "A Liberal Theory of the Good?" in *Canadian Journal of Philosophy*, vol 17.
Nicholson, Peter, 1985, "Toleration as a Moral Ideal," in Horton & Mendus, 1985.
Nordahl, Richard, 1997, "Rousseau in Dworkin: Judicial Ruling as Expressions of the General Will," in *Legal Theory*, vol 3.
Nordin, Ingemar, 1992, *Etik, teknik och samhälle: ett rättighetsetiskt alternativ*. Stockholm: Timbro.
Norton, John, 1991, *Democracy and Moral Development: A Politics of Virtue*. Berkeley: University of California Press.
Nozick, Robert, 1974, *Anarchy, State, and Utopia*. Oxford: Blackwell,
O'Neill, Onora, 1989, *Constructions of Reason*. Cambridge: Cambridge University Press.
—, 1996, *Towards Justice and Virtue*. Cambridge: Cambridge University Press.
Okin, Susan Moller, 1989, *Justice, Gender, and the Family*. New York: Basic Books.

Oldfield, Adrian, 1990, *Citizenship and Community*. London: Routledge.
Parekh, Bikuh & Pantham, Thomas (ed), 1987, *Political Discourse*. New Delhi: Sage Publications.
Parfit, Derek, 1984, *Reasons and Persons*. Oxford: Oxford University Press.
Paris, David C, 1991, "Moral Education and the 'Tie that Binds' in Liberal Political Theory," in *American Political Science Review*, vol 85.
Patten, Allen, 1996, "The Republican Critique of Liberalism," in *British Journal of Political Science*, vol 26.
Paul, Jeffrey (ed), 1982, *Reading Nozick: Essays on Anarchy, State, and Utopia*. Oxford: Basil Blackwell.
Peacock, J G A, 1981, "Virtues, Rights and Manners: A Model for Historians of Political Thought," in *Political Theory*, vol 9.
Peczenik, Aleksander, 1995, *Vad är rätt?: om demokrati, rättssäkerhet, etik och juridisk argumentation*. Stockholm: Fritzes.
Pennock, Roland & Chapman, John (eds), 1986, *Justification*. New York: New York University Press (*Nomos* 28).
Petersen, Grethe B (ed), 1990, *Tanner Lectures on Human Values*. Salt Lake City: Utah University Press.
Pettit, Philip, 1994, "Liberal/Communitarian: MacIntyre's Mesmeric Dichotomy," in Horton, 1994.
Plamenatz, John, 1992 [1963], *Man and Society* (vols I-II). London: Longman.
Plant, Raymond, 1991, *Modern Political Thought*. Oxford: Blackwell.
Popper, Karl, 1965 [1962], *Conjectures and Refutations: The Growth of Scientific Knowledge* (2nd ed). New York: Harper Torchbooks.
Popper, Karl, 1995 [1945], *The Open Society and Its Enemies*. London: Routledge.
Prostitutionen i Sverige (Report from *Prostitutionsutredningen*, SOU 1981:71). Stockholm: Liber.
Putnam, Robert, 1993, *Making Democracy Work*. Princeton, NJ: Princeton University Press.
Ramsay, Maureen, 1997, *What's Wrong With Liberalism?* London: Leicester University Press.
Rawls, John. 1971. *A Theory of Justice*. Oxford: Oxford University Press.
—, 1979 [1975], "A Well-Ordered Society," in Laslett & Fishkin, 1979.
—, 1989, "The Domain of the Political and Overlapping Consensus," in *New York University Law Review*, vol 64.
—, 1992 [1985], "Justice as Fairness: Political Not Metaphysical," in Avineri & De-Shalit, 1992.
—, 1993, *Political Liberalism*. New York: Columbia University Press.
—, 1995, "Reply to Habermas," in *Journal of Philosophy*, vol 92.
—, 1997 a, "Postscript," in Bohman & Regh, 1997.
—, 1997 b, "The Idea of Public Reason Revisited," in *The University of Chicago Law Review*, vol 64.
—, n d, "The Island of the Unborn," in J Harrison, n d.
Raz, Joseph, 1986, *The Morality of Freedom*. Oxford: Clarendon Press.
Raz, Joseph, 1994, *Ethics In the Public Domain*. Oxford: Clarendon Press.

Richards, David, 1996, "Toleration and the Struggle Against Prejudice," in Heyd, 1996.

Riker, William & Ordeshook, Peter, 1973, *An Introduction to Positive Political Theory*. Englewood Cliffs, NJ: Prentice Hall.

Rorty, Richard, 1991, "The Priority of Democracy to Philosophy," in *Philosophical Papers*, vol 2, *Objectivity, Relativism and Truth*. Cambridge: Cambridge University Press.

Rosenblum, Nancy, 1987, *Another Liberalism: Romanticism and the Reconstruction of Liberal Thought*. Cambridge, MA: Harvard University Press.

— (ed), 1989, *Liberalism and the Moral Life*. Cambridge, MA: Harvard University Press.

Rothstein, Bo, 1994, *Vad bör staten göra?* Stockholm: Studieförbundet Näringsliv och samhälle.

— (ed), 1995, *Demokrati som dialog*. Stockholm: Studieförbundet Näringsliv och samhälle.

—, 1998, *Just Institutions Matter*. Cambridge: Cambridge University Press.

Rudbeck, Carl, 1993, *Rambo och Rimbaud: essäer om kultur*. Stockholm: Timbro.

Runciman, Walter G & Sen, Amartya, 1965, "Games, Justice and the General Will," in *Mind*, vol 74

Russell, Bertrand, 1931, *The Conquest of Happiness*. London: George Allen & Unwin.

—, 1938, *Power: A New Social Analysis*. London: George Allen and Unwin.

—, 1955 [1947], "Philosophy and Politics," in *Unpopular Essays*. London: Routledge.

—, 1957, *Why I Am Not a Christian: And Other Essays on Religion and Related Subjects*. London: George Allen & Unwin.

Sabine, George, 1973 [1961, 1937], *A History of Political Theory*. Fort Worth: Harcourt Brace College Publishers.

Sandel, Michael, 1982, *Liberalism and the Limits of Justice*. Cambridge: Cambridge University Press.

— (ed), 1984, *Liberalism and Its Critics*. Oxford: Basil Blackwell.

—, 1994, "Political liberalism," in *Harvard Law Review*, vol 107.

—, 1996, *Democracy's Discontent: America in Search of a Public Policy*. Cambridge, MA: Harvard University Press.

Scanlon, Thomas, 1982 [1976], "Nozick on Rights, Liberty and Property," in Paul, 1982.

—, 1999, *What We Owe to Each Other*. Cambridge, MA: Harvard University Press.

Sen, Amartya, 1974, "Choice, Orderings and Morality," in Körner, 1974.

Sen, Amartya & Williams, Bernard, 1982a, "Introduction," in Sen & Williams, 1982 b.

— (eds) 1982 b, *Utilitarianism and Beyond*. Cambridge: Cambridge University Press.

Shapere, Dudley, 1984, *Reason and the Search For Knowledge*. Dordrecht: Reidel.

Sher, George, 1997, *Beyond Neutrality: Perfectionism and Politics*. Cambridge: Cambridge University Press.

Shklar, Judith, 1984, *Ordinary Vices*. Cambridge, MA: Harvard University Press.

—, 1989, "The Liberalism of Fear," in Rosenblum, 1989.

Sidgwick, Henry, 1981 [1907], *The Methods of Ethics*. Indianapolis: Hackett.

Simon, Robert, 1979, "Individual Rights and 'Benign' Discrimination," in *Ethics*, vol 90.

Skinner, Quentin, 1990, "The Republican Idea of Political Liberty," in Bock, Skinner & Viroli, 1990.

—, 1992, "On Justice, the Common Good and the Priority of Liberty," in Mouffe, 1992.

—, 1998, *Liberty Before Liberalism*. Cambridge: Cambridge University Press

Slote, Michael, 1989, *Beyond Optimizing: A Study of Rational Choice*. Cambridge, MA: Harvard University Press.

Smith, Steve B, 1989, "Hegel and the French Revolution," in *Social Research*, vol 56.

Smith, Tara, 1997, "Tolerance and Forgiveness: Virtues or Vices?" in *Journal of Applied Philosophy*, vol 14.

Spragens, Thomas, 1981, *The Irony of Liberal Reason*. Chicago: University of Chicago Press.

—, 1995, "Communitarian Liberalism," in Etzioni, 1995.

Statman, Daniel (ed), 1997, *Virtue Ethics: A Critical Reader*. Edinburgh: Edinburgh University Press.

Steiner, Hillel, 1994, *An Essay On Rights*. Oxford: Blackwell.

Sunstein, Cass, 1993, *The Partial Constitution*. Cambridge, MA: Harvard University Press

—, 1996, "Incompletely Theorized Agreements," in *Legal Reasoning and Political Conflict* (by C Sunstein). New York: Oxford University Press.

Swanton, Christine, 1997 [1993], "Virtue Ethics and Satisficing Rationality," in Statman, 1997.

Sydow, Björn von, Wallin, Gunnar & Wittrock, Björn (eds), 1993, *Politikens väsen*. Stockholm: Tiden.

Talmon, Jaaqov Leib, 1986 [1952], *The Origins of Totalitarian Democracy*. Harmondsworth: Penguin Books.

Taylor, Charles, 1982, "The Diversity of Goods," in Sen & Williams, 1982 b.

—, 1985, "Atomism," in *Philosophical Papers*, vol 2, *Philosophy and the Human Sciences* (by Ch Taylor). Cambridge: Cambridge University Press.

—, 1986, "Human Rights: The Legal Culture," in *Philosophical Foundations of Human Rights*. Paris: UNESCO.

—, 1991, *The Ethics of Authenticity*. Cambridge, MA: Harvard University Press.

—, 1993 [1986], "The Motivation Behind a Procedural Ethics," in Beiner & Booth, 1993.

—, 1994, "Justice After Virtue," in Horton, 1994.

—, 1995 a, "A Most Peculiar Institution," in Altham & Harrison, 1995.

—, 1995 b, "Replies," in Tully, 1995.

—, 1995 c [1992], "The Politics of Recognition," in *Philosophical Arguments*

(by Ch Taylor). Cambridge, MA: Harvard University Press.
Taylor, Charles & Gutmann, Amy (eds), 1992, *Multiculturalism and the Politics of 'Recognition'*. Princeton, NJ: Princeton University Press.
Terchek, Ronald, 1987, "The Liberal Language of Rights: From Locke to Rawls," in Parekh & Pantham, 1987.
Thomson, Judith Jarvis, 1990, *The Realm of Rights*. Cambridge, MA: Harvard University Press.
Tingsten, Herbert, 1933, *Demokratins seger och kris: vår egen tids historia*. Stockholm: Bonniers.
—, 1965 [1939], *De konservativa idéerna*. Stockholm: Bonniers.
Tocqueville, Alexis de, 1998 [1862], *Democracy in America*. Hertfordshire: Wordsworth Editions Ltd. Original title: *De la démocratie en Amérique*.
Trianosky, Gregory, 1990, "What Is Virtue Ethics All About?" in *American Philosophical Quarterly* vol 27.
Tully, James (ed), 1995, *Philosophy in an Age of Pluralism*. Cambridge: Cambridge University Press.
Waldron, Jeremy, 1987, "Theoretical Foundations of Liberalism," in *Philosophical Quarterly*, vol 37.
—, 1988 a, "When Justice Replaces Affection: The Need For Rights," in *Harvard Journal of Law and Public Policy*, vol 11.
—, 1988 b, "Locke: Toleration and the Rationality of Persecution," in Mendus, 1988.
—, 1989, "Legislation and Moral Neutrality," in Goodin & Reeve, 1989.
—, 1998, "Precommitment and Disagreement," in Alexander, 1998.
Wall, Steven, 1998, *Liberalism, Perfectionism and Restraint*. Cambridge: Cambridge University Press.
Walzer, Michael, 1983, *Spheres of Justice*. Oxford: Blackwell.
—, 1990, "The Communitarian Critique of Liberalism," in *Political Theory*, vol 18.
—, 1992, "Comment," in Taylor & Gutmann, 1992.
—, 1996. "On Negative Politics ," in Yack, 1996.
—, 1997, *On Toleration*. New Haven: Harvard University Press.
Weale, Albert, 1983, *Political Theory and Social Policy*. London: Macmillan.
Vedung, Evert, 1981, *Political Reasoning*. Beverly Hills: Sage.
Veen, Robert van der, 1999, "The Adjudicating Citizen: On Equal Membership in Walzer's Theory of Justice," in *British Journal of Political Science*, vol 29.
Weintraub, Ruth, 1993, "Fallibilism and Rational Belief," in *British Journal of Philosophy and Science*, vol 44.
Wenar, Leif, 1995, "Political Liberalism: An Internal Critique," in *Ethics*, vol 106.
Westerståhl, Jörgen, 1993, "Om statsvetenskapens förträfflighet," in von Sydow *et al*, 1993.
White, Stephen K (ed), 1995, *The Cambridge Companion to Habermas*. Cambridge: Cambridge University Press.
Wilkinson, T M, 1996, "Dworkin on Paternalism and Well-Being," in *Oxford Journal of Legal Studies*, vol 16.

Williams, Bernard, 1985, *Ethics and the Limits of Philosophy*. London: Fontana Press.

—, 1996, "Toleration: An Impossible Virtue?," in Heyd, 1996.

Wilson, James Q, 1995, *On Character*. Washington, DC: American Enterprise Institute.

Wokler, Robert (ed), 1995, *Rousseau and Liberty*. Manchester: Manchester University Press.

Wolgast, Elizabeth, 1994, "The Demands of Public Reason," in *Columbia Law Review*, vol 94.

Yack, Bernard, 1993, "The Problem With Kantian Liberalism," in Beiner & Booth, 1993.

— (ed), 1996, *Liberalism Without Illusions: Essays on Liberal Theory and the Political Vision of Judith N Shklar*. Chicago: The University of Chicago Press.

Zvesper, John, 1987, "Liberalism," in Miller, 1987.

Index

Ackerman, Bruce, 131n1, 192, 199, 202, 234nn11, 26, 235n34
affirmative action, 153–157
altruism, 158f
Aquinas, Thomas (Thomas of Aquino), 210
Arblaster, Anthony, 37n27, 38n32
Archard, David, 112n14
Aristotle, 4
Arneson, Richard, 131n5, 235n39
Atwell, John, 33, 39n47
Audi, Robert, 38n37
authenticity, 56–49, 54f, 247
autonomy, virtue of, 59, 64, 73–79, 259

Barber, Benjamin, 254n4
Barry, Brian, 61n23, 79n12, 80n27, 81n48, 128–130, 132nn26, 37, 133n42, 176, 185n102, 201, 235nn31–32, 43, 239n101, 242–254, 254nn1–2, 5–8, 10–12, 255nn15–16, 18, 28–29, 261–262
Bates, Robert, 37n12
Beckman, Ludvig, 111n4, 131n5, 255n19
Beiner, Ronald, 63–64, 73–75, 77, 79n3, 80n34, 81n47, 111n2, 112n13, 132n24, 260
Bellamy, Richard, 59, 62n60, 80n35
Bengtsson, Bertil, 181n9
Benhabib, Seyla, 233n2
Bennich-Björkman, Li, 16n4
Berger, Fred, 56–58, 61n25, 62nn48–49, 54
Bergström, Lars, 16n13
Berkowitz, Peter, 36nn2, 4, 37n21
Berlin, Isaiah, 99–100, 104, 108–109, 111n1, 113nn32, 34, 260
Binswanger, Harry, 112n16
Björkholm, Thérèse, 181nn16, 18, 182nn22, 27

Björklund, Stefan, 12–13, 17nn28, 29, 32, 182n27
Blomgren, Roger, 16n4
Brecht, Arnold, 17n26
Brink, David O, 16n13, 114n51, 238n91
Buchanan, James, 182n21, 234n24
Burke, Edmund, 237n73

Callan, Eamond, 15n3, 112n15
Campos, Paul, 234n14
Caney, Simon, 117, 125–126, 131n6, 264 n1
Carrier, Leonard, 255n22
Caygill, Howard, 132n22
certainty, 241–245, *see also* skepticism
challenge, life as a, 42–60, 164–178
Chambers, Simone, 233n2, 234nn4, 9, 21, 254n8
choice, virtue of, 73f, 76
citizen, liberal ideal of, 20, 23–26, 63–79, 189f, 232
Clarke, Simon, 238nn88, 93, 255n13
Clor, Harry, 61n24
Cohen, Gerald A, 80n21, 127, 133n41
Cohen, Joshua, 172, 185n89, 224–231, 238nn89, 92, 239nn96, 106, 246, 255n14
coherence in law, 144–147
Congleton, Roger, 182n21, 234n24
Connolly, William, 112n19, 176, 185n101
conservatism, 23, 26, 103, 218
constitutionalism, 78, 121f, 129, 190ff
cooperation, virtue of, 20, 23–26, 66, 72
Crisp, Roger, 114n53
critical attitude, 249f
cultural policy, 2, 103, 116, 141–144, 165–171

Dagger, Richard, 37n12, 63–64, 74, 77–78, 79n3, 80n37, 81nn45–46

dogmatism, 242ff
doubt, see certainty and skepticism
Dunn, John, 37n17
Dworkin, Gerald, 199, 222, 224, 233, 235n28
Dworkin, Ronald,7, 9, 14, 16n20, 41–63, 60nn1–6, 8, 61nn9, 13–16, 18–19, 22, 25–26, 31–37, 62nn41, 61–62, 73, 78, 113n41, 119, 128–131, 131n13–14, 133n46, 135–142, 143–180, 180n1, 181nn6–9, 11–13, 17, 19, 182nn23, 29–32, 38, 183nn40, 43–46, 48–49, 52, 184nn59–65, 67, 69–72, 74, 76–80, 185nn81–82, 84, 87–88, 91, 97–100, 103, 186nn104, 106, 197, 235n33, 238nn83–84, 258–261

educational policy, 2, 123, 162
Elster, Jon, 216–217, 236n67
Ely, John, 183n58, 184n62
Englund, Thomas, 15n3
equality,
    moral, 9, 32–34, 72, 197–204, 261
    in law, 137–150, 261
    of life-styles, 77, 135, 204–208, 261
    sexual, 50ff, 147f
    social, 157–164
Erixon, Dick, 61nn38–39
Estlund, David, 239n105

family, 84–91
Feinberg, Joel, 111n9, 177–178, 186n105
Fishkin, James, 16n16
Flathman, Richard, 36n3, 63, 69, 79nn2, 19
Fogelin, Robert, 16n8
Forst, Rainer, 80n40, 239n99
Frankfurt, Harry, 61n23
fraternity, virtue of, 64ff, 78
Freeden, Michael, 183n49
friendship, virtue of, 52, 107, 263
Fuller, Lon, 181n15

Gaffney, Paul, 181n10
Galston, William, 22, 36nn3, 6, 63–64, 66, 68–69, 73–74, 77, 79nn3, 7, 13, 15, 18, 258
Gaus, Gerald, 238n94
Gauthier, David, 151–152, 183n48, 238n88

Gellner, Ernest, 112n29
generality in law, 138–144
George, Robert, 184n72
Gewirth, Alan, 17n30
Glendon, May Ann, 111n2, 112n13
Godwin, William, 236n66
Goodin, Robert E, 236nn66–67
Gorr, Michael, 67–68, 79n10
Graham, Gordon, 16n17
Gray, John, 47, 56, 59, 61n20, 62nn47, 59
Griffin, James, 113n43, 114nn49, 54
Gür, Thomas, 182nn27, 33, 183n54
Gutman, Amy, 236n65, 237n69

Habermas, Jürgen, 15n2, 121, 132n21, 234n11
Hägerström, Axel, 17n26
Haksar, Vinit, 62nn53, 56, 79n3, 80n35, 184n72
Hampsher-Monk, Ian, 113n32
Hampshire, Stuart, 234n14
Hampton, Jean, 16n16, 36n4, 184n72, 239n103
Hardin, Russell, 17n22, 36n8, 132n24, 264n2
Hare, Richard, 141, 181 n14
Harsanyi, John, 113n39
Hart, H. L. A., 155, 157, 183n56
Hayek, Friedrich A, 180n4, 182n21, 218, 237n73
Hegel, Friedrich, 4, 98–100, 112n30
Hermansson, Jörgen, 80n26
historical argument, 93ff, 245
Hitler, Adolf, 91
Hobbes, Thomas, 6, 16 n14, 20, 23, 26, 36nn4, 5
Holmes, Stephen, 62n55, 111n3, 139–139, 180nn3–5, 182n26, 193–196, 234nn13–14
honesty, virtue of, 22, 33
Höög, Victoria, 36n2
Horton, John, 33, 38n36, 39n46
Hurka, Thomas, 114n57

impartiality, 66f, 200f
independence, see individuality
individuality, 44–60, 258f, 261f, 263
intrinsic values, 91f, 99f, 106

Jones, Peter, 61nn24, 27–28, 111n9, 206, 235n36, 238nn84, 91, 254n9

justice,
  principle of, 51–55, 70, 95, 196f
  virtues of, 2, 51–55, 63, 68, 69–73,
    102

Kant, Immanuel, 31, 36n2, 38n42, 212–
    213, 236n61, 237n76, 255n19
Kateb, George, 47, 60n7, 61n21
Kelly, Paul, 113n42
Kelsen, Hans, 182n21
Korsgaard, Christine, 36n8
Kreuzesbefehl, 121f
Kuhn, Deanne, 17n25
Kymlicka, Will, 16n20, 97, 105, 107,
    112n27, 114nn51, 52, 119, 132nn15–
    16, 25, 235n33

Langton, Rae, 184n68
Larmore, Charles, 120, 132n17,
    185n107, 239n100
Laursen, Christer, 237n80, 255n19
legitimacy, 8f, 63, 115, 215
Lewin, Leif, 183n43
liberal paradox, 6-11
liberalism,
  asymmetry of, 76f
  defined, 3f
  ethical, 8–11, 42
  political, 8–11, 66, 74, 77f, 258f
  negative, 9
  skeptical, 6f, 10, 243ff
libertarianism, 91–98, 128
life-styles, *see* equality
Locke, John, 20, 97–98, 171–175,
    185nn90, 93–95, 97, 255n20
Lockean proviso, 97
Louden, Robert, 36n2, 113n31
Lukes, Steven, 61n17
Lundström, Mats, 16n16, 114n51, 154,
    157, 183nn53–54, 237n73

McCloskey, H J, 17n24, 113n46
Macedo, Stephen, 21, 36n3, 63, 74,
    79nn2, 19, 80n37
MacIntyre, Alasdair, 3, 16n6, 20, 36nn1,
    2, 38n42, 39n44, 113n42, 258
MacKinnon, Catherine, 148, 182nn34–
    35
McKnight, 183n39, 184n62
Macleod, Colin, 185nn81, 88
McNaughton, David, 113n43
Manning, D J, 16n9

Marneffe, Peter de, 131n2, 132n26
Marx, Karl, 112n20
Marxism, 103, 230
Mendus, Susan, 7, 16nn7, 19, 38nn31,
    38
metaphysics, 120f, 263
Miguel, Alfonso Ruiz, 182n21
Mill, John Stuart, 20, 42, 44, 45, 48–
    51, 56–58, 61nn10–12, 25, 26, 28–
    30, 62nn41–46, 50–53, 55–57,
    129–130
Miller, David, 16n12, 65, 79n6, 184n66
Montaigne, Michel de, 248, 255n17
moralism, 175–178
Mouffe, Chantal, 133n40, 239n104
Mulhall, Stephen, 81n44, 132n26
Murray, Charles, 62n40

Nagel, Thomas, 113n44, 133n43, 228–
    229, 234n8, 235n37, 239n102
Narveson, Jan, 234n27
Neal, Patrick, 206, 235n39
Neutrality,
  dimensions of, 115–131, 260
  legal, 137–150
  principle of, 9, 219f, 241, 244, 259–
    264
  religious, 117f, 120f, 135, 263
  scope of, 126–130, 192
Nicholson, Peter, 38n34
Nordahl, Richard, 181n17, 183n41
Nordin, Ingemar, 111n1
normative research, 11–13
Norton, John, 15n1
Nozick, Robert, 94–98, 111n6,
    112nn20, 23–26, 28, 114n58, 128–
    130, 133nn43, 45

Ordeshook, Peter, 80nn22, 24
Okin, Susan Möller, 86–91, 111nn7–8,
    112n12
Oldfield, Adrian, 37n16
O'Neill, Onora, 36n2, 38n42, 39n43,
    213, 236nn55, 58, 61, 237nn76, 80

Parfit, Derek, 100, 113n36, 114n53,
    214, 218, 236nn59–60, 237n72
Paris, David C, 15n3
Patten, Alan, 37n18, 117, 131n7
paternalism, 165,172
Peacock, J G A, 36n1
Peczenik, Aleksander, 181n9, 182n28

perfectionism, 59, 101
Pettit, Philip, 3717
Pinochet, Augusto, 96
Plamenatz, John, 62 n57, 80n31, 185n92
Plant, Raymond, 155, 183nn57–58
Popper, Karl, 4, 16n10, 11, 243, 254n5, 255nn20, 23
preferences, 72, 150–153. *See also* equality
property, 71ff, 97
prostitution, 163
publicity, 188f, 208–221
Putnam, Robert, 23–26, 37nn10, 11, 12

racism, 27, 154, 156, 160
Ramsey, Maureen, 183n58
Rand, Ayn, 91, 112n16
Rawls, John, 8, 25–26, 32, 37nn19, 20, 22, 23, 24, 25, 26, 27, 28, 30, 39n45, 62nn45, 56, 63–65, 79nn1, 4–5, 10–12, 14, 16–17, 80nn20, 23, 25–36, 38–39, 41, 81nn43–44, 47–48, 94–96, 100–102, 108–109, 112nn21–22, 113nn35, 38, 116, 118, 126–131, 131nn1–3, 12, 14, 132nn19, 27, 37, 133nn38–40, 42, 151–152, 183n47, 187–239, 233n2, 234nn7, 10–12, 14–22, 24–25, 235nn37, 40–47, 236nn48–50, 52–54, 56–57, 62–64, 237nn70–71, 74, 77, 79–80, 82, 238nn85–87, 90, 92, 94, 239nn95, 97–98, 104–105, 107, 241–245, 254n9, 255n21, 258–261, 264
Raz, Joseph, 93, 96, 112n19, 113n40, 120, 124, 131n14, 132nn18, 29–30, 133n44, 182nn24, 30, 184nn62, 70, 231, 235n43, 239n108, 251, 255n24
rationality, collective and individual, 25, 70f
republicanism, 23ff
Richards, David, 30, 38n40
rights,
    of children, 84–91
    of homosexuals, 155f, 161
    individual, 20, 30f, 34
    and language, 89–91
    and neutrality, 110f, 127
Riker, Willim, 80nn22, 24
Robespierre; Maximilien de, 91–92
Rorty, Richard, 16n21
Rosenblum, Nancy, 61n20

Rothstein, Bo, 38n39, 124, 129, 131nn10–11, 132n28, 133n47, 182nn25, 27, 254n7
Rousseau, Jean Jacques, 80nn26, 31, 141–142, 181nn16–18
Rudbeck, Carl, 184n75
Runciman, Walter G, 80n26
Russell, Bertrand, 6, 16n15, 61n29, 200, 235n30, 243, 251–252, 254nn3–4, 255n27, 262

Sabine, George, 62n58
Sandel, Michael, 79nn3, 9, 81n47, 85–91, 111nn5–7, 112n11, 114n59, 132n31, 200, 234n17, 235n29, 239n103
Scanlon, Thomas, 112n25, 113n40, 254n8
Scott, Alan, 132n22
self, the, 67, 99
self-defeating theories, 107, 172, 214f
self-interest, 23ff, 29f, 216
Sen, Amartya, 80nn26, 31, 104, 113nn43, 48
Sher, George, 132n26, 185n98, 235n43, 238n88
Shapere, Dudley, 255nn21, 25
Shklar, Judith, 17n23, 113n33, 203, 235n35, 255n17
Sidgwick, Henry, 38n38
Simon, Robert, 183n58
skepticism, 6f, 12, 241, 244, 248, 262
Skinner, Quentin, 23–24, 26, 36n1, 37nn13, 14, 15, 17, 18
Slote, Michael, 114n50
Smith, Stephen, 112n30
Smith, Tara, 37n29, 38n41
social capital, 25
Spragens, Thomas, 20, 36n2, 255n20
Stalin, Joseph, 91
Steiner, Hillel, 132n19
Sunstein, Cass, 182nn36–37, 234n5
Swanton, Christine, 107, 114n55
Sweden, 2, 121, 191
Swift, Adam, 81n44, 132n26

Talmon, Jaaqov Leib, 92, 112nn17, 30
Taylor, Charles, 3, 16nn6, 16, 111n2, 113n44, 114nn56, 58, 117, 125–127, 130, 131n8, 132nn34–35, 143, 181n20

teleological theories, 99, 105ff
Terchek, Ronald, 111n2
Thompson, Dennis, 236n65, 237n69
Thomson, Judith, 92, 98, 100, 112n18, 113n37
Tingsten, Herbert, 16nn17, 18, 237n73
Tocqueville, Alexis de, 216, 236n68
tolerance, virtue of, 7, 20, 26–35, 66
Trianosky, Gregory, 113n42, 114n51
truth,
    beliefs in vs. attitudes to, 243–250
    and reasonableness, 221–233
    and logic, 250f

uncertainty, *see* certainty and skepticism
universality, *see* generality in law
utilitarianism, 101–110

Vedung, Evert, 17n27
Veen, Robert van der, 184n67
veil of ignorance, 67f, 191
virtue,
    fear of, 91f, 98f
    instrumental vs. intrinsic, 22f, 24f, 26, 33f, 41f, 65, 69f, 72, 78
    liberal, 5f, 8f, 20–36, 257–259
    environmental, 102f, 177, 224

of first- and second-order, 48f, 59, 63, 73, 78, 259
    see also cooperation, choice, fraternity, friendship, honesty, independence, justice, and tolerance

Waldron, Jeremy, 87–89, 112n10, 131n14, 185n96, 209, 235nn37, 46, 264n2
Wall, Stephen, 131n5, 211–212, 236nn50–51, 56, 237n81
Walzer, Michael, 17n24, 37n30, 38n35, 117–118, 125–127, 130, 131nn4, 9, 132nn32–33, 36, 133n48, 184n67
Weale, Albert, 183nn51, 58
Weintraub, Ruth, 255n26
Wenar, Leif, 132n20, 238n90
Westerståhl, Jörgen, 17n26
Wilkinson, T M, 169–171, 174, 185nn83, 85–86
Williams, Bernard, 3, 16n5, 28, 38n33, 104, 113nn42, 48, 206, 235nn37–38
Wilson, James Q, 37n9
Wolgast, Elizabeth, 234n3, 239n104

Yak, Bernard, 132n19

Zvesper, John, 16n7